A CONFEDERATE ENGLISHMAN

A CONFEDERATE ENGLISHMAN

The Civil War Letters of
HENRY WEMYSS FEILDEN

Edited by W. Eric Emerson and Karen Stokes

The University of South Carolina Press

© 2013 University of South Carolina

Published by the University of South Carolina Press
Columbia, South Carolina 29208

www.sc.edu/uscpress

Manufactured in the United States of America

22 21 20 19 18 17 16 15 14 13   10 9 8 7 6 5 4 3 2 1

Library of Congress Cataloging-in-Publication Data

Feilden, H. W. (Henry Wemyss), 1838–1921.
A Confederate Englishman : the Civil War letters of Henry Wemyss Feilden /
edited by W. Eric Emerson and Karen Stokes.
p. cm.
Includes bibliographical references and index.
ISBN 978-1-61117-135-8 (hardbound : alk. paper) 1. Feilden, H. W. (Henry Wemyss),
1838–1921—Correspondence. 2. Confederate States of America. Army—Officers—
Correspondence. 3. United States—History—Civil War, 1861–1865—Personal narratives,
Confederate. 4. South Carolina—History—Civil War, 1861–1865—Sources.
5. Florida—History—Civil War, 1861–1865—Sources. 6. United States—History—
Civil War, 1861–1865—Participation, British. I. Emerson, W. Eric, 1966–
II. Stokes, Karen. III. Title.
E467.1.F34A4 2013
973.7'82—dc23

2012034451

This book was printed on a recycled paper with 30 percent postconsumer waste content.

CONTENTS

ILLUSTRATIONS

ACKNOWLEDGMENTS

The successful publication of these letters would not have been possible without the assistance of a number of people who provided encouragement and direction. First, we are thankful to Faye Jensen, South Carolina Historical Society executive director, and the SCHS board of managers for allowing these letters to be annotated and published. We also would like to thank the staff of the SCHS for their assistance with this project, particularly archivist Mary Jo Fairchild. The staff of the Hargrett Special Collections and Manuscript Library at the University of Georgia provided courteous, timely, and valuable assistance regarding the use and reproduction of materials in their collections. Postal historian Joseph T. Holleman kindly offered some useful information, and author Robert B. Cuthbert was a wealth of information regarding Charleston and the Cheves family. In addition Jennifer Amy of the Florida Historical Society graciously and promptly fulfilled a request for some hard-to-find information regarding Civil War Florida. We also would like to thank Rick Hatcher, historian at the Fort Sumter National Monument, for his insightful thoughts regarding Henry Wemyss Feilden's service in Charleston and for wonderful images of Feilden's home in Burwash, Sussex. We would like to extend a special thanks to Alexander Moore, acquisitions editor for the University of South Carolina Press, who found merit in this project and provided us with needed encouragement to submit it for publication. Finally the editors would like to thank their families for their continued patience as we work to publish some of the most compelling Civil War letters still existing in South Carolina.

Editorial Method

The editors of this volume transcribed the Feilden correspondence as written from the original manuscripts, with one exception: the first letter of the correspondence was transcribed from a typescript copy. The only significant changes made to the correspondence were to adapt names and dates within the dateline to a particular style for consistency. All omissions are indicated by ellipses. In 1920 Henry W. Feilden added annotations to the letters, and these are set off from the text in bracketed italics. Feilden also underlined long passages and crossed out a few words and phrases, which are now illegible. Unitalicized words within brackets represent the editors' best interpretation of questionable words.

INTRODUCTION

On a winter night in 1863, a young Englishman completed a dangerous voyage from Nassau to South Carolina aboard a blockade runner that slipped through the Union fleet bottling up Charleston Harbor. He began his military service to the Confederacy in Charleston, the symbolic birthplace of secession. There he fell in love with a South Carolinian and dedicated himself to the defense of her state and her people. His name was Henry Wemyss Feilden (1838–1921), and his Civil War letters tell the remarkable story of a British officer and gentleman whose affinity and admiration for a fledgling nation moved him to risk his life in its defense.

Since the conclusion of the American Civil War, historians have shown an interest in the foreign soldiers who witnessed and participated in that conflict. The accounts of British soldiers, such as Lt. Col. Arthur Fremantle's *Three Months in the Southern States,* still are popular reading for those who study the subject. Yet the letters of Henry Wemyss Feilden, a widely traveled and little-known British participant in the war, have remained unpublished until now. In his unfinished biography of Feilden titled "A Noble Englishman," author Aubyn Trevor-Battye wrote the following: "In the year 1915 but two officers wore the King's uniform who had fought in the Indian Mutiny—Field Marshall Lord Roberts V.C. and Colonel Henry Wemyss Feilden. . . . The first was a man of great and deserved renown, and if the other's name was not prominent as his he had this distinction—that he alone of soldiers could wear the white ribbon of Polar Exploration, and he alone had seen service in the American Civil War."[1]

Though insightful, Trevor-Battye's introductory statement is somewhat misleading. A number of British soldiers served on both sides during America's costliest war, but it is fair to argue that few others participated in polar expeditions. Fewer still served Great Britain as frequently during wartime as Feilden, and none were still in service to their country roughly fifty years after the end of the Civil War. Furthermore no other participant in that conflict could boast of a friendship with renowned author Rudyard Kipling.[2]

Feilden's Civil War correspondence stands apart from that of other foreign participants for a variety of reasons. His letters provide needed perspective regarding the administration of the Confederacy's large and vital Department of South Carolina, Georgia, and Florida during the war's final two years. Of particular note are Feilden's description of combat operations around Charleston Harbor in 1863–65 and his detailed comments regarding conditions in Florida during an inspection tour in 1864. In addition as a Confederate staff officer Feilden gives a thoroughly realistic assessment of the military situation in South Carolina as Sherman's troops traversed the state. The Feilden letters also are noteworthy because the author led an extraordinary and active postwar career in service to Great Britain. In fact his adventure in North America was the only instance in which he served in the armed forces of another nation. In that respect he was markedly different from many foreign soldiers, both Union and Confederate, who later served as mercenaries elsewhere. Feilden's letters nonetheless provide insight into the motives and allegiance of foreign-born soldiers, who voluntarily risked their lives and fortunes to serve in the American Civil War.

By nearly any measure, Henry Wemyss Feilden lived an extraordinary life. He was born on October 6, 1838, the second son of Sir William Henry Feilden (1812–79), Second Baronet of Feniscowles, and Mary Elizabeth Wemyss (d. 1890). Through his own actions, Feilden's father instilled in his sons the value of service to country. The Baronet Feniscowles was a captain in the Seventeenth Lancers, major of the Duke of Lancaster's Own Militia, and a deputy lieutenant and justice of the peace. In August 1853 he enrolled Feilden, age fourteen, in Cheltenham College, an Anglican public school in Cheltenham, Gloucestershire. Feilden left Cheltenham in 1855 and entered the Royal Military College at Sandhurst, which he attended until 1856. As the second son of a baronet, Feilden stood to inherit little of his father's estate; the title of baronet was destined for his brother William. Feilden's father did, however, provide his second son with the means to support himself with a commission as an ensign in the Forty-Second Regiment of Foot (Black Watch) in 1856.[3]

Feilden accompanied the Black Watch when it sailed from Great Britain to help put down the Indian Mutiny of 1857–58.[4] During his later years, he spoke little of his service in India, but that conflict no doubt had a profound impact on him and all who witnessed it. Trevor-Battye, Feilden's friend and biographer, wrote, "I cannot indeed remember that I ever heard him so much as refer to the Indian Mutiny. He was only a boy at the time, and I think it had left a horror upon him. Even in his long letters home he spared his mother's feelings by giving no details of those tragic scenes or of his own dangers or hardships."[5] In India Feilden experienced the stark brutalities that accompanied the mutiny. His regiment took part in the second battle of Cawnpore, where they confronted the gruesome aftermath of the massacre of British men, women, and children who had lived in the city prior to the uprising.[6] Feilden's regiment participated in a number of other battles, and he observed the British army's retaliation against Indian combatants and civilians for their role in, or failure to prevent, the massacre of British civilians. According to Trevor-Battye, Feilden also was present at the death of legendary British officer William Stephen Raikes Hodson of Hodson's Horse, who was mortally wounded at the battle of Lucknow.[7]

After the British suppressed the Indian uprising, Feilden served as a lieutenant in the Eighth Regiment of Punjab Infantry in 1860. He was with that regiment when it traveled to China and took part in a number of battles, including the capture of the Taku Forts, during the Second Opium War. Later in 1860 Feilden purchased a commission as a lieutenant in the Forty-Fourth (East Essex) Regiment of Foot.[8] Before the year ended, however, events in North America captured the attention of the young officer.

On November 6, 1860, while Feilden was still in China, Republican candidate Abraham Lincoln was elected president of the United States without winning a single Southern state. South Carolina seceded from the Union on December 20, and other Deep South states soon followed. On February 4, 1861, the recently seceded states formed a fledgling Confederacy, and within a few months, America was embroiled in its bloodiest conflict.

Feilden found cause with the Confederacy and made plans to join the new nation in its struggle for independence. To explain Feilden's decision, his biographer surmised that "it was but natural that the gentlemen of England as a whole should side with the Confederacy, for the children of their own forefathers held closest to historic tradition, and had the bluest blood. Chivalry alone would have impelled them to sympathy with the South; they knew she was fighting against long odds." The "long odds" the Confederates faced included "overwhelming numbers," "the power of the purse," and the scarcities of needed supplies caused by the Union blockade of Southern ports.[9]

In 1860 Feilden retired from service in the British army, sold his commission, and set his sights on a new venture across the sea. To reach the Confederacy and aid in its defense, he would have to run the blockade, a thought that "fired the imagination of the youth of England."[10] In undertaking this journey, however, Feilden was not just acting out of adventurousness and chivalrous idealism; he also viewed the expedition as a means to improve his personal financial position. Perhaps using funds derived from the sale of his commission, he invested one thousand pounds in "blankets and other much needed household goods" with the intention of running the blockade, selling his goods, and then using his profits to sustain him in his new home.[11]

Feilden became acquainted with Capt. C. W. Pickering, who wished to run the blockade with his ship *Flora*. Two other vessels, the *Ruby* and the *Calypso*, joined the *Flora* in this endeavor. The ships' crews and Feilden made preparations throughout autumn, and the *Flora* departed from Plymouth, England, on December 8, 1862. The *Ruby* and the *Calypso* joined the *Flora* in Funchal, Madeira, where they took on coal for the transatlantic crossing. The arrival of Commodore T. Augustus Craven and the USS *Tuscarora* complicated their departure. Craven was searching for potential blockade runners, and the *Tuscarora* cruised outside the three-mile limit of Funchal Roads intent on capturing any British ship leaving the harbor. Local regulations were another complication. Ships were prohibited from setting sail during the hours of darkness, and those that did were in danger of being fired upon by cannon located around the harbor.[12]

The ships' masters met and decided that the *Calypso* would steam out of harbor under the cover of darkness and draw the *Tuscarora* away while the *Flora* and the *Ruby* escaped. The following night the British ships executed their plan to perfection. The ships departed amid cannon fire from the harbor's forts, which did no damage to the vessels. The *Calypso* was the first to exit the harbor, and the *Tuscarora* gave chase. The *Flora*, with Feilden and his cargo aboard, and the *Ruby* made a dash for the open sea. In the darkness the *Calypso* escaped the *Tuscarora* and then joined the *Flora* and the *Ruby*. The following day the *Tuscarora* discovered the three ships at sea and gave chase until the *Calypso*, the *Flora*, and the *Ruby* escaped into a cloud bank. All three ships arrived safely in Nassau.[13]

Feilden's voyage to the Bahamas was eventful, but he faced even greater dangers before arriving in the Confederacy. On January 14, 1863, he and his cargo left Nassau aboard a blockade runner bound for Charleston. On January 16 a severe storm struck and battered the ship until it left the Gulf Stream. On the bitterly cold and sleet-filled night of January 17, the blockade runner came within sight of South Carolina. She slipped through the outer ring of Union ships blockading Charleston Harbor and approached the bar at the harbor mouth. Nearby Union vessels sighted the ship and fired rockets to alert the rest of the blockading fleet. Instead of dashing for the channel, the blockade runner's captain panicked and turned the ship back out to sea. It narrowly escaped the pursuing cruisers and retreated thirty miles offshore to await another attempt on the following evening. The second attempt ended like the first, with the blockade runner fleeing from pursuing Union ships and expending most of its remaining coal supply. The blockade runner returned to Nassau, where it received a new supply of coal and a new captain. On January 29 Feilden and his cargo once again set sail for Charleston. The new captain was undaunted, and his ship ran the blockade through the North Channel and arrived safely in the city.[14]

Upon reaching South Carolina, Feilden sought a position in the Confederate army. He made the long journey by train to Richmond, Virginia, and arrived on February 15. There he presented letters of introduction to the secretary of war and other prominent politicians and offered himself for service. Feilden later wrote that many men, including Englishmen, were in the city seeking appointments. These had "come out to this country, and I believe with very rare exceptions they have been obliged to serve as volunteers in the Army or on some General's staff until they have proved themselves fit for something." Feilden made a favorable impression while in Richmond, and President Jefferson Davis later appointed him captain and assistant adjutant general and offered him a post in the department of his choice. Feilden chose the Department of South Carolina, Georgia, and Florida, which was headquartered in Charleston. His nomination had to be approved by the Confederate Congress, and Representative William Porcher Miles shepherded the nomination through the House of Representatives, while Senator William Lowndes Yancey performed the same service in the Senate. Feilden's nomination was approved without dissent.[15]

While in Virginia, Feilden embarked on another errand. He carried with him a box of goods intended for Lt. Gen. Thomas J. (Stonewall) Jackson from a gentleman in Nassau. Feilden made an appointment to visit the general and

Henry W. Feilden in Confederate uniform. He wrote to Julia McCord
on April 30, 1864: "As for my ugly photographs I don't think I care for
one of them and you shall have the burning of them all."

Courtesy of the South Carolina Historical Society.

arrived at Jackson's headquarters outside Richmond after traveling over miles
of muddy roads in a steady downpour. Jackson greeted Feilden warmly, and
the two spoke for some time. Feilden shared dinner with the general's staff,
and Jackson even asked Feilden to share his bed. Feilden thanked the general
but instead decided to share a tent with one of Jackson's aides-de-camp. The
young English officer departed the following day, but he took with him an
adulation of Jackson, which is apparent in the Feilden correspondence.[16]

After returning to Charleston, Feilden learned of his appointment and began his service as a staff officer for Gen. P. G. T. Beauregard. In a March 1863 letter to an aunt in England, he related the details of his trip to Charleston and commented on current events, which he thought boded ill for the North. He likened passage of the Federal Conscription Act to a "gambler staking his all on the last card."

When it came to matters regarding slavery and race, Feilden was very much a man of his time, and his opinions differed little from those of many Americans. In the same letter to his aunt, Feilden noted that he believed that the Emancipation Proclamation was a failure, since "the slaves don't want to rise, and won't, unless under the pressure of Northern bayonets." Of his fellow countrymen, Feilden wrote, "I am glad to see you all in England appreciate the Yankees. They care no more for the negro and abolition than an Andaman Islander does; they thought they could raise a servile war, but they have failed signally. If they thought by murdering all the negroes they could ruin the South, these Yankees would do it."[17] He was incredulous regarding the recruitment of former slaves for service in the Union army and asked of his aunt, "Did you notice Gen. Hunter has been conscripting all the wretched negroes that they have beguiled from the plantations into his command, and forcing them to bear arms as soldiers!"[18]

In a much longer letter written in 1863 and addressed to "Phil," Feilden described in detail the April 7 Union ironclad attack on Fort Sumter and outlined his views regarding the war's economics. Of particular note is Feilden's description of cotton cultivation in the South, the impact of the war on cotton exports, and the potential profit that he could make by selling his share of an English investment. "I know a gentleman here sold a £1000 for £5000. If I could get a certificate from Collie that I held £1000 stocks I could sell it here at an enormous price today. I was offered $150,000 for my share. I have written to Raynsford this very day per underground railroad about sending me out a certificate."[19]

On June 16, 1863, Feilden provided a Miss McCord with a pass to travel from Charleston to Greenville, South Carolina, without interference. This is the first documentation of a relationship that lasted for six decades. The next surviving letter is a fragment addressed to Miss Julia McCord in April 1864, which shows that Feilden had fallen in love. Julia McCord (1837–1920), or Julie, was the daughter of influential lawyer and editor David J. McCord (1797–1855) of St. Matthew's Parish and Columbia and his first

Mrs. Julia Feilden, c. 1875. The photograph was produced by
Cobb & Challis of Woolwich, England. The business partnership of
William Cobb and Thomas Holt Challis began in 1875 and was
dissolved in June 1876.

Courtesy of the South Carolina Historical Society.

wife, Emmeline Wagner. After Emmeline's death, McCord sent Julie and her
minor siblings to live with relatives and then married noted author Louisa S.
Cheves (1810–79).[20]

Feilden grew to know Julie and developed a close friendship with Jacob
Keith Sass (1813–65), a Charleston banker and churchman who resided in
a home on Society Street, where Julie "was almost an adopted daughter."[21]
In the April 20, 1864, letter to Julie, Feilden addressed her as "darling," a
sign that they probably were engaged. To escape the Union bombardment of
Charleston, Julie was dividing her time between Savannah and Greenville.[22]

The April 20 letter to Julie also provides information regarding operations in the Department of South Carolina, Georgia, and Florida during the spring of 1864. Beauregard had moved with a considerable body of his troops to North Carolina and then Virginia for the beginning of active campaigning.[23] Instead of accompanying Beauregard to Virginia, Feilden remained behind in Charleston to complete a detailed report of operations around Charleston Harbor since the beginning of the siege. His letters convey his disappointment. "I don't think I have any chance of getting to Virginia with him [Beauregard] for sometime though I flatter myself that he has too much regard for me to debar me from sharing the privations & dangers of the field with him. . . . You may rest assured that I shall just do what I am ordered without grumbling, and it is more probable I shall have to remain in Charleston for a long time yet."[24] Feilden's letters also demonstrate his fondness and admiration for Beauregard. To Julia he wrote, "There is not another General in the service as thoughtful as our dear General is. Before leaving he sent for all in the office, privates as well as officers and said goodbye to them. There is no doubt he has got the best military head of any man in this Confederacy and if he only gets a chance he will make his mark on the enemy this spring and summer."[25]

While Beauregard was in Virginia, Feilden came under the command of Maj. Gen. Samuel M. Jones, and his staff responsibilities kept him occupied. Feilden wrote to Julie, "I am too busy to write you anything more than a note. We are so short of men that all the clerks of the Department, Head Quarters included . . . have had muskets put in their hands and have been sent off to man the batteries on James Island. Consequently I have no one to assist me, last night I had very little sleep and again the same thing is likely to occur tonight."[26]

Feilden, though, was not content merely to serve behind a desk in Charleston. He often was on the front lines on James Island, and he participated in a number of actions, though he downplayed any danger in his letters to Julie. On May 23, 1864, he wrote, "Last night I was away down at the front on James Island and only returned this morning dead tired. The enemy landed on James Island yesterday morning and we had a skirmish with them driving them to their gunboats."[27] Five days later he wrote Julie with more details of the action. "The enemy landed in large force on James Island. . . . Though down on the Island I was not myself in any danger though I must candidly confess, that was because the Yankees ran off. I promise you darling I will not expose myself in an unnecessary manner but a man is little worthy of a woman's love who will not in a time of danger freely expose his life for the defence of her home."[28]

From late August to September 1864, Feilden wrote a series of letters to Julie that describe in detail conditions in northern and central Florida. His motives for the trip were both personal and professional. In a letter dated May 19, 1864, he wrote of a colleague who had returned from Florida, "He is in raptures about that place we bought down there. I will tell you in another letter what he says about it. Don't think I would ever go to live in such a pagan country as Fla. or take anyone I loved to such a place."[29] Though he owned land in Florida, Feilden was not enthusiastic about making an inspection tour of the state. On August 24, 1864, he wrote from Savannah, "I have got so far on my road to Fla all right and am so very comfortable here that I feel almost inclined to stay in Savannah for three weeks and then pretend that I have been in Fla."[30]

On August 25, 1864, Feilden left Savannah by train bound for Florida, and he traveled with a group of soldiers whose company he found to be less than desirable.

> My companions on the road yesterday were not very pleasant ones. They consisted of Florida reserves who were returning from Andersonville Ga. where they had taken a batch of prisoners captured in Fla. From their contact with the Yankees they had acquired very disagreeable companions and the greater part of the day was spent by them in endeavouring to catch these animals. You may imagine my feelings when a capture was announced amid peals of laughter, & thought how one of the persecuted animals might seek shelter with me. However I escaped scot free. I made friends with an old man who seemed cleaner & more intelligent than the rest, and who assured me that he had "no lice about him" and I found out that his name was [Grainger] and that he was a shoemaker by trade and a resident of Talahassee [sic].[31]

During the expedition Feilden determined that Florida and its residents lacked the refinement of Charleston and Savannah, but he found the state's climate and food to be more than agreeable. He described Lake City as "outlandish" and wrote, "Accommodation is rather scanty in this part of the world." When asked by a fellow traveler to join him at his home for water, Feilden described the man's house as "a miserable little shanty." The weather, however, was another matter. "The best part of the place is the climate. It is quite cool. I slept last night under a blanket, and no mosquitoe bar. I only heard one mosquitoe."[32] Later as he traveled south, Feilden noted, "The climate is <u>perfect</u> not a mosquitoe, not a flea or any other kind of insect. The air balmy and delicious, just scented with the smell of burning resin." Food in Florida was plentiful, unlike many other areas of the Confederacy. "Beef at 65 cents a pound and of first rate quality. Lots of syrup, sugar, butter and the finest hominy I ever eat [*sic*], &c."[33]

Feilden described in detail the areas that he inspected. He visited the battlefield at Olustee and commented on surrounding communities that Union troops had destroyed. Manifesting his scientific propensities, he made extensive observations about the state's flora and fauna. His descriptions of plantations, especially as he moved south, were less than complimentary. "The country from here became far more thinly populated and the plantations are small and poorer looking. The settlers live in the funniest of log cabins, generally one room for the whole family, sometimes two, however wealthy they may be. They have no ideas of comfort. They get everything they want without trouble and are consequently correspondingly lazy." Of locals Feilden noted, "They live in the meanest one horse cabins, have a plenty of everything to eat, thousands of cattle and stock around them, plenty of negroes, and yet they live in this savage manner."[34]

Feilden traveled as far south as Panosofkie, where he commented on the plethora of orange groves. While there he discovered a number of Indian mounds, which piqued his mid-nineteenth-century scientific curiosity. He rode to a nearby cabin, borrowed a spade, and began to exhume one of the graves. After digging for some time, he discovered the fragile remains of a young woman of rank. "The skeleton was so old that it crumbled to powder as I exposed it to the air. . . . I then set vigorously to work and disinterred the little princess Panasoffkee." Feilden removed an iron hoe, beads, a thimble and scissors, arrowheads, and a "little tomahawk which ought to have accompanied her to the happy hunting grounds." He took a number of bones, recovered the grave, and proceeded on his trip. Shortly thereafter he learned that Sherman had captured Atlanta, and he quickly headed north and returned to Charleston.[35]

Feilden's letters demonstrate his focus on personal financial gain while he served in the Confederate army. The Union blockade contributed to Confederate suffering, but Feilden benefited financially from the blockade's continued existence. When he ran the blockade into Charleston, he brought with him a cargo of items that he sold for profit to finance his new life in the Confederacy. His initial experience with blockade running demonstrated how lucrative it could be. For the remainder of the war, Feilden purchased cotton and shipped it through the blockade to be sold in Nassau. In late May 1864, he wrote to Julie, "I have got a little cotton over in Nassau."[36]

Feilden also served as a factor for English friends who ran the blockade. In a postscript composed decades later, he explained that "all my English friends in the Blockade runners, came to me for assistance, and it was no great return, if a bale of cotton was now and again taken out for me."[37] On June 30, 1864, Feilden wrote to Julie, "I have also money matters for several friends to attend to. I have some cotton to ship for other friends who have got things in through the blockade by my [medium] and of course I have all the trouble of fixing the payment &c."[38]

In a letter dated September 27, 1864, Feilden described the process of shipping cotton through the blockade for associates. "I sent out two bales of cotton but that did not quite pay for them, and as usual when you send for friends I should have been left to pay the balance had not Mr. Cobia kindly offered to send me out a couple more bales on board the 'Syren' now in port. If they get out safe it will pay for the things and have a balance to me, credit so that this winter we can send for some more little things from Nassau."[39] This trade in cotton proved to be significant for supporting Feilden and his new bride during the war's final months. Soon after returning from his honeymoon, on December 21, 1864, Feilden reported to Julie, "The only bright spot in the desert of affliction is the return of the little 'Syren' with the comforting news that she took out my bag of Sea Island cotton safe to Nassau. I will try to get another out this time. This will give us some little exchange in our hour of need."[40] On February 14, 1865, three days before the evacuation of Charleston and the burning of Columbia, Feilden wrote, "The 'Coquette' went out last night. She had on board a great big bale of cotton for me, which will fetch in Nassau some $300. I have got a small amount of sterling there to draw on, enough to keep us from actual starvation for sometime after the war ends."[41]

From October to December 1864, there is another break in the Feilden correspondence, which coincides with his marriage to Julie and their subsequent honeymoon. He returned to his duties in Charleston as Sherman's forces were enveloping Savannah and threatening South Carolina. In a letter dated January 5, 1865, Feilden wrote, "If we can't hold Charleston I am very sure that we shall not burn it up because there are now in the city and there would be left behind some 15,000 poor men, women, children & negroes, who cannot possibly leave the city in any case, for they have no place to go, and would die of starvation. . . . If Charleston is to be burnt out let the Yankees have the disgrace of doing it."[42] Two weeks later Feilden wrote to Julie about Sherman's march through South Carolina. "The people are now dreadfully scared here [Charleston], and many I am sure are sorry that they did not clear out before this. It cannot be very long before this City is attacked."[43] On January 30 Feilden warned Julie, "You must give up the idea of coming to Columbia. It is not safe now."[44]

As the Confederacy's fortunes waned, Feilden manifested some enmity toward the region's slave population. Concerning slaves, he wrote to Julie, "I am very thankful that you have none of the wretches. The more I see of them the more disgusted I am with them, and I wish they were all free tomorrow so that the lazy brutes might have to find their living by work or die of starvation."[45] He later wrote that "the experience of this war proofs [*sic*] that you can put no trust in any negro. They have invariably betrayed their masters and mistresses." With the South's impending defeat, he questioned "whether death is not preferable to subjugation by the Yankees, and the association of a negro aristocracy."[46]

Feilden's letters to Julie in early 1865 exhibit both an uncertainty regarding Sherman's movements and an informed opinion regarding the ultimate fate of Charleston and Columbia. On February 10 he wrote, "I think it is probable he [Sherman] may go to Augusta and Columbia first, and then gobble up Charleston afterwards."[47] Three days later Feilden lamented, "The fate of old Charleston is sealed. The enemy encompasses on nearly every side and a very few days more must see us evacuate."[48] The following day he wrote, "My darling, I do not know whether you will ever receive this note, as I am afraid the enemy are moving rapidly on Columbia."[49]

In a letter dated February 28, Feilden related how Union troops had occupied and burned Columbia, and he informed Julie that his most important documents had been destroyed. "I hope Mr. Sass got off safely from Columbia. I am afraid he must have been unable to save the tin box containing the title deeds of our house and my other papers."[50] In a later letter, he spelled out the extent of the loss. "The trunk we lost in Columbia had only one valuable thing in it viz a tin box containing my papers, the title deeds of my house, stocks, bonds, & letters & some valuable records however as you say it is a trifle in these times."[51] Regarding funds for his wife, he instructed Julie to write "to Theodore Wagner and tell him to let you have some, and that I will give him exchange on England or Nassau for the amount. But I hope you be able to get on all right. I expect I [lost all.]"[52] Feilden participated in the long retreat from Charleston to North Carolina, witnessing battles in Cheraw, Averasboro, and Bentonville. His service to the Confederacy ended with the conclusion of hostilities in Goldsboro, North Carolina.

Though Feilden surrendered with the rest of Johnston's forces on April 26, 1865, he still had one small role to play in the conflict. He traveled to Greenville to join Julia around the time that Union troops belonging to Maj. Gen. George Stoneman raided and pillaged the city on May 2, 1865. After the raid Sheriff William T. Shumate attempted to keep order in the city, which was located perilously close to deserters and outlaws (outliers) residing in the nearby mountains. On May 23, 1865, Shumate received word that a band of outliers was approaching Greenville from Anderson District. To protect the town, Shumate organized a posse of Confederate veterans, which "consisted of two or three former colonels and a number of other officers and men," one of whom was Feilden. Armed with "pistols, muskets, and a few hunting pieces," the group moved to a high ridge south of town. Hearing horses approach, the men moved to both sides of the road to ambush the riders. The Confederate veterans opened fire on the horsemen, who actually were Union troops of the Thirteenth Tennessee Cavalry, which had been pursuing Jefferson Davis and had earlier sacked Anderson, South Carolina. The Union cavalrymen returned fire with Spencer repeating rifles, and Feilden and his colleagues fled. The Union troops captured a colonel and two others who, without the intervention of the colonel of the Thirteenth Tennessee, would have been hanged. Feilden later recorded, "Thus endeth my participation in the affairs of the former colonies."[53]

By spring 1866 Henry Wemyss Feilden had spent nearly three and a half years in South Carolina. He had served in defense of the Palmetto State during its most destructive war, and he had met and married the daughter of a prominent South Carolinian. The young couple suffered significant financial losses when Columbia burned, and like many of the state's residents, they began their postwar lives with few resources. To compound matters, they faced the previously inconceivable thought of living in a state controlled to a great extent by Northerners and former slaves.

An obvious challenge for Feilden was to eke out a living for himself and his young wife. He labored as a teamster and attempted to build a business transporting goods to market for those who could afford the service.[54] After this business venture failed, he worked on the railroad. Of this period Feilden wrote that he "tried various methods of catching something, but only succeeded in catching the (confluent) smallpox on the 7th of May 1866. I was dreadfully ill—nearly died. Both of us being in bad health, and finding nothing to be done in America, we determined to return to England."[55] Julie's bad health was probably related to a failed pregnancy. While he was working on the railroad, Julie was "expecting an addition to the family."[56] No child is mentioned in the surviving correspondence, so Julie presumably miscarried.

In late June 1866, Feilden and Julie left Charleston bound for New York aboard the *Emily B. Border*. On July 12 they departed New York aboard the *City of London* and arrived at Feniscowles New Hall, the home of Feilden's father, on July 25, 1866.[57]

Feilden resumed his military service soon after his return. In January 1867 he rejoined the British army as adjutant of the Eighth Battalion of the Lancashire Volunteers. Near the end of 1867, he became paymaster of the Eighteenth Hussars, and in February 1868 he and Julie sailed for India to join his unit. Feilden's time there, however, was short. The heat affected his heart, perhaps as a by-product of previous campaigning, and he was invalided home at the end of 1868.[58]

Feilden's Civil War letters demonstrated interests other than those of a military or financial nature. After returning from India in 1868, he focused much of his attention on his growing penchant for natural science. He participated in a number of ornithological expeditions, including one to the Outer Hebrides during spring 1870 and one to the Farol Islands from May to June 1872.[59] His scientific interests led him to make the acquaintance of Cambridge professor Alfred Newton, who instructed Feilden in research methods and introduced him to other scientists, including Sir Joseph Hooker, who served as president of the Royal Society.[60] Through these early expeditions and relationships, Feilden developed an enhanced knowledge of scientific inquiry and positioned himself to participate in an expedition that would significantly enhance his reputation and define his later career.

While gaining a reputation as a budding naturalist, Feilden remained an officer in the British army, and his duties took him from England for prolonged periods of time. He became paymaster for the Twelfth Brigade, the

Henry W. Feilden in the uniform of the Eighteenth Hussars. He became
paymaster for this regiment in late 1867. The reverse of the photograph
is inscribed "For Miss Murden." It was taken at the photographic
studio of G. H. Hay at 191 Regent Street in London.

Courtesy of the South Carolina Historical Society.

Royal Artillery in 1873, and he served in Malta for fifteen months after his
appointment. During his duty in the Mediterranean, Feilden occupied his
spare time with the study of the region's flora and fauna.[61]

Upon returning from Malta, Feilden received a letter from the Admiralty
informing him that he had been appointed naturalist to the British Arctic
Expedition in search of the North Pole under the command of Sir George S.

Nares.[62] The expedition was the first major British exploration of the Arctic in the thirty years following the loss of the Franklin expedition. This Arctic expedition included HMS *Alert* and HMS *Discovery*, and the ships and crews sailed from Portsmouth on May 29, 1875, with Feilden aboard the *Alert*. The expedition remained in the Arctic until its return seventeen months later in October 1876.[63]

Feilden's contributions to the expedition were considerable. On August 19, 1875, he ascended Cape John Barrow with other members of the expedition and found a stratum of limestone replete with numerous fossils, which was one of his earliest discoveries.[64] Feilden surveyed three hundred miles of coastline in Smith's Sound, made valuable zoological observations, and collected more than two thousand specimens that returned with him to England. He discovered Miocene flora of Grinnell Land, which later appeared in Oswald Heer's *Flora Fossili Arctica*. In 1878 a detailed account of the expedition, titled *Narrative of a Voyage to the Polar Sea during 1875–6*, was published. It included a section titled "Notes on Natural History," which Feilden edited.

Feilden's efforts did not go unnoticed. Nares enthusiastically commended him in his official report of the expedition. Regarding Feilden, Nares wrote, "I will merely state here that no one moment has been lost by this indefatigable collector and observer. He has, by his genial disposition and ready help on all occasions, won the friendship of all, and I feel confident that their Lordships will highly appreciate his valuable services. I am only doing him justice when I state that he has been to this Expedition, what Sabine was to that under the command of Sir Edward Parry."[65] The Lord Commissioners of the Admiralty took note of Nares's report and recommended to the secretary of state for war that Feilden be awarded a CB (Companion of the Order of the Bath) in the Civil Division. They soon discovered, however, that Feilden was ineligible because under the terms of the royal warrant, a paymaster was not eligible for a CB.[66]

Feilden continued his military service for a number of years, but he always found time to partake in scientific endeavors wherever he was stationed. He was sent to South Africa and served with the Sixth (Inniskilling) Dragoons during the First Boer War in 1881.[67] After the conclusion of hostilities, he stayed in Natal to observe bird life. In 1888 he was stationed in the British West Indies and spent a summer studying the fauna of Barbados. He was an active member of the Committee of the British Association for Scientific

Research in the West Indies, and he published in the *Journals of the Geological Leniea* and other scientific publications. Despite his significant scientific accomplishments, Feilden was denied admittance to the Royal Society.[68]

In the early 1890s, Feilden retired from the Royal Army and settled with his wife in Norfolk, where he became a magistrate. He befriended Thomas Coke, the Second Earl of Leicester, and hunted and fished on his estates.[69] He did not, however, retire from scientific endeavors, and he spent time searching for rare birds in Scotland and Scandinavia. This life of leisure continued until 1900, when the Second Boer War began. Not content to remain in England while his country was at war, Feilden became chief paymaster to the Imperial Yeomanry in South Africa. For his service in that conflict, he was mentioned in dispatches, received the Queen's South Africa Medal with three clasps, and finally was awarded the CB (Military Division).[70]

In 1901 Feilden inherited a William and Mary house known as Rampyndene, located in the Sussex village of Burwash, from his uncle John Leyland Feilden. There Feilden became close friends with Rudyard Kipling, who lived nearby.[71] Life at Rampyndene was much quieter for Feilden than his early years. Trevor-Battye describes Feilden as "an elderly gentleman in an old house in the street of a sleepy little Sussex village attending the Bench, working in his garden, writing papers, collecting butterflies, shooting pheasants, catching brook-trout, a father to the village and beloved by all."[72]

Amazingly Feilden offered his service to his country once again in 1914, though he had reached the age of seventy-six. With the outbreak of World War I, Feilden worked for six weeks in the Army Pay Department and later served alongside Kipling as a recruiting officer for Sussex.[73] At the end of the war, Feilden returned to his quiet life with Julie in Burwash.

Julie died in 1920, and Feilden was heartbroken by his wife's passing. Their marriage, though childless, had been a happy one. When looking through her personal possessions, he came upon the letters that he had written to her decades before as a young Confederate officer in South Carolina. Prior to her death, Julie told Feilden that she had kept his correspondence and instructed him to read the letters before destroying them. Feilden followed her instructions, and as he mourned her death, he read the stack of Civil War letters that his wife had neatly bound with twine and carried with her in their travels around the world. Feilden destroyed nearly half of the letters after reading them, "as they were only intended for our two pairs of eyes." Of the rest Feilden wrote, "Still I think some of my letters are of a little historical interest."[74] The following year, in 1921, Feilden joined his wife in death at the age of eighty-three.

Since Feilden's death a number of historians have unsuccessfully attempted to write a history of this fascinating and accomplished Englishman.[75] Feilden's friend Trevor-Battye completed two chapters of a biography before he died, and he provides readers with considerable insight into how other men viewed Feilden. Trevor-Battye's comments mirror those that appear in Kipling's autobiography, *Something of Myself.* Of Feilden, Kipling wrote: "I was honoured till he died by the friendship of a Colonel Wemyss Feilden, who moved into the village to inherit a beautiful little William and Mary house on the same day we came to take over 'Bateman's.' He was in soul and spirit Colonel Newcome; in manner as diffident and retiring as an old maid out of *Cranford;* and up to his eighty-second year could fairly walk me off my feet, and pull down pheasants from high heaven."[76] When asked to describe Feilden by one of Julie's South Carolina relatives, Kipling replied, "He was the gentlest, gallantest English Gentleman who ever walked."[77] Based upon the accounts of those who knew Feilden best, few if any of his contemporaries would have questioned those sentiments.

Upon his death Feilden left behind a significant number of letters and papers. The majority of these are housed in the collections of the South Carolina Historical Society. The bulk of the letters were written by Feilden and addressed to his wife, Julia. These items first came to the attention of the South Carolina Historical Society in a letter dated July 8, 1920, from Feilden to famed Charleston Renaissance author John Bennett (Bennett's wife, Susan D. Adger Smythe Bennett, was one of Julia's nieces). Referring to Bennett as "the literary genius of our family," Feilden asked him if he would like to receive the remaining letters. Feilden forwarded "samples" of the letters to Bennett.[78]

On July 25, 1920, Bennett replied to Feilden's letter and noted that the sample letter was from General Beauregard to Feilden. Bennett, an officer of the South Carolina Historical Society, wrote, "I shall be only too glad, sir, to receive from you any letters and papers you shall choose to think of no interest to your immediate English heirs, but which you think may possess personal or historic interest to us."[79] Feilden died in 1921 prior to forwarding any other wartime correspondence to Bennett.

In 1949 Susan Smythe Bennett became aware of the continued existence of the Feilden letters from Herbert Ravenel Sass, another Charleston author. Sass had been contacted by David Rankin Barbee, an amateur historian and former managing editor of the *Asheville Citizen.* Barbee was interested in Feilden's service and contacted his niece, Mrs. Winifred Feilden, for information. Mrs. Feilden informed Barbee of the Feilden letters and loaned them to him for the purpose of writing a biography of the Englishman. Before returning the letters to Mrs. Feilden, Barbee had the University of Virginia Library microfilm them in case they should be lost or destroyed.

Through David McCord Wright, Julia Feilden's great nephew, officers of the South Carolina Historical Society sought to have Mrs. Feilden donate the letters and papers to the society. She agreed with their request and mailed the items to Wright, who donated them to the society on June 6, 1950. There the Feilden manuscripts joined previously donated Feilden correspondence to Louisa McCord Smythe, Julia Feilden's half-sister, and to John Bennett. Since that time the materials have remained in the society's collections in Charleston.

Another collection of Feilden material can be found at the Hargrett Rare Book and Manuscript Library at the University of Georgia. That collection was compiled and donated by Ella Mae Thornton, Georgia state librarian. Like Barbee, Thornton hoped to publish Feilden's story, but she ultimately gave up and donated her research materials to the Hargrett Library. Materials in that collection include correspondence from Thornton to Mrs. Winifred Feilden regarding Feilden materials. Of greater significance is the typescript copy of Aubyn Trevor-Battye's incomplete biography of Feilden. There are undoubtedly other Feilden materials in the United Kingdom, but his known surviving Civil War letters can be found in the state to which he committed his life and his fortune one hundred and fifty years ago.

THE ADVENTURE BEGINS

March 4, 1863–May 28, 1864

Henry W. Feilden to Mrs. Eliza Feilden
Charleston, March 4, 1863

My dear Aunt,[1]

As I have a chance of sending this letter to England by a private hand, as at present I am quartered in Charleston in a nice house, and reposing comfortably after some very hard times, I think it is only proper to send home a short account of my doings since coming into the Confederacy, and as I can't write to all of my kind friends in England perhaps you would be good enough to pass this epistle on to any whom you think may be interested in its perusal.

Before commencing I may say that the likeness and autograph of Beauregard and the letters of Stonewall Jackson I should like to show you but the same time preserve for me, as I value them highly, and they are perhaps more interesting to me than to those who have not a personal knowledge of these eminent men.[2] Please put them alongside of my other little valuables that you have so kindly taken charge of for me.

I know not exactly where to commence in my late adventures, the rough journal that I keep is alongside of me, but it strikes me that in the multitude of events and scenes that I have passed thro' and witnessed during the last three months, I run a very good chance of doing justice to none of them. You won't care to hear me retail what you can read in Encyclopedias of a voyage across the Atlantic, of the beautiful West Indian Isles, of the people and products. I am tired of going to sea myself, I am sick of seeing new places, and

never did I feel happier than at the present moment when I find myself staying in an elegant mansion in Charleston, with some English friends around
me, and enjoying without a shadow of restraint for a day or two <u>dolce far
niente</u>.[3]

You will want a few words as regards the Blockade running; I ought to be
able to say something about it, as I tried three times and was fired at unmer-
cifully each time. One sees, though, such momentous events pass here daily
that one feels almost ashamed of descending into simple egotism, and an
account of one's own doings.

We sailed from Nassau on the 14th day of January bound for Charleston.
On the 16th we got with our ship into one of those mighty Atlantic gales in
which you think all the winds of heaven have been let loose, and our slight
craft rises on the mountainous billows and then tumbles helplessly in to the
great green valleys of water, then shivers and shakes as if she were not quite
sure whether her wisest course would not be to take a header altogether to the
bottom. Then you can remember and appreciate the words of Horace, "That
man's breast was bound with brass and triple oak who first ventured his frail
bark upon the tempestuous ocean."[4] The gale moderated, though, on the following day as we got nearer the land and away from where the Gulf Stream
with its strong current from the Caribbean Sea was battling and struggling
with a N.E. gale. It was a bitter cold night, that 17th January, so cold that it
seemed impossible to get warm, the teeth shook in one's head, the sleet and
rain poured down, and about one o'clock in the morning it required all the
excitement of seeing in the [hazy] distance the South Carolina shore and
then, shortly after, the low black hull of one of the blockading squadron to
bring one to life again. Then anxiety is pictured in every face. Does she see
us? No! We are past her! Half a mile ahead the Channel look-outs whisper
'two more forward.' We are past them—is the fickle Goddess to shine on us?
The illusion is soon dispelled; a bright flash, a roaring and shrieking monster
passing overhead, and the loud report of a gun, lets us know that the fleet is
awake. The rockets from the squadron illuminating the darkness of the horizon are thrown up on all sides, more guns are fired, more shot pass about,
we are approaching the bar that guards the entrance of Charleston some four
miles or so from Fort Sumpter [*sic*], inside of which the hostile fleet never
venture. Ten minutes would make us safe, but as we approach more ships
are seen lying right in the narrow channel over the bar through which we
must pass. The Captain hesitates. 'I don't think it would be right to venture

there,' he says, gets a little nervous, turns the ship's head round and runs out to sea again followed by a howling pack of cruisers; but speed and good luck and the darkness favor us, and daylight finds us some thirty miles from shore, tossing about again in the Gulf Stream. The same programme is gone through the next night, and then we have to return to Nassau for coal; the Captain is changed, and on the 29th of Jan, we try it again under the new auspices. This time no hesitation. 'Charleston or beach her!' says her skipper, and an hour's run through the North Channel sees us safe under the guns of Fort Beauregard, and the Yankees have again had a useless expenditure of powder and shot, rockets and blue lights.

One's first idea after speaking to the people of the South for a short time, is that they are an intolerable set of boasters, but though such is their character to a superficial observer, yet when one sees more of them, and knows what they say they intend to do, that never will they give in as long as life courses through the veins of a Southern man, that they have beaten the Yankees in every stand-up fight under the most disadvantageous circumstances, one must admire them.

The more I see of the Southern ladies, the more I hear of their actions, of their grand heroism, of their sacrifices, of their sufferings, the more I am lost in astonishment. Words cannot express my admiration of them—as the President justly styled them in his address—"our incomparable women." The war could not have gone on without them; from the delicate lady to the hardy peasant wife they have all sent without a murmur their husbands, sons and those they hold nearest and dearest to the war. They have tilled the fields, they have clothed the troops, they have nursed them in the hours of sickness, and above all they have prayed unceasingly to the great Ruler of the Universe, to the God of Battles, to fight for them and theirs for liberty and freedom, and strange, incomprehensibly strange, would that man be who could deny the hand of an all pervading Providence in the successes of the South, and who doubted for a moment that the Lord of Hosts was fighting on their side. To read the blatant arrogance, the entire dependence upon self, on human force, that emanates from the Northern journals, compares so unfavourably, for instance, with the President's proclamation ordering Friday next to be set aside as a day of solemn fast and humiliation, and thanksgiving, throughout the entire Confederacy. The issue of this great struggle I can foresee; though blood may be poured out like water, though many tracts of country may be fertilized—as around Richmond—with dead men's bodies, though the

North may bring three million of men into the field, the South shall never be vanquished, for as a people they rely on God, and that nerves their arms for still more deadly strife. I am digressing, however, from the plain historical thread of my story.

On the 31st Jan, the Ironclads went out from Charleston and damaged the Yankee fleet considerably. Of course we were all much interested in the event, and the capture of a ship of war carrying 9 guns up one of the rivers the day before raised the spirits of the Charlestonians.[5] I stayed about a week longer in the place, visiting the famous localities, making friends and enjoying Southern hospitality, and then started for Richmond bearing with me letters from England of introduction to some of the principal men, and further fortified with an extra budget from my Charleston friends.

The rail journey of 500 miles to Richmond is very long and very tedious as you may imagine; the rails and rolling stock are in very bad order owing to no importation through the blockade of materials, and the speed of the trains has to be greatly moderated to prevent accidents. However I arrived in the capital of the Confederacy on the 15th of February.

The city is one great camp, indeed the whole country is, everyone is a soldier, and everyone is trying for military distinction. The demand for appointments as officers is enormous, so many thousands have extraordinary claims on the Executive that it is impossible to do one half of them justice. I saw at once that my chance of getting a military appointment was very small, and indeed I could not expect otherwise. I paid a visit to the Secretary of War,[6] presented my letters to him and other influential men, was told that if possible something would be given to me, and I received from all of them that kindness and courtesy so distinctive in the Southern gentleman. A good number of Englishmen live here, prior to this, come out to this country, and I believe with very rare exceptions they have been obliged to serve as volunteers in the Army or on some General's staff until they have proved themselves fit for something. I thought of doing the same, when the other day I was gratified by the Secretary of War informing me that the President had appointed me Captain in the C.A. and Asst. Adjt. General, with the choice of going to any Department I chose. I chose Charleston as we daily expect the whole force of the Yankee Armada to be thrown against this portion of the State, and I am now here as Asst. Adjt. Gen. in the Inspecting Department, waiting for the fight, with a very good position, good pay, and above all quarters with some English gentlemen connected with the Blockade business, in a beautifully furnished house and with an excellently provided table, rather different from what we have been living on for the last month or so—coffee made out of rye, or else water, crackers and old bacon or tough meat. The people of the South are suffering very much from want of good food. In all my undertakings connected with this voyage I have been fortunate, very fortunate; I hope I am grateful for it.

I find it very difficult to carry on a connected story; I am so pleased with my meeting with the celebrated Stonewall Jackson, so anxious to let you know about him, that I cannot write any further without bringing him to your notice.

I brought a box of goods for him from a gentleman in Nassau, and the General asked me to come to his camp and see him when I was in Richmond.[7] I left the city one morning about 7 o'clock, and about 10 landed at a station distant some 8 or 9 miles from Jackson's—or, as his men call him, 'Od [sic] Jack's'—camp. A heavy fall of snow had covered the country for some time before to the depth of a foot, and had formed a crust over the Virginian mud, as famous in this country as our [Baleclava] mixture. To crown this, the day before had been mild and wet, and the day I went to camp the rain came down with redoubled fury, as if it was proud of showing the earth's dirty face, and dissipating the white mantle of snow. You may imagine, sooner than I can describe, my morning's walk. I stumbled through mud, I waded through creeks, I passed through pine woods. Wet through I got into camp about 2 o'clock and made my way to a small house—the General's Head Quarters. I wrote my name, gave it to an orderly and was immediately told to walk in.

The General rose and greeted me warmly—he is so simple and unaffected in his ways and habits. I cannot illustrate this better than by telling exactly what he did—he took off my wet overcoat with his own hands, made up the fire, brought wood for me to put my feet on to keep them warm whilst my boots were drying, and then began asking me a great many questions on many subjects. We had a very pleasant conversation till dinnertime when we went out and joined the members of his Staff. At dinner the General said grace in a fervent, quiet manner that struck me much; there is something about his face that you cannot help reverencing. He is a tall man, well and powerfully built but thin, with a brown beard and hair; his mouth is very determined-looking, the lips thin and compressed firmly together; his eyes are blue, dark, with a keen and searching expression in them; his age is 38 and he looks about 40. I expected to see an old, untidy-looking man, and was surprised and pleased with his looks.

After dinner I returned to his room and he again talked to me for a long time. The servant came in and took his mattress out of a cupboard and laid it on the floor. As I rose to retire the General said, 'Captain, there is plenty of room in my bed, I hope you will share it with me.' I thanked him very much for his courtesy, but said goodnight, and slept in a tent, sharing the blankets of one of his aides-de-camp. In the morning at breakfast I noticed the General said grace before the meal with the same fervor as I had remarked before. An hour or two after it was time for me to return to the Station.

This time I had a horse, and I turned up to the General's Head-quarters to bid adieu to him. His little room was vacant so I stopped in and stood before the fire; I noticed my great coat stretched before the fire on a chair. Shortly after the General entered the room. I was saying goodbye, and as I finished he said, 'Captain, I have been trying to dry your great coat, but am afraid I have not succeeded very well.'

That little act shows the man, does it not! To think that in the midst of his duties, with the cares and responsibilities of a vast army on his shoulders, with the pickets of a hostile army almost within sight of his Quarters, he found time to think of and to carry out these little acts of thoughtfulness! He is the darling of his men, the pride of them all; they never seem to tire of talking of him. I am told by officers of his staff that if ever a man breathed who was perfectly pure and virtuous it was Jackson; no one seems to think that he could do a wrong as a Christian. I believe his moral character, like that of General Lee, is spotless, as far as a human man's can be.

Another gentleman who had been a considerable time on Jackson's staff and accompanied him in several of his battles, told me some curious anecdotes about him. He said that one day, in the midst of a fierce battle, he rode up with some news to Jackson who was sitting on a horse watching apparently the discomfiture of the enemy. As he approached nearer he perceived the General's eyes were fixed not on the flying foe, but earnestly gazing up into the skies, his lips moving and one hand stretched up as in the attitude of adoration. He said he felt it would have been almost impious to intrude on such a scene; he waited quietly until the General noticed him and calmly received the information he brought. The gentleman remarked, 'If ever I saw a man pray, Jackson was praying then.' He was not the only person who told me this; another Aide said that in the midst of a battle he had seen a grandeur and majesty in Jackson's eye and appearance, and that it made him feel afraid to speak to him or disturb him.[8]

I must stop telling you of this favourite of mine; I must merely add that he is a man of great endurance, he drinks nothing stronger than water, never uses tobacco or stimulants, has been known to ride for three days and nights at a time, and if there is any labour to be done he takes his share of it.

My dear Aunt, I began my letter at 10 this evening, I look at my watch and find it is quarter past 2. I have my duties to attend to tomorrow and shall only have 3 ½ hours' sleep, so adieu for tonight.

March 5th

I have been at Church today, the Governor of S. Carolina[9] has proclaimed it as a day of prayer. I enclose you this morning's paper, it may interest you to read the leading article. I am off tomorrow with the Inspector General to examine some troops at Secessionville, a town some ten miles from here.[10] I'll add a little to this budget as long as I can, but at any moment we may be called out to fight, so I feel glad to have a long letter in readiness in case anything in the shape of a Yankee bullet comes in contact with my head. I think it is very little use explaining or attempting to demonstrate the great military manoeuvres now going on, as events change so rapidly here one's ideas on every subject. For some time we had an idea that there was a peace party in the North sufficiently strong to detach some of the States, and to battle against Lincoln and his unconstitutional acts, but the passing of the Conscription Act and Finance Bills by the Yankee Congress,[11] thus giving Lincoln the power of an autocrat for another year, has dashed these hopes to the ground, and the South is prepared to battle on a more gigantic scale this Spring than heretofore. One cannot help being struck with the prodigious energies and power of the Yankees; defeated and over-defeated, the hydra-headed monster reappears in larger numbers, and with increased material of war. Their resources are tremendous, but the Conscription Act, is, I think, like the gambler staking his all on the last card; if it fails the North is ruined. The Emancipation scheme has fallen flat; it is nonsense, the slaves don't want to rise, and won't, unless under the pressure of Northern bayonets.[12] Did you notice Gen. Hunter has been conscripting all the wretched negroes that they have beguiled from the plantations into his command, and forcing them to bear arms as soldiers![13]

I am glad to see you all in England appreciate the Yankees. They care no more for the negro and abolition than an Andaman Islander does; they thought they could raise a servile war, but they have failed signally. If they thought by murdering all the negroes they could ruin the South, these Yankees would do it.[14]

I see little chance now, though I thought differently some time ago, of the war ending this summer—until Lincoln retires from office—but it cannot be carried on in its present prodigious form, unless the Yankees meet with some great success, sufficient to turn them mad in the North. Richmond, Vicksburgh [*sic*] and Charleston are the points to be assailed; the taking of any or all of them will prolong the war. If the Yankees are repulsed at these three points surely they must see their madness in carrying on the war.

March 10

I am finishing off this scrawl as the gentleman who is taking this to England leaves tomorrow. We are living here very comfortably and enjoying ourselves, although every day we expect to be attacked by the Yankee Armada. The weather here is lovely, the camellias are in full bloom in the gardens, and many other flowers. The beautiful cardinal birds sit on the boughs of the trees and awake me at the open window in the morning, and the people are the kindest I ever met. . . . If I can only get through this war without being wounded or shot, I shall have been fortunate. I do think getting on the staff of such a man as Beauregard is enough to make one pleased—and being made the Asst. Adjt. Gen. . . .

Your ever affectionate nephew,
H. Wemyss Feilden

Henry W. Feilden to "Phil"
Charleston, April 16, 1863

My dear Phil, I have already sent you a line or two previously I hope you may have received them. I have not received a letter but one from [Henty] since I came into the Confederacy. I have written a very large number home. Devil take the Yanks, if they burn my letters at New York. I never was more amused in my life than reading this morning on the Telegram boards the accounts given by the New York papers, of the crushing & ignominious hiding we gave the far famed Monitor fleet here <u>outside</u> Charleston harbour on the 7th.[15] In it those infernal liars say it was a great success that they entered Charleston harbour, a most deliberate lie. They never came within a half a mile of the first obstructions across the mouth of the harbour. They say that 500 guns played on the "<u>Keokuk</u>,"[16] and on the iron clad fleet. To show you the fallacy of that only about a third of the guns in Fort Sumter played on them. Sumter is a pentagon like this:

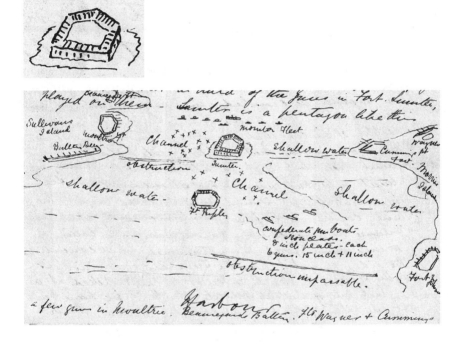

Feilden sketched this diagram in a letter of April 16, 1863, in which he asserted that the enemy ironclads did not enter Charleston Harbor as it was claimed in New York newspapers. "They never got further than you see them in my plan, and if they had come inside they would only have fallen a prey to those ready to receive them for all those crosses represent torpedoes to galvanic batteries on shore which blow them sky high when they get in."

Courtesy of the South Carolina Historical Society.

They never got further than you see them in my plan, and if they had come inside they would only have fallen a prey to those ready to receive them for all those crosses represent torpedoes to galvanic batteries on shore which blow them sky high when they get in. I believe Fort Sumter bears on its walls & casemates the heaviest weight of metal that was ever hurled against a fleet, and the weight of metal it is able to throw from the face parallel to the Channel will upset if it can't break any Ironclad that human ingenuity ever invented. The Yankees may say that the <u>Keokuk</u> was their worst ship. If so it was very strange that they put her in foremost, and that she was the only one that ventured within half a mile of the front of Sumter, and in 5 minutes after Col. Rhett[17] concentrated the fire of one battery on her, she was broken up. I don't believe now in the invulnerability of the monitors. As for the Ironsides[18] she is no better than our Warrior or Blackprince,[19] and any of the ships built on that plan would be crushed in a quarter of an hours fire, if they came within half a mile of the weight of metal that can be thrown from Sumter. I am convinced that artillery will hold the day against the Iron ships. It is all very well firing at a target with one gun, but I should like to see where that target would be if 30 or 40 guns of the same caliber were fired instantaneously at it. For instance we can [take] this for an example of a battery of 20 15 inch guns, fired simultaneously and concentrated on the side of a ship like the Ironsides or Warrior, is 8000 lbs of iron, or nearly 4 ton of metal, impelled at a very high rate of initial velocity. Nothing we have built can stand such a discharge. I don't think the Yankees can capture Charleston do what they will—and no stone is left unturned, that military, naval, & engineering skill can command to render the place impregnable. In 6 weeks more the unhealthy season will come on, and the scoundrels will die on this coast like rotten sheep. Richmond is given up, that attempt to travel to Jordan . . . is given up. Vicksburgh & Port Hudson are safe.[20] They seem to be concentrating all their strength to smash Joe Johnstone & Bragg in Tennessee & Tullahoma.[21] Gen. Johnstone is a great man & I have hopes that he will be too many for them. In another month nearly the whole of Abraham's army will have a right to disband. That is the critical moment. If they take their rights, if they disband, if Abraham cannot carry out his Conscription Bill the war ends. If neither of these things happen, then the war will enter into its greatest & bloodiest form & peace can only come with the complete exhaustion of one side. Never, never, never can the South compromise. The whole population, loathe the Yankees with a more bitter hatred than Poles have to the Muscovites, Lombardy to the Austrians; they know that the fate of Poland in chains would be preferable to the South overcome by the Yankees. We have heard them, the leaders of the administration express their sentiments on the platforms in New York, that now Union was impossible, & that the Southern States as Brute Butler[22] expresses it, must be brought back to Washington, bound in chains to the bright car of victory. The Southern people know what they have to expect. Everyone is cognizant of it from the President to the poorest backwoodsman in Arkansas; & therefore fight more desperately than any people ever did before. However long the war may last, the Southern people cannot be beaten. The food question is a grave one, certainly our worst, if ever we are conquered it will be for want of food & transport. But the administration is alive to this, and the country is awake and this harvest will with the blessings of providence be a bounteous one. So much has been & so much is being planted. Don't believe the lies the Yankees tell about the attack on Charleston. In brief it amounted to this. In two hours & a half engagement, the vaunted Ironclad navy that was to [run] down Sumter with their prows, was whipped, the <u>Keokuk</u> sunk, the frigate Ironsides seriously damaged. One monitor was disabled and towed off to Port Royal & the other I. hurt. They did not dismount a gun. They did not kill a man on our side, though some were killed through accidents & the Forts received no more damage than was fully repaired the next day. I think I shall have tired you out with these military views of mine, but I know the old soldier is strong in you, as well as myself. The next page is to be filled with my views on business, cotton and monetary transactions in general.

Now for the dethroned hoary headed monarch, King Cotton. The old rascal will hold his head high for many a long day though he is in trouble. The facts I have to lay before you is this. The crop in hand throughout the states is day by day decreasing from destruction, waste, from age, exposure & climate and export through the blockade. At the beginning of the year, or if I am correct last autumn the crop throughout the states was estimated at 3 millions and a half. I now estimate it at 3 millions of bales, of which the Government hold 500,000 for the security of their cotton loan. Another 500,000 is held by European merchants and the remainder two millions by the planters. This year about 300,000 bales will be planted at the outside perhaps less. As the spirit of patriotism, is strong amongst the planters, and instead of growing as much cotton as the legislature allows they will probably plant less. Therefore whenever peace comes the crop must be small, & if the war continues for any number of years, the crop here will be reduced to the minimum and the question arises whether the negroes won't be run off in such numbers as to prevent for many years the raising of an average crop. As for the Sea Islands crop that is knocked on the head at any rate for another year. No crop of Sea Islands has been raised since Hilton Head, Port Royal & the Sea Islands were occupied by the Yankees in '61.[23] Every bale in this country has been bought up by strong English & French hands and the amount in the aggregate is very small. And if the Yankees made peace tomorrow as it is now too late to get a crop put in the ground of this kind of cotton. Besides all the plantations have been destroyed and the negroes run off. Therefore there is no chance of Sea Island cotton going down in the market come what may. During the last 2 months middling cotton has run up one hundred per cent. I have seen upland sold here lately at 45 cents per lb. At the same time exchange on England is sold at 500 % premium, which renders cotton cheap if bought in bills on England. You must not suppose that the present rate of exchange presents any fair criterion of the depreciation of the paper currency. Exchange here is a fancy class of goods. There is very little to sell, and when parties sell it they know that the buyers are necessitated to have it, and force up the price to an enormous rate. I have a firm conviction that the South will be triumphant and 6 months after peace exchange will fall very greatly and the fortunes made by the holders of this paper currency will be enormous. I have based these conclusions on long and diligent enquiry into this matter, and feel convinced that I am right. On this basis I rested several letters which I wrote to Raynsford in regard to selling my share as Collie's venture. I know not whether he ever received them or if he was able to manage it. The venture has been most fortunate. I know a gentleman here sold a £1000 for £5000. If I could get a certificate from Collie that I held £1000 stocks I could sell it here at an enormous price today. I was offered $150,000 for my share. I have written to Raynsford this very day per underground railroad about sending me out a certificate. Goodbye old fellow, in haste.

Yours very sincerely
H. W. Feilden

Travel pass issued to Miss Julia McCord:

HEAD-QUARTERS
Department of S.C., Ga., and Fla.
Charleston, S.C. June 16, 1863

Miss McCord has permission to pass from Charleston to Greenville S. Ca. without interference.

Recommended of Maj. Gen. Sam Jones
H. W. Feilden, A.A.G.

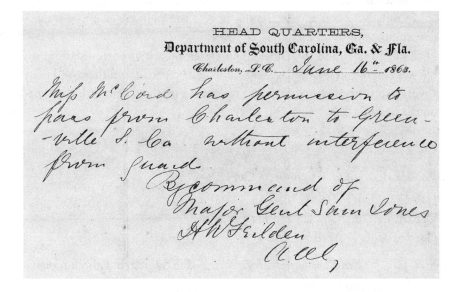

Travel pass issued to Miss Julia McCord and signed by Captain Feilden on June 16, 1863, which may have been the day they first met.

Courtesy of the South Carolina Historical Society.

Fragment of a letter dated April 20, 1864, from Henry W. Feilden in Charleston, S.C., to Miss Julia McCord:

. . . The General[24] sent for me however before he left introduced me to General Jones[25] and told him that I was the officer he had selected to remain with him. On saying good-bye he told me that he wished me to remain here for the present as long as he was only temporarily assigned to the army in North Carolina; but if he was relieved from this command (Charleston) he would most certainly send for me to return to his staff. This was very kind of him I thought, and I am much obliged to him for it is indeed pleasing to see one in his position so careful in regard to the wishes of those with whom he is associated. There is not another General in the service as thoughtful as our dear General is. Before leaving he sent for all in the office, privates as well as officers and said goodbye to them. There is no doubt he has got the best military head of any man in this Confederacy and if he only gets a chance he will make his mark on the enemy this spring and summer.

I firmly believe that we are going to beat the Yankees terribly and that a few months must end the war.

I will come round the house about eleven oclock tomorrow darling and see you before you leave. Have you still made up your mind to go on Friday. I will have your passport made out for you so that you cannot be bothered on the [journey].

Travel pass issued to Miss Julia McCord:

HEAD-QUARTERS
Department of S.C., Ga., and Fla.
Charleston, S.C. April 21, 1864

Miss Julia McCord has permission to proceed to Savannah without molestation from guards or sentries.

By Command of Maj. Gen. Saml. Jones
H. Weymss Feilden
Capt & A.A.G.

Henry W. Feilden to Miss Julia McCord,
c/o Robert Habersham,[26] Savannah, Ga.

Charleston S.C., April 29, 1864

My darling you must think me a perfect ingrate not having answered all your dear kind letters, but if you only knew how I am worked you would excuse me. I have been writing since 8 till 5 o.c. and have merely taken one hours rest to eat dinner and send a few lines to you. I am so glad Mr. Sass[27] has written to you. You will get his letter tonight or tomorrow and I saw Herbert [*Sass*][28] address a letter to you yesterday so darling you will hear something about us everyday. I am quite determined when I get relieved from this duty to take 30 days leave and spend it with you in Greenville. I heard from Genl Beauregard today. He is well. He said nothing of my joining him but gave the directions to prepare some work for him [*Report of the operations Siege of Charleston. H.W.F.*] which will oblige me to stay here. I don't think I have any chance of getting to Virginia with him for sometime though I flatter myself that he has too much regard for me to debar me from sharing the privations & dangers of the field with him. I know dearest you think differently with me on this point so I will not make you unhappy by talking or writing any more on the subject. You may rest assured that I shall just do what I am ordered without grumbling, and it is more than probable I shall have to remain in Charleston for a long time yet. You won't object to this I know.

You must excuse me not sending you an answer to your nice letter which I received the day before yesterday and liked so much. I cannot at this moment collect my ideas sufficiently to answer all the questions as you would like them answered. I have only one thing to say and that is you must have no doubts of my love for you darling. You must think me cold and inattentive not writing to you everyday, not divining all the questions that you intend to ask and thus save you the trouble of having to put them on paper. But I can assure you dearest Julia that I would not thus neglect you if I did not consider the claims of the office prior to anything that gives me pleasure. Do forgive me and write often. I will repay you for all when I have time to devote myself to you and with best love believe me to remain

Your ever affectionate
H. W. Feilden

P.S. Don't repeat to Herbert what I wrote about Harriet Lowndes.[29] I will tell you sometime what I mean. I have not called on Mrs. Elliott.[30] She is in town. I wrote her a note saying my business prevented me from calling.

☘

Henry W. Feilden to General P. G. T. Beauregard

Charleston, April 29, 1864

General

I have the honor to acknowledge the receipt of your letter of the 25th inst directing me how you wished the report of the occupation of Morris Island to conclude. I will endeavour to carry out your instructions to the best of my ability. I have had a clean copy made by Mr. Hincks[31] of the original report and was retaining it for General Jordan's[32] return, as I should like it to be looked over by him.

It will be I am afraid some time before I can conclude the report as you desire for I can assure you the office work does not seem to have decreased since your departure, with the exception of Mr. Gilchrist[33] attending to the court martials. I am the only A.A.G.[34] and though in the office from 8 A.M. till 12 P.M. with the exception of dinner hour I cannot get through all the work as I should desire to see it accomplished. I merely mention this to plead as an excuse for me if you think I am dilatory in attending to your instructions. But I will promise you not to delay a moment when I am relieved by General Jones's staff. I trust that you are in good health and that you are collecting a good command around you. The greater portion of Hagoods Brigade has left and I will endeavor to hurry up all the detached and detailed men which can be collected. You are doubtless aware of this however. I will not occupy your valuable time by further correspondence but conclude by saying if you can find a position for me on your staff which doubtless you have had to remodel I shall be very glad to occupy it. Of course if you consider my service more useful here I am content to remain. I find General Jones a very nice gentleman and get on very well with him.

General if half the good wishes and prayers that I hear breathed for your success come to pass you will indeed be fortunate. I can assure you that your loss from Charleston is deeply regretted. Believe me with respect to remain

Your obednt Servant
H. W. Feilden

Private

P.S. From conversation with deserters and reports of our scouts I am inclined to believe that the enemy are rapidly depleting their forces on this coast as well as Fla. All accounts agree that they are off <u>for Va.</u>

Henry W. Feilden to Miss Julia McCord
Charleston, April 30, 1864

Your nice long letter of the 29th received this evening. I have got through most of my work and now take up my pen to scratch off a few lines to you before going to bed and I shall send this note down to the mail agent by a messenger in the morning for the Post Office has closed long ago. I am sure dearest you will look very pretty and beautiful to me, any way that you arrange your hair but I expect myself that I should like it best long, however cutting your hair short will do it a great deal of good and make it grow better in future. I will endeavour to come down to Savannah for a day and have an inspection of this new fashioned method of arranging hair. Don't be alarmed about my overworking myself. The business of the office is already decreasing. The pressure arose from the great number of changes that were made in the troops belonging to this Department. Some are going to Va. some to N. Ca. and others to Tenn., but I expect when that is over we shall have a very quiet summer. The enemy have been shelling Fort Sumter all day both from the land batteries on Morris I. and the Monitors, but the telegraph cable is not working so up to this time we have no news from the Fort. I am waiting up to receive the report. I don't suppose any harm has been done, though I am told the Yankees made the dust and [bricks] fly in the poor old Fort. I shall answer your letter regularly tomorrow but the truth is that several of my clerks are sitting writing round me and I don't care for reading your letter when other people are [talking] around. So you must be content with this scrawl and expect a nice letter from me on Monday.

I heard from Genl Beauregard yesterday. He told me of a lot of things he wanted me to do but said nothing about my rejoining him. Indeed he gave me work to do that will detain me in Charleston even after I have finished my duties with General Jones. So for the present you need have no fear of my leaving for Va. I liked your letter received this evening very much. Don't mind what your practical sister says but cross and recross your letters as much as you like dearest. You may rest assured that they are valued by me. I will tell you when I see you about Harrie Lowndes and my reasons for not liking her. You will be astonished at what I tell you, but please keep this a secret and don't mention it on any account to Herbert.

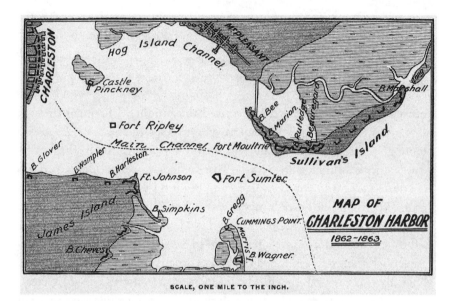

Map published in *Views of Fort Sumter* (1899) by John Johnson, who was the chief Confederate engineer at Fort Sumter. He was one of five members of the board appointed by General Beauregard to compile a "military history of the siege of Charleston, S.C." Captain Feilden acted as recorder for the board.

Courtesy of the South Carolina Historical Society.

You can hardly understand what a pleasure it is to me receiving your letters. They come at night and I put them on one side until I have waded through all the official letters and written & answered all that require immediate attention, then your letter lies before me and makes me go through my work with redoubled vigour, for I am buoyed up with the thoughts of reading and rereading it before going to bed. I really don't care one bit about going to the Brewsters. I have not been there since you left & don't know when I shall go. The old gentleman[35] comes daily to the office and asks me as often to come up to tea and "call upon Annie." He is a vulgar old fellow and I don't covet his acquaintance very much, especially as he comes into the office during my busiest hours and occupys [*sic*] my time with his horrid cases.

You have heard I suppose that Mrs. Elliott is in town. I have not as yet found time to call upon her but wrote her a few lines today, to say that I intended doing so the first moment I had to spare. I do hope they will be able to do something for her children. As for my ugly photographs I don't think I care for one of them and you shall have the burning of them all.

I think I can arrange in a short time to get down to Savannah for a day or so. I should much like to hear Bishop Elliott[36] preach and your idea of my coming on a Saturday and returning on a Monday would suit exactly. Will you give my kind regards to your sister and thank her for me for her kind invitation. I shall not be at all alarmed about coming into a house with seven ladies in it when you are there to take charge of me. I have never written to Miss Malvina.[37] Is it not shameful. I have begun two or three times and then tore my letters up as I never liked them. I am almost afraid she will take a dislike to me on your account. And now I must conclude this very unsatisfactory letter darling. There is very little in it and it is hardly worth calling an answer to your long delightful letter which I have only half read and intend taking home to finish before going to sleep. Don't be afraid dearest of my love to you fading. You are so good & kind I am only afraid I don't show my love to you sufficiently, but wait till I go up to Greenville with you and I shall be as attentive to you as you can desire and now my love good-night and believe me to remain your fond

H. W. Feilden

What name have you decided to call me?

Letter from Henry W. Feilden to Miss Julia McCord
in Savannah, parts of which are missing:

Charleston, May 6, 1864

. . . Cousin Frank Miles[38] he is a gentleman that I like very much. Do you know that I have been always most polite to the Miles' in any business that I have had with them, because they were connections of yours. Any one who had anything to do with you I could not help liking.

So you have quite made up your mind to call me Harry. It is a very pretty name, though they always give that name to wild boys in story books. I hope however that I will turn out one of the exceptions that prove the rule. You can have no idea how delightful your letters are to me, but never force yourself to write. . . .

[PORTION MISSING]

By the way I must tell you that I went out to a little fete yesterday. Mr. Bull had a picnic at Ashley Hall.[39] The General was invited with his staff. He was too unwell to go but he insisted on my going so I rode over there in the afternoon and I spent rather a pleasant time. I daresay there were some 70 or 80 of us present. We had a very good band and a good deal of dancing and eating. I picked up a rather nice girl there a Miss Annie Heyward.[40] Her father she told me lived near Pocotaligo. She told me she thought she knew you. I have not been round to old Brewster again. He paid me another visit this morning and said he expected me not to miss the strawberries, which I shan't most certainly.

Is it not dreadful to think that all day yesterday when I was at the picnic our brave fellows in Va. were fighting throughout the whole long day.[41] Again today Lee has been engaged with Grant fighting fiercely. We know no particulars except that the news is cheering. God grant that we may beat them, but though I feel very sanguine and very hopeful yet I cannot help thinking and praying for those devoted men who are now pouring out their heart's blood for us like water on the banks of the Rapidan. It is almost too dreadful to contemplate. I would not mind so much if I was there myself and could run the risk of being killed or wounded, but at this distance off to read the telegrams, and know that at the very same moment battle is raging is dreadful.

And now darling pet I must say good night to you. This is a dull stupid letter I know, but it will be better than nothing, so goodbye dearest Julie and believe me to remain ever

Your loving
Harry

*Fragment of a letter, Charleston, May 9, 1864,
from Henry W. Feilden to Miss Julia McCord:*

. . . you may depend darling that I shall be overjoyed to see you at the depot. You will find me dreadfully bashful when I get to Savannah. I know the eyes of love are proverbially blind, and you have doubtless been telling your sisters and nieces that I am a wonderful character, and when they see the "Simon Pure"[42] they will be very much disappointed.

As soon as I can get a spare day I am going to Mr. Russells[43] and exchange the books I got, for I am sure you won't like them and I will get something nice for your library.

I am very sorry that Mrs. Cheves's[44] feelings should have been shocked in the manner you describe; it must have been very painful to her, but as you say it is the fashion to be as hard hearted as possible nowadays. And we get so accustomed to dine with a friend one day & bury him the next that the generality of people think very little about death and eternity nowadays.

When the war is over and persons and families can sit down calmly and contemplate their losses then the community will become aware of those who have gone from amongst us never to return. At present the excitement of war is too great for any of us to appreciate the terrible losses in valuable lives that this country has suffered.

You are quite right darling about "Macaria."[45] It is not to be read through by anyone I think. I have tried desperate hard but got caught in the stars, and could go no further. For goodness sake don't try and wade through the book because I sent it to you.

Is Bishop Elliott going to preach on Sunday next?

Henry W. Feilden to Miss Julia McCord
Charleston, May 19, 1864

Darling I received your letter last night and I send you a few lines just to show that I have not forgotten you. But I am too busy to write you anything more than a note.

We are so short of men that all the clerks of the Department, Head Quarters included (Herbert as well) have had muskets put in their hands and have been sent off to man the batteries on James Island. Consequently I have no one to assist me, last night I had very little sleep and again the same thing is likely to occur tonight.

I was out at 4 o.c. this morning and rode over to James Island & back 14 miles before breakfast in order to get Herbert his breakfast so you see I have not deserted him quite.

The news from Va. is very cheering. Genl Beauregard has reopened the line via Petersburgh & we are now in direct communication with Richmond which is a great comfort to us all.

I had a telegram from Mr. Sass this evening. He is in Columbia and will be down on Saturday.

You must not think me inattentive dearest. You know I love you more than all the world beside and would not behave in this manner to you if it were not that the crisis is so urgent and demands every man's whole attention.

I am so glad to hear that your cold is better. Do take care of yourself. Please give my kind regards to Miss Mary[46] and remember me kindly to all the others. I regret extremely that I was not able to stay longer in Savannah. I liked your family so much, what I saw of them.

Col. Lay has come back from Florida. He is in raptures about that place we bought down there.[47] I will tell you in another letter what he says about it. Don't think I would ever go to live in such a pagan country as Fla. or take anyone I loved to such a place. You shall live wherever you like my darling. And so with fondest love believe me to remain in great haste

Your ever affectionate
Harry

Henry W. Feilden to Miss Julia McCord
Charleston, May 20, 1864

Your nice letter of the 19th just received darling. You can have no idea what a pleasure they are to me after the labours of the day are over and my sole enjoyment of the day is to answer them because I think it gives you a little pleasure to receive mine.

I am glad to think you went to church to return thanks for our great successes to the Giver of them. I have not been able to do so myself but in my own heart I have done it frequently. Today we received a New York paper through a Flag of Truce. It is full of the most extravagant falsehoods. A copy of the summary was sent to Savannah so you will see it in the Papers tomorrow morning. On the strength of this news the deluded Yankees outside Charleston fired a salute of 100 guns the day before yesterday.

I found your brother Ned [*Parker*][48] extremely agreeable when I traveled with him in the cars coming here. Miss Nina Moses[49] is the cousin of a clerk who was in my office. The young man had gone off on 60 days sick furlough before the note came so that he was doubtless at her graduation and made her heart glad. I am so forgetful that I have never sent yet the "Lays of Ancient Rome."[50] The fact is I am nearly distracted at having sent off all my clerks. Poor Herbert [*Sass*] wrote me a sad letter this evening saying that he was quite sick from having to stand sentry during the heat of the day. [*on James Island*] I am very sorry to hear it but though it may seem very unkind in his estimation I did not order him back as he requested me, because there is a right and a wrong way of doing things. If he is sick he ought to go to the Doctor and he would send him to the city. I have no right to make any distinction in his favor and consequently have not answered his note. I am afraid he will think me very cruel but though I am as fond of him as if he were my own brother yet I cannot do what is not right. I would not do it for my own brother. I tell you this because Herbert may think me unkind and may tell you so hereafter. But though I am very sorry for him and would gladly take his place if I could. Yet duty must go first especially in these times. You know dearest I would not do an unkind thing to him but you know also I feel conscientiously in these matters. Oh! that we could have peace and happiness once more, darling. How happy we should then be together. I can scarcely realize it even in my thoughts.

If Savannah agrees with you darling you ought to stay there. The company of your sisters and nieces will do you good after your long dull stay in Greenville. I have never received a line yet from Miss Malvina. I am very sorry about it. If she only knew how I was worked here and had as bad a headache as I have tonight she would not blame me for not writing oftener. I wish very much darling you could come and assist me in some of my work. It would make it very agreeable I can assure you and I think it would then become a matter of pleasure and not of duty.

I don't expect you will enjoy your day on the Ogeechee[51] very much if those sandflies that we made the acquaintance of at Bonaventure[52] have any relatives on the plantation that you are going to. Goodnight darling, and God bless you my own dear love and believe me to remain

Your ever affectionate
H. W. Feilden

Kind regards to the ladies & Miss Mary.

Henry W. Feilden to Miss Julia McCord
Charleston, May 23, 1864

My own darling you must think me very unkind and careless not writing to you for two days. My reasons are that on Saturday night it is no use writing as there is no mail agent on the cars for Savannah on Sunday. Last night I was away down at the front on James Island and only returned this morning dead tired. The enemy landed on James Island yesterday morning and we had a skirmish with them driving them to their gunboats. They are at it again this afternoon. I am not afraid of their effecting anything but they keep me nervous and uneasy. We had a nice little force on James Island and I was anxiously longing for them to attack us last night but they did not give us the chance. We had five wounded none killed yesterday. The guns are booming away at Secessionville as I write but you know that is no novelty in Charleston.

I had a few lines from Miss Malvina today. She is very far from well. She says she has not heard from you since I was in Savannah. I can't help feeling ashamed of my conduct to you dearest. It seems so unkind. I do long to be all in all to you, to attend to your every wish and want, and hundreds of plans that I propose for and about you are nipped in the bud because I have not time in which to carry them out. But when I have a little time to myself I will endeavour to make all this up. I don't suppose there ever was a newly engaged man who behaved so badly to his darling as I have done and I really feel that I am shamefully inattentive to you, but do forgive me Julia. All last night whilst I was sitting out on the ground, I thought of you darling and felt happy to be able to render my small mite in defence of your country. If the Yankees had only come we would have made them suffer terribly.

I saw a letter yesterday from DuBose Porcher[53] to Mr. Sass. He is engaged to be married to a young lady Miss Marion Parker I think. He seemed so happy and was asking Mr. Sass where he could get a wedding ring made. You see he is better off than we are darling. He is not in the army and can stay at home and be domestic on his plantation. I do wish and long dearest that I could ask and think about our getting a wedding ring made but I think it would be foolish to do so until we see how this fighting ends in Va. You will trust me dearest won't you to love you ever as I do now, whatever happens. If I am alive you will be protected darling and have some one who will think of nothing else for the rest of his life but making you happy.

I never think of you darling but as my own dear wife and the knowledge of your love keeps me up altogether. I really am quite hard worked, and almost wish that I could get ill so that I could have an excuse for leaving my office and return with you to Greenville.

I am going to have my will made pet in which I shall leave you everything for you are the only one in the world that has any claims on me. Don't think me foolish Julie in writing like this but I might get killed someday and if so I should feel as if I was leaving a wife behind in you and it is my duty to attend to your wants.

Herbert has come back from the island. [*James Island*] He was not near so unwell as I expected and I have no doubt his three nights of roughing it on the Island will do him good. I have got a little cotton over in Nassau, which I ordered to be sold and if you will send me a list of some things that you want I will send over for them. [*All my English friends in the Blockade runners, came to me for assistance, and it was no great return, if a bale of cotton was now and again taken out for me.*]

I am sure you want some muslin now. Write me a nice letter and say exactly what things you want in the muslins, the number of yards and colors. Be sure and send me a list of plenty of things & I will get you all I can, and in great haste darling good bye & believe me I remain your ever affectionate

Harry

P.S. Don't delay sending the list or I shall be vexed with you Julie.

Henry W. Feilden to Miss Julia McCord

Charleston, May 28, 1864

Dearest Julia I am going to try and write you a nice long letter tonight. It won't go tomorrow morning as I have no one to take it to the railway and it won't get off before Monday, but as I have finished my work early tonight I take up my pen in good earnest. I have got your nice long letter of the 26th before me, and will read it over and answer it in detail, but first of all I must tell you how we are getting on here.

The work in the office is gradually getting lighter, so many troops have gone to Va. that there is less correspondence and everything is very quiet, so that in future I hope to be able to pay you the attention that you deserve darling. The news from all quarters is satisfactory. You will have seen before this letter reaches you that Johnson [*sic*] has at last turned upon the enemy in Northern Ga., and that Major Genl Pat Cleburne[54] has given the enemy opposed to him a very severe handling. My own opinion is that General Sherman[55] will get very badly worsted, and that before long we shall hear of him retreating, defeated and disgraced. Everything from Va. is cheering and if the same gracious protection is continued, as has been formerly, we may without boasting place implicit confidence in a grand final triumph. I cannot help thinking that a higher power has turned the Yankees mad in order to destroy them. In all these battles they have attacked us in our entrenchments and have been repulsed with terrific slaughter. If they will only continue that style of fighting we must ultimately destroy them. [*To cheer the poor women. H.W.F.*]

I saw a note from Miss Malvina. She is uneasy that you have not written to her lately. I am not behaving well to her. I have not answered her last letter but the fact is dear Julie she expects me to write and tell her of you and my feelings toward you, and I cannot do it. To me it is a sacred subject and I can't bear to speak to anybody in the world about it except yourself. I do tell a few of my thoughts to Mr. Sass however. I walked down to the Legare St. house[56] this evening. It was a lovely afternoon. We sat for some two hours in the verandah, a delightful breeze blowing across the Ashley River. He sat in a rocking chair & I lay on the ground. We formed a great many plans, one of principle [*sic*] ones was to get a nice house, for you darling. And we decided that it must not be too far away from Legare Street, so that Herbert could run in and out and take tea with us, and that you might be able to get comfort from Miss Malvina whenever I behaved badly, and you were angry with me (which I trust may never be). I will try and get you a nice little house, not too large a one for it would only make us incur unnecessary expense, but I have one in my mind that I think will just suit if I can only purchase it. I really look forward to the war ending this year, and if so and we are spared to one another we shall be able to settle so comfortably in Charleston. I will go into some business and work very hard, and then I shall have you to comfort and inspire me. Then you will be able to amuse yourself with all your old friends and acquaintances, dearest Julie. If I can only make you as perfectly happy as we mortals can expect to be, I shall have no other wish on this earth, and I will always endeavour to repay you for your love and confidence which you have so kindly and affectionately bestowed upon me. I do not understand why all these blessings have been given to me. I do not deserve them and ought to be very grateful to God for it all. Tomorrow is Sunday. I suppose you will have the benefit of hearing Bishop Elliott. It is so pleasant to have Sundays come round and to hear our church service read. It makes me feel thoroughly happy for the rest of the day. Last Sunday I was extremely anxious. The enemy landed in large force on James Island and for a few hours the impression on my mind was that it was intended for a real attack and not for a feint to prevent us sending off troops to Va. Though down on the Island I was not myself in any danger though I must candidly confess, that was because the Yankees ran off. I promise you darling I will not expose myself in an unnecessary manner but a man is little worthy of a woman's love who will not in a time of danger freely expose his life for the defence of her home.

The young lady that Dubose Porcher is going to be married to is Miss Marion Palmer, and I understand that the 5th of July is fixed for the wedding day so that no chance is to be given to the Fates to interfere. It strikes me that it will be a very difficult thing for a young lady to make up her trousseau in these times.

When do you think of returning to Greenville. I really think you had better stay in Savannah until the weather becomes too hot. As yet the officer I expect to assist me has not arrived but I hope he will come soon. I will let you know whenever he makes his appearance. There is another point however of difficulty in my going to Greenville which is this. For some weeks past, ever since active operations commenced in Va., we have been most stringent in granting leaves to officers, & are only giving them in case of urgent necessity. The idea has crossed my mind whether it would be right or proper in me to take a leave of mere amusement to myself under these circumstances. This however is a case which we can talk over when you pass through and that must be guided by circumstances. One thing is certain. I shall leave it entirely in your hands to say yes or no and I am very sure you will do whatever is right.

General Jones is coming to dine with us tomorrow. He is a very nice gentleman. I am glad you liked his photograph. Whenever I have time to go down to the Mr. Cooks'[57] I will get a few more photographs for it is very pleasant to have an album that can afford amusement to others as you say yours does.

Will you remember me very kindly to little Langdon.[58] I have taken quite a fancy to that boy. He is such an intelligent little fellow I wish I had him here to talk to me this evening. His mother will have to make an Engineer of him. I am sure he has great natural aptitude for it. I hope Miss Mary is getting on with her painting. I was such a short time in Savannah it was impossible to see everything. Does Miss Emma like the Lays of Ancient Rome. She ought to. The first twenty verses of "Horatius" and a portion of "Virginia" are perfectly splendid and when I see troops going into action I cannot help repeating to myself some of the verses from the "Lays" which come in very appropriately.

I think dearest you had better not say anything about my promotion to any one as though recommended by my Genl. The worthy people at the War Dept. may not view my claims or services in the same light as we do. Though I do not think there is much chance of their refusing it. Personally I do not care whether they do or not.

I dined with Col. Lay at Mrs. Robert Lucas[59] the other evening. She is a very nice person. She asked me why it was that Herbert never came round. She said "tell him that though I have none of my Flat Rock friends to attract him yet I have a very sweet little girl." The reason why I bring this remark of hers into the letter is that it was a prelude to something she said about Adele.[60] She thinks, (I could very plainly see), of her a good deal as you do.

It seems very hard that we should be so close to one another and yet not be able to see you. If you are going to stay much longer in Savannah I really must run down again and see you. The General is a very kind hearted man and I am quite sure would like me to go. He appears so fond of his wife that he must have a feeling of charity towards persons like myself.

Mrs. Jones is still in Va. and has had a battle fought very close to her home. I believe almost on the Genl's farm. You may imagine how anxious he must have been whilst the Yankees were in that part of the country. Frank Miles is still in the city staying with the Crafts though I understand that he has applied for service in Virginia. He called to see me one evening but unfortunately I was away at the office as usual.

I hope my own dear Julie that you were not vexed with me for what I wrote to you the other day. If you are scold me well & I shall not misbehave in future. You will not think this a very interesting letter for I have very little to write about that is amusing and somehow or other I am dreadfully sleepy. Bye the way a little bit of private news. My poor friend Genl Jordan has been relieved from command at Pocotaligo by order of the War Dept. Whatever may be the General's faults I have no reason to complain of him. On the contrary [I] have always found him my consistent friend. The War Department has behaved in a scandalous manner to him.

So now good night darling and with best love believe me to remain your ever affectionate

H. W. Feilden

Defending Charleston

June 15–August 24, 1864

Henry W. Feilden to Miss Julia McCord
June 15, 1864

Dearest Julie, I cant come this morning tho busy, will endeavour to come during the day. I did not get home till 3 oc this morning. Those telegrams I received kept me going till three. I looked at my little portmanteau this morning and think it will hardly suit you as well as a box which I am sure Mr. Hanckel[1] will find for you. I will call in about 12 oc and show you how to pay for those things from the Bee store.[2] I have asked Silas to carry over two boxes of cigars & an ambrotype which please take up to Greenville for me. Goodbye darling.

Yours ever
H. W. Feilden

Henry W. Feilden to Miss Julia McCord
Charleston, June 17, 1864

Dearest, I hope you arrived safely at Greenville. I am sure you must be dreadfully fatigued with your journey. I am only afraid that you may lose by it all the good that you have derived from your visit to the Low Country.

I can vouch for myself that I never felt more tired than last night. When I went to bed during the last two preceding nights I had only been in bed four hours. You must have been terribly tired with the long trip to Greenville. I hope you found pleasant companions at Columbia and that Herbert was attentive and did not lose the tickets on the way. I sent off Mrs. Cheves parcel today by Express and wrote as well. Last night a note came to you from [Mrs] Genl Robertsons[3] cousin Theodore and I took the liberty of opening it as we presumed it contained no secrets. As I imagined it was only a request to you to attend to some shopping for her and to get 10 yds of muslin. I went to the Bee sale about it but could not get what she wanted so I wrote and told her, they expect the muslins however in a few days and I will look after it then.

Now for a little bit of scandal. I hear that Mr. Riordan (Herbert's great ally) married and levanted yesterday morning with Miss Minnie Whaley.[4] I have heard no particulars so don't say anything about it out of the family for I don't know the rights of the story. Rumour says that it is not the first time that Miss Minnie has run off so we need not shed tears for the hapless maiden, as I suppose she is pretty well hardened by this time to the effects of public opinion. Herbert was very informant [*sic*] about her previously having eloped, then her Father brought her back, but this time she has had the good sense to get married before starting.

[Colonel] Lay is laid up this afternoon. The injury he received to his knee was a very severe one and he has taken no care of it. Today he is threatened with erysipelas in the injured leg, and consequently is on his back in bed.

I hope Herbert understands that I don't want to see his face for a fortnight. Major Stringfellow[5] has come and he appears to be a very nice pleasant gentleman. I am at liberty to come up to Greenville whenever <u>you like darling</u>, but would prefer to do so after Mr. Sass and Herbert leave. You will give my kind love to them, Miss Malvina the children. I shall bring up the little ones fans when I come up.

Will you tell Mr. Sass that it is understood that Judge Campbell[6] is to be the new Secretary of the Treasury. I do not know what amount of financial talent he brings to bear on the question, but he is unquestionable [*sic*] one of the clearest heads in the Confederacy and the very epitome of honesty and rectitude. Mr. Memminger's[7] slippery policy will I think be dropped.

Everything is looking very well for us though I have no doubt but there will be a series of bloody battles [*north and*] south of Richmond before Grant becomes totally used up. [*What I wished, not what I thought. H.W.F.*] And now my love excuse a short note and believe me to remain your ever affectionate

H. W. Feilden

2

Henry W. Feilden to Miss Julia McCord
Charleston, June 18, 1864

Dearest Julie

I write you a few lines before the mail closes to let you know that I am off tomorrow morning to Savannah. I am ordered down to Ga to inspect the condition of a regt which is in an unsound condition. I suppose Savannah will be my headquarters for two or three days. I shall have a very pleasant time I have no doubt and will call upon Mrs. Cheves. I am very glad of a change of air. I want it sadly, and now that Major Stringfellow has come I can leave the office without any compunction. He appears to be a highly intelligent and well informed officer.

I am sorry to inform you that Col. Lay is very far from well. He has been attacked with his old complaint and is now in bed quite sick. He has regularly laid himself up with too hard work. It is extraordinary that people will not take care of themselves. I have been scolding and remonstrating with Col. Lay on this same front for weeks past. I am extremely glad that Bishop Lay[8] will be here this evening. He is staying here on his way to Augusta.

Will you give my love to Mr. Sass and tell him that I read his letter to [Lt] Col Lay enclosing an extract from a Columbia paper relative to imprisoning the Federal officers in Charleston and disapproving of the course. I am somewhat amused with Mr. Sass's inconsistency. Two months ago at his own table Mr. Sass urged the very course which Genl Jones has taken most strenuously and Herbert coincided with him.[9] My argument then and now was the homely adage that "two wrongs can never make a right." And my idea was laughed at by Mr. Sass who then considered it perfectly right and proper to confine prisoners under fire and advocated their being brought here. Mr. Sass cannot forget this conversation for it was mooted by me more than once at his dinner table. My own belief is that the idea originated with people in

Charleston who have been crying out long enough for retaliation but shrink from it when they are called to put a finger to the plough. The result of the course now adopted, I always foresaw and as constantly predicted and expressed my belief weeks ago at Mr. Sass table that the Yankees would be justified in pinning an equal number of our officers on the batteries of Morris Island (and entre nous I used the same argument to the Genl).

Not that I don't consider the brutalities of the Yankees entitle us to exercise the most stringent acts of retaliation. Yet we had kept the escutcheon of our young Confederacy so pure and so unsullied that I had hoped that the future historian would not be able to bring a single act unbecoming a great people against us.

Now that the step has been once taken I advocate and shall insist as far as my influence can go on a stern system of retaliation if our men are confined in the batteries on Morris Island to be killed by our guns. Let an equal number of Yanks be placed outside the parapets of Sumter, and if they put our men on the Gunboats and attempt to run in with them, as the silly editor of a Columbia paper suggests, gibbets must be erected on the shore and the Federal Genls hung in view of their friends.

It is not a pleasant alternative to look to, but if the system is once inaugurated I advocate its continuance to the bitter end. Things are progressing favorably for us in every quarter. We have no news from Petersburgh but Uncle Robert Lee is supposed to be there with a portion of his army so there is no fear for the result.[10]

The entire destruction of Sherman's army is a thing to be looked for. The accounts I receive from Johnston's army are most encouraging. Our army is understood to be larger better clothed armed and fed than Sherman's. His force is decreasing daily ours increasing. The splendid victory of Forestt [*sic*] will relieve Miss. and Genl Lee & Forestt [*sic*] will ere long be in Sherman's rear, unless he retreats soon. I do not think he will ever reach Chatanooga [*sic*] with 20,000 men. We are quite safe here and can hold our own. The enemy have sent away troops from here to the north quite lately. [*I am afraid that in this, truth was subordinated to the hope of cheering the poor women refugees.*]

You will find this a very stupid letter I am afraid my own dear darling. I am writing in a great hurry. I am looking forward very anxiously to receive letters from you. I will write as often as I can when away in Ga.

I shall not be long in coming to Greenville. What happiness that will be. Give my love to Herbert & Miss Malvina and don't forget the children and believe me to remain

Your ever affectionate
H. W. Feilden

Henry W. Feilden to Miss Julia McCord
June 19, 1864

My dearest Julie

I write you a few lines before I leave this morning for Savannah in order that you may not miss receiving a note from me.

We have Bishop Lay, Mr. Courtenay and Mr. Wilson staying with us. I am sorry to go off just when the Bishop comes and he is going to preach both morning and evening. I would not travel on Sunday either were it not that the business I am off on is very important and will not bear delay. I will write to you fully from Savannah.

Bishop Lay has given me a letter for Bishop Elliott which he wants me to deliver in person this evening. I shall be very glad to see Savannah again. All my associations with Savannah are connected with you darling. I shall be so delighted to come up to Greenville. I really am not in the best of health and I am sure a month in the country air will do me good. I look forward with pleasure to this little trip to Ga. I hope darling you are well and all at Greenville. I do long so for letters from you. I shall get one when I return to Charleston.

Excuse this very short line my own darling and believe me to remain

Yours ever affectionately
H. W. Feilden

Note from Henry W. Feilden, addressed to Miss Julia McCord,
Greenville, S.C., June 24, 1864

Telegraph me when you arrive safely in Columbia. If there is no one to meet you give your checks to [driver] of Congaree House[11] and he will look after your baggage.

Ask Mr. Sass whether my two boxes have arrived and if so try and have them sent on to Greenville.

Tell Mr. Sass to buy for me 50 bushels of salt and ship it to Greenville. It will be our only medium of getting supplies in a short time.

You have some $10,000 in the Bank. Use it for your personal expenditures. It will continue to depreciate until it is worth nothing. When in Greenville offer to pay for part of the expenses. Stay a few days in Columbia and if you can live with a friend there do so and watch the course of events.

Tell Mr. Sass that I urgently advise him to pay a visit to Charleston instead of Greenville this Xmas. Affairs are very threatening and it is absolutely necessary that he should attend to his affairs here.

H.W.F.

Henry W. Feilden to Miss Julia McCord
Charleston, June 30, 1864

Dearest Julie I am quite disappointed that you have received no letters from me up to Monday. I wrote from Savannah and since my return I have never missed a day. It is not my fault darling. I hope ere this time you have been deluged with them. I have received no letters from you for two days past so I suppose you are repaying me for my negligence. Yesterday we had quite a large dinner party at Mr. Theodore Wagners.[12] Genl Jordan, Genl Robertson, Mr. Sass, Col. Lay, Genl Jamison,[13] Capt [Gayer], Dr. Ogier[14] and Mr. Hanckel. We had plenty of ice and excellent champagne and altogether a very pleasant dinner party. The steamer "Fox" returned safe from Nassau yesterday but it brought no more of Genl Jamison's book[15] so I shall have to come up to Greenville without one for you. Mr. Hanckel read me a letter from your cousin Miss Julia Wagner[16] in Baltimore that came in the <u>Fox.</u> It spoke of you and was a very nice cheery letter considering her circumstances and that she had lately been called before a Military Commission to answer for her Southern proclivities but was let off after an examination. It is very strange if you have not received your sister Mary's and my letters from Sav. I gave them myself to Genl McLaw's[17] orderly in the barracks to post, and I don't want to suppose he would have forgotten to do so. I am really unhappy that you should have been so much annoyed.

Then again I suppose any letters for Herbert did not arrive in time to tell him to stay till Friday. Verily the mails are very troublesome. It is some weeks since we have had any mails from Richmond and consequently our office work is very slack. I am going down this morning with Col. Lay to pay a visit to the Federal prisoners. If I have time this evening I will write you an account of my visit to them and tell you what they are like. I don't look forward to the visit with any great pleasure as it is extremely hot and I want to put on my best apparel to show that we are not quite ragged yet in the Confederacy.

Johnston's victory over Sherman is I think a more important one than the papers lead us to suppose.[18] We killed and wounded a number of Yanks without much loss to ourselves, and gradually Pillow[19] and Forrest are working toward Sherman's rear. If his communications with Chattanooga are cut he will have to retreat or starve, and it will be as terrible a rout for the Yankees as the road from Moscow was to the French. Gold is still advancing quickly in New York. Miss Julia Wagner said in her letter that every article of consumption was now three times dearer than before the war. It must soon have an effect upon the [market] of the North. Unless some terrible misfortune happens to us such as the loss of Richmond or Atlanta we shall have peace before the end of this year. The New York papers show that the great mass of the people are as heartily sick of the war as we are.

We have no news yet from Richmond. I don't suppose that anything decided has taken place because the news of victories or defeats travel [*sic*] very fast. We have had telegrams from Richmond [direct] frequently but no [fresh] news. This is a miserable letter to send you. No news and so cold unloving dearest but I am writing it with a whole crowd of people round my desk asking me questions and wanting things done.

I do hope Miss Malvina is better. Please give her my love and the same to the children, and believe me to remain

Ever your affectionate
H. W. Feilden

Henry W. Feilden to Miss Julia McCord
Charleston, June 30, 1864

My darling I am going to victimise with you [*sic*] another letter so that you may not feel Herbert's loss as badly as you otherwise would for I presume he leaves Greenville tomorrow. We have still no news from Virginia which makes us anxious but we hope when it does come it will be something cheering. The Western news is still good. Early this morning the enemy attacked Cheatham's lines but were repulsed again with slaughter.[20] Our loss only <u>one</u> killed and nineteen wounded. Gold is advancing "hand over fist" as sailors say, in the North.

The mail has just come in and brings your lone one, and Herbert's of the 27th. Yours is a charming one & H's delightful. It is no use attempting to answer his as I shall see him probably on Saturday evening. I have merely skimmed over your note, darling, (I mean letter) and shall keep it as a bon bouche for after tea. I am going back to the house to take tea about 8 oc this evening a thing I have done but once during the last few months, but the reason is that Bishop Lay and Dr. Quintard[21] have come down and I wish to enjoy their company. The Bishop tells me that Bishop Elliott's funeral sermon at Augusta over the remains of Bishop Polk,[22] was one of the most brilliant and effective displays of oratory he ever heard. I hope it will be printed and will bring you up a copy in return for the "water lappers of Gideon."[23]

The old mastodon [*fossil*] bones arrived this evening from Savannah by Express. I will guarantee the old gentleman never traveled by railway car before. Dear old fellow if I could only put on his skin and make him alive again and send him down King St. how he would astonish the natives of Charleston. [*These were bones I got out of the phosphate beds.*] Your sister Mary is very charming woman and I am sure we shall be very fond of one another in a peculiar way. She is very original and I delight in that character and we agree so completely in our interest in Geology that we have one point to talk about without any fear of disputing.

I went down and called on the Federal Genls [*prisoners*]. I met them, Genl Seymour, Genl Schaller, [Wessels], [Scammond] & Hickman.[24] I have rather an objection to Yankees as you know, but truth obliges me to admit that Seymour is a very pleasant gentleman, well educated, well informed and smart as a steel trap (excuse this vulgarism but it is expressive). I had an hour's pleasant conversation with him. He told me several things which elucidated the report I am now writing of the siege of Charleston, and gave me information I wanted with great frankness, took out his pencil and paper and made me drawings of positions of projectiles and portions of guns. Told me the effective force of the enemy under his command on different occasions &c. I hardly ever met a Yankee before, never a Yankee general and thought that the contact would make one's flesh crawl but strange to say I could not blow Seymour from a gun or hang him without a good deal of repugnance. Indeed I felt more inclined to ask him to dinner and show him around Charleston. I think it would be an excellent thing if you would write now and again to your cousin Theodore[25] he would certainly appreciate it and with all his [business] he delights in getting private letters but he has one idiosyncracy [*sic*] and that is giving them to everyone to read who comes into his house, so never send anything of a private nature to him.

He gave us an excellent dinner yesterday. I think I told you that champagne and ice flowed right royally. It really was refreshing [in] this hot weather.

I have been quite unhappy darling for some time past thinking of you getting no letters from me and meditating in your heart, "I think I had better give this idle extravagant gentleman up." You are a dear funny little pet writing to me about the grey cloth and say that you would like me to wear it all. I imported some sixty seven yds, and as four yds is ample for a suit I should have to get some 17 coats, vests and pantaloons made to oblige you and carry about a wardrobe of about ten thousand dollars worth [*Confederate money*] of Confederate grey cloth. Do tell me darling how much it takes to make you a winter cloak. I suppose <u>ten</u> or <u>twelve</u> yds will do. If you don't tell me the exact quantity I shall bring up that amount so that there may be no fear of your having to cut your jacket too short.

I think what you say about Adele is about true and I shan't let Mr. Sass make himself conspicuous in that quarter. There is nothing that old Mother King[26] would like better than to have the good pious Lay Bishop[27] (not Bishop Lay) running around her establishment. She is so thoroughly whicked [*sic*] that she would delight in entrapping good innocent Mr. Sass, but I will look after her.

I am thinking of sending my application for leave tomorrow for [20] days but there are several most important things that I have to look to. I have now lying in the Bank some $25,000 Confederate money which I have drawn from England for the purchase of a house and I don't want to leave it there doing nothing and losing interest. I have also money matters for several friends to attend to. I have some cotton to ship for other friends who have got things in through the blockade by my [medium] and of course I have all the trouble of fixing the payment &c. Then there are many things about the Department which I feel in duty bound to attend to. First and foremost I must organize an expedition to drive the deserters and tories from the mountains and in the neighborhood of Greenville. For the last six weeks I have endeavored to prepare such an expedition but owing to constant drain on our resources from Virginia and Genl Johnston's army I have had to desist. Now "coute qui coute"[28] something must be done so as to keep you all safe this fall. Please don't say anything about this for it would leak out get magnified and people would say that an army was going to be sent up. And now dearest goodbye and God bless you and believe me to remain ever

Yours affectionately
H. W. Feilden

Henry W. Feilden to Miss Julia McCord

Charleston, July 2, 1864

My darling we have been busy here all day. The Yanks landed on James Island this morning and drove in our pickets and captured two light field pieces. They are now in line of battle in front of our works on James Island but I think by night we shall have a sufficient force concentrated to give them battle and whip them out. Another lot of the scoundrels have landed on John's Island so they mean to give us some trouble before they are done for.[29] They must not eat their 4th of July dinner in Charleston that is certain. I am in excellent spirits and believe by the blessing of God that we shall whip them. Don't be afraid on my account. If it <u>were otherwise</u> I should have been on the Island now but I think of you darling and shall not go until I am ordered to do so. [*This is not quite the truth for I went, but no use alarming people.*]

I expect Herbert back this evening. I have got a 25 days leave in my pocket and would have left on Monday for Greenville if the Yankees had not paid us this visit, but we certainly never can tell what a day may bring forth. If we whip the Yanks tonight I daresay I shall be able to leave on Tuesday. I am so busy darling that you must excuse a short note. Don't be alarmed about the state of affairs. The Old City is safe yet. Give my kind love to Miss Malvina and the children and to Miss Victoria[30] my very kind regards. And to you my own darling Julie more love & kisses than I can write.

Your ever affectionate
H. W. Feilden

Henry W. Feilden to Miss Julia McCord
Charleston, July 4, 1864

My darling is it not disappointing that instead of being en route to Greenville I should be kept day and night at work on account of these horrid Yankees. They have given us a great deal of trouble and I daresay will give more before they quit but so far we have been very successful and I hope that God will still be gracious to us and protect us. We have inflicted considerable loss on the enemy, calculated by Genl Taliaferro[31] to be about 600 in killed and wounded & captured on James Island. We took 140 prisoners yesterday at Fort Johnson.[32]

All yesterday afternoon and evening our troops on John's Island were busily engaged with the enemy who landed there in considerable force and attempted to advance, but our men kept them at bay and this morning Genl Robertson & Maj Jenkins[33] telegraphed that all was quiet in their front and that everything was right.[34] I have no doubt your brother Ned was engaged but he has not been hurt or else we should have heard of it.

Parker & Jenkins are two first rate men and will make a good fight any day of the week. Do you notice the Yankees always take Sunday for the fighting day. You thought darling that I was talking nonsense when I asked you to leave Savannah and go to Greenville but you see I was right after all. The enemy have been longer making the demonstration than I expected. Dr. Quintard preached three times yesterday and gave a very admirable doctrinal sermon last night.

Herbert gave me your nice letter dearest which by the way I have not answered properly, and also the little silver mug which I shall guard like the apple of my eye and bring up with me. If the Yankees run me off you may depend upon it I shall save the silver mug but I don't think there is much fear of that. [*This is a little silver mug which she had in Europe (Switzerland) in 1857. I still have it.*]

I have had so little sleep for the last few days that my brain is quite addled and I cannot write a respectable note.

What a relief it will be darling for me to get up to Greenville and have some rest.

Mr. Sass has not been very well for the last few days but I think he is better today. Herbert came back with a bad head-ache which he is now recovering from. Why did you not tell me what shopping you wanted done for you. Write as soon as you receive this and it will not probably arrive too late for me to receive it, as I hardly hope to get away even if very successful over the Yankees in less than a week. And perhaps my visit may have to be postponed for some time. I can't leave with the Yanks rapping at the door. Of course no decent minded man would do such a thing. Give my love my own dear darling to all and with a great deal for yourself

Believe me to remain

Your ever affectionate
H. W. Feilden

Henry W. Feilden to Miss Julia McCord
Charleston, July 5, 1864

My darling I send you a few hasty lines to inform you that things are progressing favorably here. I expect we shall have our lines assaulted on James Island this afternoon as the telegrams report them advancing in line of battle. We feel very confident and in excellent spirits and I sincerely believe we shall handle them very badly if they attempt it.

I expect you will think me darling a poor correspondent in comparison with Herbert who is writing everyday to you, but I am up the greater portion of the night and busy during the day. I think we have got arrangements on hand that will rid us of our foe by the end of the week, so don't be afraid for old Charleston. The Marion Arty[35] are all right. We are in constant communication [by wire & signals] with Genl Robertson and he reports no casualties in that company which is very gratifying. We are having lovely weather a little too warm though & it must be dreadfully trying to our poor fellows fighting on James Island.

I really do not feel in the humour to write you a proper letter dearest so you must be content with this little note and trust to me making up for it when I come to Greenville. I am so sorry for your disappointment. I am sure you will feel it a great deal but it really cannot be helped.

Johnston has fallen back from Marietta to the line of the Chattahoochie [*sic*] River.[36] Private letters received today from that army represent that the step has been expected by the army and that the troops are in the highest spirits. I believe that ere long Sherman will be very badly defeated. Everything in Virginia is progressing very favorably so you must all keep up your spirits. [*I could not depress the women with my real thoughts. H.W.F. 9/7/20*]

Give my kind love to Miss Malvina. Tell her that I feel quite ready and able to fight with her when I come up to Greenville. And believe me my own darling in great haste

Yours ever affec.
H. W. Feilden

Fragment of a letter from Henry W. Feilden to Miss Julia McCord
Charleston, S.C. 4 A.M. July 9, 1864

Dearest yours of the 6th I have this moment received. It came last night but I did not come down to the office until this morning. I am writing however to keep you out of suspense and will endeavour to have this sent off by the cars this morning.

You are an excited little darling. You must not run off with the idea that I am in constant danger. I feel quite ashamed of myself after reading your letter to think that you are in such a state of mind about me and I have been sitting safely in an office since the fighting began, never intending to expose my life until ordered to do so, which will not be this summer I imagine, unless the

Yankees take the city of which I see very little chance at present. We are having some very hard fighting around here and the enemy outnumber us considerably and have the advantages of a powerful fleet, but I think that we may safely rely on God's shield, which has heretofore been so graciously raised over the Old City. If they intended taking the city they ought to have done it a week ago. We are going to attack the enemy on John's Island this morning after daybreak. I suppose they are just at it now, but I do not hear the voice of the cannon and the musketry yet. I feel very confident that we shall play havoc with that portion of the enemy's forces that are on John's Island. On the 7th there was some very severe skirmishing there, and we lost several men from the 1st Ga. and 2nd S. Ca. I am glad to say none of the Marions were killed and only one slightly wounded. Yesterday they were equally fortunate. You will be very sorry to hear that poor William Porcher was killed.[37] I think you must know him. He comes from St. John Berkeleys. He has been very often at Mr. Sass'. He was killed on John's Island on the evening of the 7th and his body was sent to our house yesterday. Good Mr. Sass had been down to the depot for it, and brought the remains up, and when I came home to dinner I found the body downstairs on a table. He must have been killed instantly, the bullet passing into the body between the shoulders not far from the spine. The poor fellow had left a good clean shirt behind at the house, and as Silvy said she little thought when he left it behind with her, that she would have to dress his dead body in it.

Mr. Sass got a coffin and carried the body down to St. Luke's church in the evening and it leaves in the freight train this morning for St. Johns, so that his relations will have the melancholy pleasure of burying him at home.

The more I see of Mr. Sass the more I like him

Henry W. Feilden to Miss Julia McCord
Charleston, S.C., July 10, 1864

My darling yours of the 7th received on Saturday night and many many thanks to you for the same. I do not believe darling for one instant that anybody in Europe loves me as you do, rest quite contented on that score. I wish you would remain quite easy on my account. There is no fear of my getting into danger. It is very seldom that an A. A. Genl is obliged to expose himself individually and hardly ever when he is on the staff of a commanding Genl. I have put up for you in this letter today's extra in which there is an account of the fight that took place yesterday on John's Island.[38] The enemy are bombarding Sumter very heavily and I should not be surprised if they endeavoured to attack it before morning. This letter will not go until 6 oc tomorrow morning so I will keep it open till the last moment, as I am sure the movements of the enemy will keep me up all night. I think we shall repel the enemy there as elsewhere. These Yankees are most tormenting fellows. They keep us running our small force from place to place to meet them. It is perfectly wonderful how we manage to repel them. A gentleman from the office Mr. Adams is going up to Greenville shortly. I shall send you by him your little silver mug, [*It is the one she had in Europe 1857, and carried in Switzerland. It is in the drawing room cabinet now. H.W.F. 9/7/20*] your likeness, the grey cloth and the children's fans. Not that I am at all afraid of our losing the Old City. We have broken the back of the attack though the enemy's powers of annoyance are incalculable. You may depend upon it I shall come up to Greenville whenever I can but at present I see no chance for it. I will let you know whenever a prospect arises. You must not bother yourself on my account. When I do come you will enjoy it all the more in consideration of the delay.

The Newspapers will be full of good news tomorrow and I will endeavour to send you one by the railway cars in the morning.

July 11th 2 A.M.

Darling I was called away this evening from your letter by the indefatigable Yankees who again endeavoured about 9 oc last night to [carry] Fort Johnson and Simpkins[39] by assault. They came in barges but were repulsed. I hope plenty of them were killed. It was too dark for us to see what damage was done, but judging from the number of guns fired some considerable killing ought to have been effected. I am quite convinced that with the blessing of heaven we shall be able to hold the Old City. The Yanks have tried every imaginable road this time and have been foiled on each. Genl Foster[40] will get tired of this work soon, and if he does not his men will for he has kept them running and fighting for the last ten days.

You are very kind dearest thinking of me day and night. You can have no idea how it lightens a man's work to think that there is one who loves him truly and dearly. It is such a comfort Julia to know that I am really and truly loved. How much I shall have to tell you when I get to Greenville. You must not expect me every night. I shall write and let you know the day before I leave Charleston.

You have no idea what terrible accounts the Virginia gentlemen have received in their late letters relative to the atrocities of the raiders in that state, burning and desolating houses, committing terrible outrages on women and children, tearing the clothes and jewelry from their persons, and committing every sort of villainy.[41] Dearest you ought to be thankful that up to this time this State has been spared these terrible wrongs. I would rather die a hundred deaths than you should run the risk of such things. We are not suffering down here as the Virginians are. In fact we know nothing in S. Ca. of the horrors of war. I am <u>afraid</u> I shall still have time to attend to your shopping and to Herbert as well. You may depend upon it that I shall take good care of him under any circumstances and of Mr. Sass too. They are both better. Mr. Sass has been lately a little low spirited but our sturdy defence of Charleston has reawakened his hopes. Herbert has certainly improved in health. I hope you are keeping pretty well. I know from the way that you write that you are far from being altogether well. I wish my own love that I was up in Greenville to nurse and attend to you. You should be so petted that in a very few days you would be quite strong. I myself have improved greatly since the Yankees came and I think am getting stronger and fatter each day under the pressure of business. Okra soup and tomatoes have come in, and I eat enormous amounts of hominy and milk for breakfast. I can eat the latter mixture at any hour of the day or night. You would be quite pleased if you were down here. Do you remember how brave you were the evening you went past the jail and how you enjoyed being under the fire of the shells. Well you could have your wishes in that line gratified to any extent, for the enemy keep up an incessant fire day and night. I have no doubt that this war will tell severely on most of us. The reaction when we sink down into peaceable pursuits will be very great, but you kind hearted ladies will have to make allowances for this generation, and if they get old prematurely remember that they served their country well, and you will have to take care of the decrepit husbands.

I was talking to Major Jenkins a few hours ago and he says that brother Ned fought his guns well and bravely on Saturday.[42] I am extremely glad that he escaped untouched.

I shall be very glad to see Mr. Wm. Lowndes[43] when I come up and you will have to introduce me to the present object of Herbert's adoration. By the way I think you introduced me to Harrie when I was in Greenville.

What a miserable time of it poor Mrs. [Daisy] has with her children. I don't think it is quite wise of you, delicate as you are going amongst children who have diphtheria. Some physicians say that it is infectious, though I don't believe it is, it would be better to run no risk. [*Of course I knew better.*]

I saw Capt. McAlpin[44] from Savannah today. He says the people there are not a bit scared. If it was not that I can hardly keep my eyes open, and have thousands of mosquitos flying and feeding around me I should write this morning to your sister Charlotte.[45] In the event of the enemy turning their attentions from here to Savannah I should have to go there at once and in that case Mrs. Cheves would have some one to attend to her. I do not think that they will try Savannah this summer. By the time they have done with Charleston they will have had enough.

I had a nice chat with Frank Miles and judging from appearances we were mutually pleased with one another. Do dearest continue saying your prayers for me. I require them all. And now good bye. I hope you will enjoy reading this letter and believe me my own darling

Your ever affectionate
H. W. Feilden

P.S. Love to Miss Malvina, Miss Victoria and the children.

General P. G. T. Beauregard to Henry W. Feilden
Near Petersburg Va., July 16, 1864

Dear Capt.

I thank you for your interesting letter of the 7th inst. giving an account of the attack & repulse of the enemy on Johns & James Islands. I congratulate the gallant officers & men engaged in those creditable engagements. They have added another bright page to the defence of Charleston. I hope they will always meet with the same success in repelling the attempts of our vandal foes against that [now] historic city. I would be happy to hear from you as often as your time will permit, especially when the opportunity shall present itself of communicating again such good news as those contained in your letter of the 7th.

We are progressing slowly here, but I hope surely, towards our object of defeating that persevering drunkard[46] in our front. Unfortunately he has ceased his former system of assaults, which was reducing fearfully his army in numbers & morale. He has now resorted to regular approaches & numerous Batteries but thus far with very little success.

With my kind regards to Genl. Jones I remain, Yours very truly

G. T. Beauregard

P.S. Will you have the goodness to send me by Dr. Choppin[47] that Report of the landing on Morris Island & if not completed, send all the papers with it, & I will have it finished here.

G. T. B.

General Samuel Jones to General Samuel Cooper
Copy
head quarters
Department of South Carolina, Georgia and Florida
Charleston, S.C. July 20, 1864

General,

. . . I further recommend that Captain H. Wemyss Feilden A.A.G. Dept. be promoted to the rank of Major in the same Dept. Captain Feilden is an officer of very high order of merit, who has seen much active service in the British Army serving in India and has been long an officer in your Dept in our service.

When Genl Beauregard left this Dept and took many of his staff officers with him, Capt Feilden was the only officer left with me in the A.A. Genl Dept proper; and until the recent arrival of Major Stringfellow all the duties of that office devolved on him. He performed them with good judgment, intelligently and promptly and with untiring attention day and night. It was a period of great activity owing to the many changes made in the Dept, and required constant attention and watchfulness.

Capt Feilden is in every way worthy of the promotion which I hope he will receive and be allowed to remain on duty with me.

Respectfully
Your obednt Servant
(sg) Sam Jones
Major Genl
Genl Sam Cooper[48]
A & I Genl C.S.A.

Henry W. Feilden to Miss Julia McCord
Savannah, Ga., Aug 24, 1864

Dearest Julie

I have got so far on my road to Fla all right and am so very comfortable here that I feel almost inclined to stay in Savannah for three weeks and then pretend that I have been in Fla. I had a very pleasant ride in the cars. My companion was a Judge Baker[49] the senator from Fla. I had met him in Charleston & hope to see him again in Lake City. He is a very pleasant gentleman. I had telegraphed to Mr. Battersby[50] that I was coming to stay with him and when I arrived at the depot I found his carriage and two nice gray horses in it, and a couple of servants to meet me. I got my horse and servant out of the cars and went up to the house. Mr. Battersby's house is very nice inside. The furniture is very good and all the arrangements admirable. I was put into the best bed room that I have seen in the Confederacy. Off the room was a dressing room with a good bath in it with hot and cold water. The dressing table and washing stands were mahogany with nice marble tops and the chair in the room was white & gold. Very handsome almost too pretty for a bed room. A large bed with the loftiest and largest mosquitoe [*sic*] curtains (and best of all no mosquitoes). You will perhaps think me very foolish noticing all these things but I am so fond of pretty house arrangements. Well after a bath and changing my clothes I came down to tea and then again I was delighted. The table was a large oval (the prettiest shape) and all the children some 4 or 5 and several ladies were there. Mrs. B. made tea herself in a handsome silver teapot & there was plenty of silver plate on the table, and of course an excellent tea.

Mr. B. has got some very pretty English water color drawings. I was to have gone on to Quitman[51] this morning, but I thought it would be better for me to delay a day or two and call upon Mrs. Cheves, as I am in no particular hurry and as Mr. [Anderson] told me that he had asked Genl McLaws to meet me at dinner today and would give me some of the best Burgundy and Madeira I ever drank. I am just going to breakfast. Will finish this letter afterwards.

H.W.F.

10 P.M. I have been so busy all day I have only got home. Spent some time with your sisters. Off tomorrow at 6 oc for Fla.

H.W.F.

3

WARTIME FLORIDA

August 26–September 14, 1864

Henry W. Feilden to Miss Julia McCord
Quitman, Ga., Friday, Aug. 26, 1864

My precious darling before riding over to Madison Fla this morning some 26 miles off I sit down to write you a letter and let you know how I am getting on. I wrote you a hasty note from Savannah but my time there was so fully occupied that I could not do you justice. In the first place I must inform you that I hear all the Yankees have gone back to their dens and that Florida is quiet again so there is no chance of my getting into any difficulties there. I expect though that I shall have a very pleasant trip. You will want to hear how I got on in Savannah so I will begin an account of my small adventures up to this time. I told you how comfortably fixed I was with the Battersbys. Well after breakfast on the 24th I called on your sisters and had a nice long talk with them all. Your sister Mary says that she is coming up to the wedding, and Mrs. Cheves says we must pay her a visit this fall. I afterwards went to call on the Genl, and in the afternoon went to Mr. Andrew Lows.[1] Col. Edward Anderson & Mr. B. were there. We got the very best of good wine &c. Curiously enough Mr. Low began talking to me about my Grandfather.[2] He said that he had not seen him since 1839, when he was quite a young man traveling in England for orders for cotton. He said that he was so much struck by old Sir William's courteous old school manners that he described him to us just as if he had seen him yesterday, and it agreed exactly with what I remember of the old gentleman—even to the white choker & the gilt buttons on his coat. I called again on your sisters in the evening and found out that the Wilsons, Miss Annie Lesesne went to stay with in Charleston, was old Wilson,[3] Mr. Sass' porter at the Bank and the young lady would insist on staying in Mr. W. house though there was no one to take care of her except W. Wilson to whom she is engaged. Is it not a queer proceeding!

I left early in the morning of the 25th by the Albany & Gulf Board for this place. Mrs. B. was up however to make my coffee and give me breakfast. I was given a good lunch, cigars and a beautiful rifle to take with me to Fla. and was sent off on condition that I should stay a couple of days with them at Montgomery on my return from Fla. Mr. B. says he will give me a splendid days fishing.

My companions on the road yesterday were not very pleasant ones. They consisted of Florida reserves who were returning from Andersonville Ga. where they had taken a batch of prisoners captured in Fla. From their contact with the Yankees they had acquired very disagreeable companions and the greater part of the day was spent by them in endeavouring to catch these animals. You may imagine my feelings when a capture was announced amid peals of laughter, & thought how one of the persecuted animals might seek shelter with me. However I escaped scot free. I made friends with an old man who seemed cleaner & more intelligent than the rest, and who assured me that he had "no lice about him" and I found out that his name was [Grainger] and that he was a shoemaker by trade and a resident of Talahassee [*sic*]. He told me some interesting particulars of the private life of the late Prince Murat[4] who used to live near Talahassee [*sic*]. He made shoes, cigars and worked in the garden for the old prince.

I got to this place in the evening about 9 oc and put up at a house kept by a one armed old gentleman called Russell.[5] He used to keep an Hotel on the Indian River in Fla. Has been a sailor and also lost an arm in the Florida war. He knew Genl Jordan, Ripley, Genl Seymour and others very well, and this morning he asked me if I was not an Englishman as I reminded him of Sir Francis Sykes & other English gentlemen who used to go to Indian River to shoot, in my way of talking.

You will thus see darling up to this time I have seen nothing very new or interesting. The road from Savannah here is nothing but a wilderness of swamp, pine barren & saw palmettos. I saw multitudes of cooters,[6] and one alligator.

And now darling I wonder how you are and that you won't be vexed with me going to Fla. I know I shall come back very well and strong. I shall be back in Charleston D.V.[7] by the 20th of September. When you see Mr. Sass in Greenville I hope you will tell him that you will be married on the 6th of October. That will put an end to all my wanderings for I wont be able to travel without you. I hope Mr. Edward Miles[8] is better. Please give my love to all and believe me darling Julie to remain your ever fond

H.W.F.

Mr. Battersby says if you are anything like what Mrs. Cheves[9] was 20 years ago you must be very pretty. He said that then he could have fallen down and worshipped at her feet. I said you were a great deal prettier. H.W.F.

Henry W. Feilden to Miss Julia McCord
Lake City, Fla., August 28, 1864

My darling I am afraid you will think that I am not a very good correspondent. I wrote to you however on the 26th from Quitman Ga. I hope you received that letter. I left Quitman on old Billy my horse that same day and had a long hot ride from that place to Madison a station on the Fla railroad. I got in there about 5 oc and put up at the house of a Mr. Russell who takes in travelers. There is no regular hotel there. I found in the house a cousin and some other relatives of Col Lay's one of them a rather pretty young lady. Accommodation is rather scanty in this part of the world. I had to sleep on the parlour floor and wash in the passage in the morning, all the women of the establishment passing by, but it seemed to be the "Modus operandi" of the place, and "when in Rome do as the Romans do." The road from Quitman to Madison was a very solitary one, 26 miles through nearly a wilderness of Pine, swamp, and goffer [*sic*] holes. Here & there I came to a plantation. I stopped at the prettiest one, and went to the door & asked for some water which was given me, and the lady of the house sent for a bucketful for my horse. There were two nicely dressed young girls peeping through the windows and I heard one say to the other, "I think he is afraid to ask to come in." I certainly must have a very diffident and modest appearance. I did not stay longer however than to give my horse water, but as I was leaving the gate a little negro came running after me with a watermelon in his arms. I asked him who sent it and he said the young ladies. It was an excellent one & Billy & I discussed it with great gusto.

I also met a man riding through the woods and he came and spoke to me and he asked me to come to his house & have a drink of cool water, so I turned off the road and went to his farm. His house was a miserable little shanty, but he was a good natured fellow as he wanted me to stay dinner with him. As I was only 6 miles from Madison I declined his offer.

I left Madison at 1 oc on the 27th & got to this place (Lake City) at 5 oc. Considering what an outlandish place this is, the running of the cars was remarkably good. We passed over the Savannah River, a stream of almost romantic recollection to me, for I believe it was the residence of the poor nigger who is supposed to have invented the "Old Folks at Home"[10] a ditty which I learnt in the nursery and which at one time I believed to be the model of all true poetry. That was however when I was about four years old, & could appreciate those lines.

> When I was playing wid my Brudder
> Happy was I.
> Oh! take me to my kind old Mudder
> Dere let me live and die.

When I got to this place I took by servant, horse and baggage to Genl Jackson's[11] house which is one of the nicest in the city. We should call it a village in England. The Genl was asleep but I was kindly welcomed by some of his staff. As soon as the sun went down they asked me to join them bathing, so we all got our horses and rode to a lake about three quarters of a mile from the village. It is a very pretty one, the banks fringed with fine old oaks covered with long moss. Near the edge of the lake is a bath house, filled from a clear cool spring that issues from the hill side. It is fitted up both as a plunge and a shower bath and you may imagine how I enjoyed it after a long hot ride in the cars. The only fault about it is that it is rather shallow but it is made to accommodate ladies and children as well as gentlemen. I saw some of the fair sex coming from the bath in the General's ambulance. There are plenty of ducks and small game around here and they say plenty of shooting. If I had only my gun & plenty of time I would enjoy myself greatly. The best part of the place is the climate. It is quite cool. I slept last night under a blanket, and no mosquitoe bar. I only heard one mosquitoe.

I am not sure that the climate is very healthy. It appears to be too damp but I am well provided with quinine.

There is also plenty to eat down here. Beef at 65 cents a pound and of first rate quality. Lots of syrup, sugar, butter and the finest hominy I ever eat [*sic*], &c. I think what with outdoor exercise & plenty to eat I shall come up to Greenville looking very well. The mails here are very erratic in their courses. A letter sometimes takes seven days to come here from Charleston. I asked you when I left Charleston to write to me here. I think I shall return to Charleston about the 20th of next month, so I think you had better not write to me here after the 12th of Sept but after that time leave off writing until the 17th and then address to me at Charleston. I expect on my return to our city to find a letter from you saying that you expect me up in Greenville by the 6th of Oct.

Things are very quiet in this portion of Fla since the defeat of the enemy and capture of the greatest part of his Cav by Capt Dickerson[12] on the 17th of this month. I shall stay here a few days and then I shall take a trip towards Jacksonville and then down in the Peninsula. During that time I shall be away from all the mails & civilized life.

I have stopped here and gone out with the Generals over the hospitals. There is no Episcopal church here so I thought the next best thing to going to church was to visit the sick men. I have just returned after a very pleasant visit. With the exception of two or three cases they all looked well both Confederates & Yankees and I saw several reading their bibles.

I look forward to a very busy three weeks and some roughing but I am sure I shall enjoy it very much.

I only wish my darling that you were enjoying yourself as much as I am doing. I hope you will when you come to Charleston & do don't disappoint me dearest about the 6th of October. The hope of it is keeping me up.

Has Mr. Sass got to Greenville yet if so you must talk to him about your arrangements in the house at Charleston. I am afraid dearest that you will think this a very short and dull letter but the fact is that I have got to write to Genl Jones and it will soon be dinner and bath time and I must close my letter. Please give my love to all and believe me to remain your ever affectionate

H. W. Feilden

Henry W. Feilden to Miss Julia McCord
Lake City, Fla., September 1, 1864

My darling I wrote to you on Sunday the 28th and have not been able to write since as we left early on Monday morning and went to the front as far as Baldwin in order to see how things are progressing in the neighbourhood of the enemy, and only returned yesterday evening.

I must give you a little account of our trip as perhaps it may interest you. We left Lake City by the cars at 8 oc in the morning with our horses. The party consisted of Genl. J. K. Jackson and his staff. We ran some 21 miles on the road towards Jacksonville until we got to the trestle near the St. Marys River, from there to Jacksonville now occupied by the enemy. The railroad has been completely destroyed by the Yankee raiders but we are now busy in repairing it. . . . The Yankees occupy Fernandina & Jacksonville but have the principal part of their forces at Magnolia. Our picket lines I have marked by an imaginary circle shown by little crosses. I think this little sketch will show you our position down here better than a great deal of explanation so I will return to my narrative. A few miles beyond Lake City we passed the battlefield of Olustee.[13] Nothing is visible to show that only six months ago a fierce battle [*action*] was fought there in which hundreds on both sides were killed and wounded. Some of the pine trees are scarred and broken by the artillery fire and here and there a few bleached horses' bones mark the place where the Yankee artillery held position. By the broken down depot there are several rough graves with still rougher wooden head boards. This part of Florida is very monotonous in appearance. On each side of the road spread interminable forests of pine, the trees not nearly so close together as the woods in South Carolina. The ground is perfectly level with here and there a pond or lake generally fringed with moss covered oaks. The undergrowth is a long wiry kind of grass and saw palmettos. Large herds of cattle roam and feed in these woods and are so much at home that several times we had to stop the cars and whistle awfully before they would leave the line. The salamanders, a kind of rat also have a fine time here and the gofers [*sic*] and a species of land turtle abound in the woods making holes into which ones horse is very apt to fall.

We mounted our horses at the St. Marys trestle and rode six miles to the camp at <u>Darly Still</u> which is the headquarters of the little army of East Florida, under the immediate command of Colonel [Tarney]. Here we had dinner excellent beef and good corn bread with tolerable water. After dinner we remounted and rode seven miles to Baldwin passing here and there dead horses and numerous graves which show the effects of the guerilla warfare which is constantly being carried on in this devastated country. On all sides the wretched little farm houses are in ashes and the little corn patches left uncultivated, or destroyed by one party or the other.

Baldwin used to be a small town at the junction of the two railroads, but now not a vestige of it remains. Here and there the black charred heaps show where houses once stood. At different intervals it has been held by both ourselves and the Yankees and the only thing left behind by either side are dead horses and mules, and worn out clothes, and boots, and shoes. The smells and the flies were intolerable and the latter bit in swarms on our horses sucking their blood and irritating them to such an extent as to make them nearly frantic.

From this point looking towards Jacksonville as far as the eye could reach the destruction of the road was complete. The method of destroying railroads is ingenious and unless you have seen it you will wonder how it can be so expeditiously and effectually done. The cross ties are torn out and placed in a heap, and the rails are then placed across and the cross ties fired. The heat of the fire makes the iron hot and the weight of the ends makes the solid bars curl up when cold like bows. . . . By this simple method of destruction the cross ties are consumed and the rails are irredeemably spoilt for that purpose.

Our pickets were some eight miles in front of Baldwin but as the day was drawing to a close we had no time to visit them and look the enemy up. We returned to the camp at [Darly Still] and had supper by the light of the blazing pinetops. I enjoyed it immensely. The climate is <u>perfect</u> not a mosquitoe, not a flea or any other kind of insect. The air balmy and delicious, just scented with the smell of the burning resin. The night was dark, or the woods made it appear so, though the heaven was unclouded. But every now and then some new camp fire would spring up and illuminate that portion of the forest throwing a bright glare to the top of the surrounding trees and throwing the back ground into still greater obscurity. To the old American campaigners all this appears very commonplace but to me very beautiful.

We had a good supper, lit our pipes, smoked then coiled up in our blankets and had a delicious sleep, being so tired. At dawn on the 30th we got up and breakfasted shortly after.

About 8 oc Genl Jackson reviewed the troops and then we rode back to the St. Marys trestle, took the cars which were waiting for us and returned to Lake City, had dinner, and about an hour afterwards went out to the bath house and bathed and swam until we all got so cold we could stand it no longer, then home. In the evening I went with Captain Moreno[14] of Genl. J. staff and called upon Mr. Gilchrist to whom I have a letter of introduction. He had two tolerably nice daughters. The Captain brought his guitar and as he sings very sweetly we passed a pleasant hour. I almost expected that one of your letters forwarded by Herbert would have come by this time.

My plans for the future are as follows, to go to West Florida this week with Genl J., stay a few days at Tallahassee, visit St. Marks and other places, then I shall return to Lake City and proceed on a diplomatic tour to the peninsula of Fla. Throughout this state but especially on the coast there are large numbers of deserters and desperadoes who have fled from our armies and hid themselves in these almost inaccessible wilds. They issue out from their strongholds at times and commit all sorts of depredations aided and abetted by their Yankee allies. Force has been tried against them and in one instance families of women & children were captured and led by our authorities to Tallahassee. This measure proved ineffectual. The General now wishes to apply the policy of reconciliation and I shall go down amongst them as an ambassador. I think with good care we may have some success, but they will be a hard crowd to deal with. I will write to you more fully on the point soon.

And now my own darling I have told you of my proceedings. Let me ask a little about yours. I hope you are not vexed with my coming down here. I am sure you are not for you would not like me to remain quiet in Charleston as I was doing nothing. I shall return D.V. about the 20th so do not write to me here after the 12th of this month, but address to Charleston. Please give my love to all, and believe me to remain dearest Julie your ever affectionate

H.W. F.

General P.G.T. Beauregard to Henry W. Feilden

Near Petersburg Va., September 5, 1864

Dear Captain,

I beg to thank you for the "Report of Operations on Morris Island during the Months of July, August & September 1863" which I have been able, at last, to revise & correct before sending it to Richmond. It is lucid, concise & to the point, giving, I think, a very fair & full account of the operations referred to. I shall have a clean copy of it made for the files of the Dept of So. Ca., Ga & Fla as well as of my letter to Genl Cooper, explaining why the report had to be made so full.

I thank you for the copy of my correspondence with Major Genl Gillmore[15] relative to the firing on Charleston in the dead of night, whilst its population of unsuspecting women & children were fast asleep, but I think there is another letter of about the same date, which goes more fully into the merits of the case quoting extensively military authorities. I do not now remember whether it was ever sent, but it was surely written. Should it be found in the letterbook, may I request you to send me a copy of it.

I regret to find that the defender of Forts Powell, Gaines & Morgan[16] profited so little by the example of Wagner, Sumter & Moultrie. I hope Genl. Whiting's Forts[17] will do better than Genl. Maury's,[18] when they come to be attacked by Farragut,[19] in about one or two months hence.

Please inform Genl. Jones & the authorities of Charleston, that I believe firmly their city will also be attacked in the autumn by the combined fleets of Dahlgren[20] & Farragut, if the latter be successful at Wilmington. Hence the rope obstruction near Sumter should be repaired, or renewed if possible. Piling, with rope obstructions & torpedoes, should be put across the Cooper River entrance of Hog Island to the city, & across the mouth of the Ashley, leaving, for the passage of boats, openings which could be closed up at any moment. If sufficient rope & piling cannot be had for the Ashley, then, increase the number of guns commanding the anchorage from the mouth to the new bridge. Be assured that without these additional obstructions, Charleston will not be safe against the daring & impetuous attacks of Farragut.

We have just heard of the fall of Atlanta. It is a serious blow, but not a mortal one. It must incite us to new exertions & sacrifices. Conquer we must & shall!

We are holding our own here with success, watching a good opportunity for striking a decisive blow. God grant that it may be a successful & crushing one. This army is in fine spirits & condition. All the members of the staff are well.

(In haste) Yours very truly
G. T. Beauregard
Capt. H. W. Feilden
A. A. G.
Charleston S.C.

Henry W. Feilden to Miss Julia McCord

This letter has nothing in it that you cannot either read or let Miss M. or Miss V. read.

Lake City, Fla., September 11, 1864

My darling Julie I returned from my travels yesterday and found three letters awaiting my return to Lake City. One was forwarded by Herbert, two came direct from Greenville, one dated Aug 26th, the other Sept 2nd 64. You can imagine how I valued your dear letters, and that though very tired having ridden 100 miles into Lake City without resting I neither eat, [sic] drank or washed until I had read them through.

When I am on an inspecting tour I generally keep a journal and I think as I have nothing to do today I had better give you a short description of my journey. It may amuse you darling. I can assure you that I was delighted with it and it has made me feel so well and strong. My face and hands are burnt the color of a hickory nut, and I have the appetite of a Western hunter. I intend to leave this place tomorrow morning the 12th. I shall be at Quitman (D.V.) the same day, Savannah on the 13th where I shall post this letter and I think stop 2 days with the Battersbys, and then on to Charleston; but now I had better return to my original programme and give you a sketch of visit to the far famed Lake of Panasofkie[21] and what I saw and did there. To commence with, I got up early on the morning of Friday the 2nd of Sept., packed up a change of under linen in the saddlebags and had my good horse Billy brought to the door by 7 oc. My companion on the journey was to be one of

Genl Jackson's couriers. He came in and breakfasted with me and we started at 7.30 for Gainesville 50 miles off. The courier's name was Richard Long,[22] a private in the 5th Fla Batt. He is the only son of a Lady in Tallahassee, the richest widow I presume in the State of Fla. This young man is also wealthy, has over 200 working negroes on his, or rather his mother's plantations. He is a grandson of the late Gov. Call[23] of this State. Long was a merry bright young fellow about 19 years of age, had been a good deal in Texas where he has large possessions, had seen a good deal of the world, an excellent appreciation of his own merits and capabilities, a tremendous fund of talking material and a tongue that never ceased wagging except when he was asleep. I was extremely fortunate in getting such a good companion for he made the roads appear much shorter by his anecdotes of Florida, backwoodsman life &c. Well we left Lake City at 7.30 oc and rode along through the hot pine woods in the direction of Gainesville. You know very well that a traveler can't give much of a description of these forests, one mile is just like another. Long interested me by telling me the names and habits of all the birds that we met. He has a natural turn for the subject and gave me a great deal of information about their nesting &c. Some 23 miles from Lake City we came to one of the curiosities of Florida namely the natural bridge over the Santa Fe River. These bridges are of very frequent occurrence in this state; the substratum is composed of Limestone geologically speaking of very recent formation, for I noticed fossil shells in it, of the same kind as now exist in the surrounding seas. This Limestone is full of immense fissures or cracks beneath the surface which join one another and spread over large areas of the state, and are supposed by many to have a complete chain of connections one with another. At the Natural Bridge I am describing the Santa Fe River comes down a rapid looking stream some 50 yds wide and apparently very deep. From where you look at it by the road side you see it enter into a marsh full of Cypress trees and a stranger would not notice anything particular about it, except that as the road crosses the river at right angles one would wonder why the river never appeared again. If I had not been told of the natural bridge I should have thought that the river turned off in some other direction for after it disappears in the marsh there is not the slightest sign of it until it comes up again quietly, smoothly, and as perfectly composed as if nothing extraordinary had happened, some 3 miles on the other side of the road.

There were many venerable Turtle sitting on the logs near to this underground river who I daresay take constitutional walks daily up and down the tunnel. 3 miles beyond the bridge we stopped at a farmers named Dills to get dinner. This was about 1 oc. In this country though the fare is plain there is plenty of it and the poorest have a sufficiency to eat and to give away. As the Bill of fare throughout all the places I visited was the same I may as well tell it once and for all. Corn meal coffee at breakfast, dinner and supper, hunks of beef fried in grease dignified by the name of beefsteaks, plenty of sweet potatoes which take the place of wheat bread, molasses, hominy, & corn bread, and some bacon. In a few very civilized houses I saw butter & butter milk but it is rather the exception than the rule. Though nearly every person owns large herds of cattle, it makes no difference what meal you arrive at, they are all the same in quantity and quality and you are expected to eat a great deal. At dinner at Dills house a sailor called O'Neil from the gunboat lying at Savannah came in and joined us. The poor fellow had eighteen days furlough and was off to see his wife on Manatee River, away down in the peninsula of Florida. By walking some 40 miles a day he would get down there in time to spend two days with his wife and family, and then have to return to his duty. As I met him once or twice afterwards in my travels I mention his name here. After dinner Long and I resaddled our horses (one has to feed and saddle ones own horse and make ones own bed in Fla) and got to Gainesville about half past eight oc at night. I felt extremely tired with my 50 mile ride not being accustomed to so much of it at a time. I rode up to the house of Major Hamilton the Q. M. there. He is a South Carolinian and a very nice gentleman. He made me dismount, told me to bring in my blanket, and we sat down to supper; afterwards the candle went out and I rolled into my blanket and slept soundly till day break.

Shortly before my visit Capt Dickinson had captured a large number of Yankee horses from raiders and Major Hamilton had some 60 on hand so Long and I left our good horses with the Major and started Southward with two Yankee nags. About 5 miles from Gainesville we passed over Paines prairie.[24] It is a beautiful tract of green grass land some [14] miles long and 3 broad, covered with herds of cattle and horses. Here and there little clumps of live oaks rise from the prairie like islands in a lake, and the marshes were covered with storks, cranes, spoonbills. I saw the beautiful roseate spoonbill here for the first time. 16 miles from Gainesville we came to the little town of Micanopy. The country in this county "Marion" is a great improvement on anything that I had then seen in Fla. The ground is principally rolling hammock covered with live oak and hard timbers. When cleared it makes fine sugar lands, much more valuable than the pine woods. There are also good looking plantations in this part of the country but I understand that it is looked upon as the garden spot of East Fla and is settled up with people from the Carolinas & Georgia principally South Carolinians. 28 miles from Gainesville we stopped at the plantation of Mr. Owens[25] of S. Ca. He was from home but the ladies of the house came into the piazza and met us. We asked for a little buttermilk, but they were very anxious for us to stop for dinner which would be ready in an hour. This would have delayed us too long so at last they compounded by saying they would let us off if we would have a little lunch. This was agreed to & in a short time a table was spread, in the piazza. Some very nice sliced ham and some cold meat was brought out, hot rice, vegetables, beautiful butter, buttermilk and curds, and last but not least two kinds of cake. One of them a sort of seed cake was excellent, and I shall never forget Mrs. Owens delicious cakes. They had also the good taste to go into the parlour whilst we were eating, and let us gobble up as much as we could. The best of the [place] was [that] when we were leaving they invited us again to stay to dinner assuring us they would get it ready in half an hour. This however would have been too great an undertaking after the cake so we declined it and went on. We then turned off and rode to the house of Captain Chambers and the South Carolinians with whom I had some business. He was desirous of getting dinner prepared for us also, but we let him off with buttermilk and peach brandy. Capt. C. is a nice hospitable man and when we were leaving saddled his horse and accompanied us some 6 miles on the road to Ocala. We got to that place about 9 oc. in the evening. By that time the effects of the cake had worn off and I enquired of mine host whether he would give us anything to eat. He reckoned not as the cook had gone to bed, and we had best do the same. I did so without a mosquito bar and was glad to find none of the wretches about. I got up at daybreak on the morning of the 4th saw the horses fed, and brought them round. I asked the host if we could get some breakfast. He reckoned not as it was too early. We got some honey from him, and breakfasted off peach brandy and honey, an admirable compound which I advise you to try as soon as you can. Captain C. had made me take a bottle of peach along with me from his house, but the greater part of it had leaked out into my saddle bags, and with the essence of Tobacco juice had as you may imagine greatly improved the color of my only change of linen. 3 miles from Ocala we stopped for <u>real</u> breakfast with a

Mr. Ramidge, a settler from South Carolina. We got a good meal and went forward. The country from here became far more thinly populated and the plantations are small and poorer looking. The settlers live in the funniest of log cabins, generally one room for the whole family, sometimes two, however wealthy they may be. They have no ideas of comfort. They get everything they want without trouble and are consequently correspondingly lazy.

At 12 oc. we got to Col Somers[26] plantation, the last really civilized place this far south. The Col was at his summer residence on Lake Ware, but his overseer's wife gave us an excellent dinner and we started on. The road now lay through the dreariest of pine woods, for miles no sign of cultivation. About 4 oc. there came down a tremendous shower of rain. We were soon wet to the skin. The rain got into the saddle bags. Our boots got so full of water that in the pauses of the storm, we had to get off our horses and hold up our legs to let the water run out of our boots. Long had a little fever in the morning and this ducking made him worse. His horse also began to give out, and showed premonitious symptoms of blind staggers. I took the knife you gave me and bled him which did him a little good. Just as darkness came on we came to a settler and asked him if we might put up for the night. He said we might with pleasure if we liked to rough it. We were very glad of this. A big fire was raised in the one room which made up the house and we soon pulled off our clothes or nearly all and began drying before the fire. There were four men besides ourselves, two or three women & some children, and some four beds. Long and I had one bed, the women slept in another next to us. Where all the men were I never enquired. As soon as I had supper I turned in, and went to sleep. I could hear as I fell off dozing, Long telling the men long yarns before the fire. At daybreak I got up so as to give our fair friends in the neighbouring bed a chance to complete their toilet, and I hinted to Long that he had better do the same. With pleasure he replied, but unfortunately until you can find my clothes I am blockaded under the sheet for the old man when I went to bed last night took everything I had to dry before the fire. I got Long his clothes and we went out of doors and chatted with the men when the women got up and cooked breakfast. This is an example of the Floridian people. They live in the meanest one horse cabins, have a plenty of everything to eat, thousands of cattle and stock around them, plenty of negroes, and yet they live in this savage manner. One thing I will say to their credit the beds and bed linen and the mosquito bars were scrupulously clean, but that only makes it more singular that they should live in the way they do.

After breakfast on the morning of the 5th we rode to Sumterville distant some eight mile [*sic*] from where we had stayed the night and went to the house of Mr. Branch.[27] He had the best house in the village made of planks of logs and glass windows and four rooms. This is the nearest place inhabited by Christians to the Lake of Panasofkie, and was for the present the terminus of my journey. Long by this time had turned right sick so I handed him over to Mrs. Branchs tender mercies who sent him to bed. I went down to a Mill about a mile off where I found Mr. Branch, introduced myself to him, told him what my errand to this part of the country was for. He was very glad to see me and invited me to his house, and said that he would take great pleasure in showing me the lands. He came originally from South Carolina but had been down some 30 years in these parts of Fla. He is a fine looking man of 50 years, a regular specimen of a goodhearted shrewd backwoodsman; walked, rode & shouldered his rifle as if he were 25. Mr. B. is very much superior to the usual run of the settlers, as his wife informed us he had traveled a vast deal, "indeed all over the world except one place and that she did not remember the name of." On examination I found that Branch had been a good deal about in Fla., Ga. & S. Ca. from which state he originally came and had also visited New York and New Orleans.

I chatted with Branch at his mill until about 12 oc when we returned to his house. He is evidently the gentleman in these parts and as the neighbours pass they all drop in to see Mr. Branch. When we got to the house there were two visiting there, one old fellow called Brother Miller, the presiding elder of the Methodist congregation, and a man called Perry, evidently well to do, fat and devoted to Brother Miller, as he listened to him with the greatest respect and attention, and treasured his remarks, as if they had issued from the Delphic oracle. I wish I had the power of description, you would have enjoyed the scene. When we returned I found Dick Long had got out of bed and was sitting on the piazza floor telling yarns to old Brother Miller and his shadow. The shadow was evidently astonished, mouth open & eyes staring he listened admiringly to all Long had to say. Brother Miller with his gold spectacles on and his hands clasped on his very prominent stomach, his toes just touching the ground was evidently a little annoyed. He did not seem to like Long telling tales so quickly and taking him up so shortly. Brother Miller was evidently accustomed to have it all to his own undisputed way in the conversation line. I sat down in my shirt sleeves and listened in delight to the arguments. It appeared that Mr. Branch's sister in law had been taken very ill that morning and was expected to die and sister Martha's dangerous illness was Bro Miller's favorite theme. He talked long and sententiously about doctors, gave us his views on the setting of <u>fracturated</u> bones, and told us how a friend of his, a very great doctor, had taken a man who had cut his throat from ear to ear severing both wind pipe and <u>goggle</u> (perhaps he meant gullet) & both arteries, and for the sake of experiencing (perhaps experimenting) had sewn the man up and that he was alive and doing well. He seemed much discouraged when Long told him he did not believe a word of it. The conversation then turned again to poor sister Martha. Brother Miller spoke in a very affecting manner about it, and sagely remarked that we must all die and that he must be resigned to the will of God. I thought this all very proper and quite in keeping with the old humbug, but what was my astonishment when the old fellow let the cat out of the bag in one bound, by finishing off with Oh! Mr. Branch, if sister Martha dies I'll lose that 4 pounds of wool she promised me a few days ago. Just at this juncture we were called to dinner by Mrs. B. and set to work as hard as we could.

After dinner I went and bathed the whole afternoon in a nice clear pond with one or two of the young savages of the neighbourhood. They seemed much astonished at my using soap.

Sure enough poor sister Martha died and next day, 6th Sept, Branch and his wife had to go to the funeral and again I had to put off visiting the far famed Panasofkie property. I was handed over to the care of a Mr. Tomkins[28] who was to show me a good days fishing. I went with him and certainly on his farm had a days sport I seldom ever saw equaled. I caught fish as fast as I threw in the bait, and soft shell Turtle and all sorts of creatures, but the most extraordinary part of what I saw was Tomkins residence. He was a jolly bluff generous fellow in excellent spirits, seemingly very well contented with the world in general, possessed of some 30 negroes, many thousand head of cattle, any amount of land and plenty of money, with a large family. And yet the man lived in a little log hut some 14 feet square, all the family together, what with the beds and the spinning wheel there was just room left on the floor for his sick son to be stretched out on a mattress. Tomkins to show me his skill in surgery operated on his own son. He got a blunt lancet and hacked and lanced the poor lads stomach. He then got an old quinine bottle, filled it with lighted paper and applied it to the wounds as an impromptu cupping machine.

We had a big dinner but no butter though the cows were around in hundreds, and no forks, but as fingers were made before forks I made an excellent dinner. The younger children were playing in front of the house aged 2, 3 & 4, perfectly naked, but at dinner time they sat around the table in their nurses laps on the floor and were clothed in little pinafores tied in front. I recommended Tomkins to have the soft shell Turtle I had caught converted into soup but he indignantly repelled the idea of eating "them critters."

But I must cut my story short or you will never wade through it all. On Wednesday the 7th I started with Mr. Branch and rode to the Panasofkie lands. I was more than pleased with them and they quite come up to Major Lay's description. The orange groves were still covered with the yellow fruit of last year and I eat [*sic*] any amount of them. When the railroad is made to Tampa it will pass within 5 or 6 miles of this ground and it will be a very valuable property, but I hardly think with the description of the surrounding society that you might have to meet, that you will be very anxious to be the first settler at Panasofkie. I will say no more about these lands because if I do so I shall be trespassing on Lays peculiar province which is to blow and gas about them. But alas as Brother Miller would say human happiness cannot be unalloyed. My days pleasure was entirely spoilt, my whole trip made miserable by a sad loss. You will be extremely sorry about it I know. I am really vexed and mad about it. I have lost the ring you gave me, and I will tell you how it happened.

There are several Indian Mounds on the ground and one little one I was anxious to open and look into. I rode to a small cabin and borrowed a spade from a poor woman and returned to the mound. I dug vigorously for half an hour and at last came to some human remains. I found them to be that of a young woman, probably some chiefs daughter. The skeleton was so old that it crumbled to powder as I exposed it to the air. From a little piece of sentimentality on my part (which I wish had never crossed my mind) I took the ring off my finger and dropped it into the pocket which holds my watch. I then set vigorously to work and disinterred the little princess Panasofkie. I first took out her little iron hoe which had been buried with her, then round where her neck ought to have been were any quantity of beads. I took a lot of them away then I found her thimble and scissors, her arrow heads and little tomahawk which ought to have accompanied her to the happy hunting grounds. I knew she was quite young because her back teeth were not cut and her front teeth just coming up. Evidently she must have been pretty or they would not have expended so many beads on her.

I was in high glee with my performance, took as many of the articles as I wanted, filled up the grave, shouldered the spade, remounted & went to the squatters cabin. The woman brought me a basin of water. I washed my hands, and now I said I'll put Miss Julies ring on. I wonder what she will say when I tell that I have been robbing little Indian princesses of their effects, but imagine my horror when I put my fingers into my pocket and felt for the ring. No ring there. I pulled out the lining and found a hole in it. The truth at once flashed across my mind. It had slipped into the mound and I had buried it up. When I first discovered my loss I made such an exclamation that the woman thought I was ill, and the more when I frantically tore off my boot & stocking to see if by any good fortune the ring had slipped in them, but no. Well for me to go and hunt for the ring was absurd. It was getting late and I had to go home. I told the woman if her children would find the ring I would send them $100. She promised me that they should do all they could to find it. I went home in very bad spirits to Mr. Branchs. Next morning I started homewards. The B's would not let me pay for anything, indeed my trip down the peninsula cost me nothing more than the hotel bill, some $16 at Ocala. (I am now going to dinner will return and finish this scrawl.)

H.W.F.

[PART OF THIS LETTER MAY BE MISSING.]

Long had not been able to leave his room during the time I was at Branchs but he said he was well enough to start on Thursday the 8th, so we left at 7 oc in the morning and said adieu to Panasofkie and got that evening to Ocala. Distant between 40 or 50 miles there I heard rumours of the fall of Atlanta and many other bad reports. I was extremely anxious to get back to Lake City. I tried to go to sleep but could not do it. Got up about 3 oc in the morning of the 9th, fed the horses and started at daylight for Gainesville. I stopped at the Owens one hour for breakfast, had a very nice one, but made no other halt till I had made the 50 miles to Gainesville. There I got a cup of coffee from Major Hamilton, had Billy my horse saddled and went off at once for Lake City. I rode through the wilderness and wilds and reached Lake City on the morning of the 10th doing my last 100 miles in twenty four hours and only being out of the saddle for two hours during that period. Of course I had to leave Long behind. I no more could have ridden one hundred miles without resting when I came down here than flown, and yesterday when I came in I got off my horse, read your letters, washed & eat [*sic*] breakfast and did not feel as if anything extraordinary had happened. If I leave this place tomorrow morning for Savannah it will be best for me to carry on there and add a line or two in that city. But no I had better write you a whole letter from Savannah. It will look better. I suppose you are very low spirited about the fall of Atlanta. I think it will all turn out for the best. I daresay some portions of this letter will amuse the children & Miss Malvina or Miss Victoria. I will write to you from Savannah a different letter all to yourself.

Hoping dearest that this will find you quite well believe me to remain ever affectionately yours

H. W. Feilden

[Now let me add the sequel to the lost ring. About 2 years after we had left S. Ca. and returned to Europe, a small package came to me from Fla. and in it was the lost ring! The children had sifted the mounds until they came across it. I sent the reward or rather its equivalent in sound money to the finders. I have the ring on my watch chain now!! H. W. Feilden 8th of July 1920]

Henry W. Feilden to Miss Julia McCord
Savannah, Ga., September 14, 1864

My darling I arrived here all safe last night. I called on your sisters and they told me that you had written to them lately and that your letter arrived yesterday. I wrote on Sunday last to you from Lake City giving a long account of my Fla. trip which I hope will interest you. I daresay I shall find letters from you in Charleston. I was unable to bring my horse with me from Quitman by passenger train. He has to come on by freight train & will not arrive till tomorrow evening. Horses are too valuable to leave by themselves to travel on the roads so I shall remain here till Friday morning the 16th and go to Charleston that day. I daresay Major Stringfellow will be right glad. Until I get there and see how things are progressing I can write nothing definite about coming to Greenville. You may imagine how anxious this makes me dearest. I cannot bear keeping you in a state of suspense and bother but you may rest assured Julie that it will not be my fault, if you are. I will do all I can to put things right. I am also much annoyed about the loss of that ring. I really <u>do feel it</u>. I am going off in a few minutes to the stores to see if I can find such a thing in Savannah. I read your good advice carefully in regard to the non-flirting policy. I only spoke to two young ladies in Florida and that was for about ten minutes so I do not think I can have offended you much. You must divest yourself of the idea that I am a flirt. I am quite sure that ere long, you will scold me for not being attentive enough to young ladies.

I don't feel in very good spirits about our affairs in Georgia. I think that there is a lack of energy shown, but of course until I get into the office, and see how things are really being carried on I cannot say much. I have returned from Florida personally in excellent health and spirits. I wish you could see me before office confinement spoils me again. My complexion is as clear as possible. The lower part of my face and hands are burnt the color of mahogany and I really do look well. I could eat, drink, sleep, walk, ride or run with any man in the Confederate States. I suppose the visit Mr. Sass paid to Greenville has cheered you all up. I hope it did. I am very glad to find that Miss Victoria has [turned] so loving to you, but don't be taken in darling with her. I told you when I was in Greenville that this would follow. I have often seen the same thing happen, as soon as you leave the family, Miss V. will vow that you are sweetest dearest most loveable darling that ever existed, and though she tells you how sad parting with you will be yet she would be extremely sorry to hear that you were to [remain].

Mrs. Cheves asked me last night how I got your dress and who choose [*sic*] it. I never let on a word. She said it reminds her of a dress in which she saw Alboni[29] appear in Paris as Prima Donna of some opera. [*A beautiful moiré antique white silk dress that I got through the blockade. H.W.F.*]

Things are not as bad as they look darling throughout the Confederacy. I believe that the end is approaching very rapidly of all these troubles. I give myself credit for greater foresight than most people and entre nous, I still believe that Xmas dinner will be eaten in peace in Charleston. [*I had heard from the (word unintelligible) circle that some feelers between Washington & Thurlow had been going on.*] You will perhaps think me inclined to lunacy but I don't wish you to be put me down as quite insane, so I would advise you not to promulgate these views of mine. If I was with you I would tell you my reasons. I am staying here with Mr. Battersby [*British Consul. H.W.F.*] I went last night to his house. He and his family were out of the city at Montgomery. There was only an unmarried lady keeping the house but she insisted on my staying there and I sat up talking with her till late. I know Miss Julie will be anxious to know who this young maiden was or else she will be getting jealous, but your alarm will be unnecessary. She is Miss [Hartridge], Mrs. Battersby's aunt aged between 50 & 60. A very agreeable old lady. Battersby came in this morning. I am going out to Montgomery this evening and coming back tomorrow to be ready for the cars on Friday morning. Adieu darling and believe me to remain your ever affectionate

H.W. F.

4

DEPARTMENTAL CHANGES

September 16–October 19, 1864

Henry W. Feilden to Miss Julia McCord
Charleston, September 16, 1864

My darling Julie I arrived today from Savannah all right and well, and found everyone in a state of ferment about the Yellow fever which they have in the city. I shall be very careful of myself dearest and use every precaution to avoid catching it. I think myself if it assumes a virulent form, the General will remove his Headquarters to some healthier place. Don't be alarmed darling on my account. I shall take every care of myself and then trust in God for the result. I enclose you dearest a portion of a letter I received from my Mother today. You will see that it refers a good deal to you. I hope you will be contented with the expression of my Mothers feelings. The reason that she applies the term <u>nameless</u> to you is that when I wrote I never mentioned your name but simply said I was engaged to a charming young lady. I also heard from my sister Blanche.[1] She says she hunted two days in London before she could get a parasol to come up to my idea of perfection, but she found it at last and with the gloves from [Pine's] store will be sent off on the 30th of August, or rather were sent off on that date so that we may expect them in less than a month. My mother said she would ask Mr. Prioleau[2] in Liverpool to forward the box to me.

I found a nice long letter from General Beauregard awaiting my return. I enclose you the letter as I am sure you will value it. To me it is a great pleasure corresponding with such a man as General B. and some day or other his letters will be very valuable and interesting.

This appearance of the Yellow fever in an epidemic form in the city puts all our little calculations out of the question. I most certainly would not think of bringing you to the city until it is perfectly healthy and this will not be the first [frost]. Perhaps six weeks from now. Sorry darling, you must try and make the best of a rather gloomy state of affairs.

You must excuse a dull letter this time as I am quite tired of hearing people on all sides talking and talking about this horrid old fever. And it is enough to make one dull to hear all their gloomy forebodings.

I saw Mrs. Cheves and your sister Mary last night in Savannah. Mrs. Cheves was not very well. I had a very pleasant day with Mr. Battersby at Montgomery. He has an extremely nice house there, and I enjoyed myself very much.

I don't feel altogether in as good spirits as usual but I daresay I shall be better tomorrow morning so good bye for tonight and believe me to remain

your ever affectionate
H. W. Feilden

Sept 17th 64

Dearest I was so stupid last night as to forget to thank you for the beautiful tobacco pouches you sent me. I think they are perfectly lovely and I am very much obliged to you darling for them. Mrs. Cheves promised to send me a box of wine in a few days. There is however no prospect of it being consumed for at least 6 weeks. But darling as far as I am concerned I don't grumble, for I am confident that these matters are arranged by an all wise and just providence, and that battle and pestilence are sent to the old city for some very good reason. Herbert is very well and says he does not care for fever. Col Lay is also well but I think a little alarmed. I am very well but will get out of the city just as soon as I can do it with propriety. Mr. Sass is the same as ever. I expect to hear from you today direct from Greenville. I hope you received my long Lake City letter and that it amused you. Please give my love to all in Greenville. Mr. Sass says you were not looking very well. Try darling and take care of yourself. Goodbye.

your ever loving
H.W. F.

❧

Henry W. Feilden to Miss Julia McCord
Charleston, September 19, 1864

My darling I received your long letter of the 16th this morning. A little gloomy in its tone but I was delighted all the same to receive it. I did not write to you last night or rather during the day as I had to go up on a special train to Summerville to see Genl Jones who happened to be there for a night he having taken Mrs. Jones from the city. I am only afraid that you will think from my silence that I am dead. Now don't be a bit alarmed about me. The good people of Charleston are the greatest alarmists I ever saw and I don't believe there is much sickness in the city. When it becomes dangerous I will quit and go with some of my office to Summerville, so don't make your mind uneasy. I am so busy darling I cant pay the attention I should like to you. I know Farragut will attack us this fall, [words crossed out]. I am working all I can to get obstructions, Torpedoes and guns. Charleston will fall when attacked if great energy is not infused into our military circles. I will do all I can. I write to Genl Beauregard this evening and will urge [words crossed out].

You cannot think how I love your tobacco pouches. The velvet one is too pretty. I have locked it up for use when you come.

It is almost useless my saying again that it is utterly impossible for me to come up on the 6th of Oct. I find the office crowded with work, and on no account should you come to the city when fever is about. I don't believe myself that there will be any epidemic this year.

As for our affairs in general they certainly look rather gloomy, and I for my part have given up speculating. I feel though quite happy and contented. If we lose everything it is God's will and we must not repine, and we can only say "Thy will be done" and wish it from our hearts. I only hope I may be spared for you dearest and believe me to remain

Your ever affect
H.W.F.

P.S. Will write a long letter tonight.

Henry W. Feilden to Miss Julia McCord

Charleston, September 22, 1864

Dearest Julie you will think that I have very little business to do if I write so constantly to you, but the fact is it is the only pleasure I have now to look forward to. I received your letter (a little one) dated the 18th this morning. It evidently ought to have been dated the 19th for it has the Greenville post-mark of the 20th on it and I have already had a long letter from you dated the 18th and it arrived last night the 21st but I did not receive it till this morning as I was not down in the office. I expect all your letters will arrive in time from Florida. They are beginning to drop in slowly now. I have not seen Mr. Elliott in Charleston. I wonder very much he has not been here to see me if he is here. I should like very much to meet him again. Your cousin Wm. [*Porcher*] Miles[3] is in the city. I met him a few minutes ago in the street. He is looking very well, and asked after you, congratulated me, and desired me to call on him which I shall do as soon as possible. General Beauregard telegraphed today that he would be in the city on Sunday. I shall be charmed to see him once again. By direction of your cousin Theodore I telegraphed to him that Mr. W. [*Wagner*][4] would take pleasure in accommodating him whilst he was in Charleston. I imagine the General will do so. I presume the General is en route to take command of the army of Tenn. What would you say darling if he were to offer me an appointment on his staff. I should have to refuse it because you could not follow me to Tenn, and you can stay with me in Charleston. I am not altogether pleased with the condition of things down here. The General is very kind and courteous with me, but Stringfel-low is rather a boor in my estimation. Lay is a good fellow but meddling and rather shallow in some things. Well they bother me a good deal sometimes, particularly Lay now that Stringfellow is away. He has got much less common sense than S. and if I do anything, and he is passing by, he is sure to drop in and give his advice, and alter the whole thing. Well I submit to it quietly, as he is my senior officer, but I have been all my life in the army and these men are but youngsters at it. Herbert is in a very bad temper with me. Today, I found that Warwick[5] and Stringfellow had been in the habit of letting him open the mails, make what decisions he liked on some of the papers, and then the papers he did not like to act on he brought to them. A system so unsoldierly and so subversive of military discipline could not last a moment in any office where I had control. I think I told you yesterday, that I issued an order that the mails on arrival were to be placed on my desk and not to be opened except by a commissioned officer attached to these Hd. Qrs. I came down earlier than usual this morning. Herbert was not in, so I gave the mail to be endorsed and receipted by another clerk. He generally does it. On Herbert's appearance, he came to me and said something about my doing this. I then told him that as long as he was out of the office he might do what he liked in speaking to me, but in this office I was master, and that he would just have to what I told him, and that I would submit to none of my clerks questioning my authority. The fact is Julie these American boys pass beyond anything I ever saw for cool impudence. An English young man would no more dream of questioning the authority of the Captain in charge than fly. I expect Herbert will behave better now. But this is what I feel about this office. The moment I leave it or am not in charge there is less management about it than in any other office I ever saw.

I was only saying to Mr. Sass the other day how dreadful it would be if the Yankees were to come and burn your moiré antique. I really do think it would break my heart as well as yours. I am afraid Miss Malvina will have a real lonely time of it this winter with Miss Victoria. I am afraid it will be a sad winter for many but we must try and keep up our spirits. The end of these troubles is approaching, and the war will come to a close before very long. The danger from shells is one of the greatest humbugs under the sun. I am rather a timid man, but I have no more fear of a shell hurting any of us, than you good people in Greenville. I have now a large fragment on my desk which the clerks in the office presented me with. It came over the Hd Qrs on Sunday the 18th burst and this fragment flew into our yard. They may fire again for a year and never do the same thing. Our little house is so far down town so small and so out of the way that the Yanks never think of meddling with it. I believe it is in the very safest part of town. Did I tell you that I dined with cousin Theodore this afternoon. I have had so many interruptions to this letter I don't remember what I have already written. The mail is just in, a long letter from you. I will take it home and answer it, and enclose it in this. Goodbye. Your loving

H.W.F.

On my return to the house with your letter in my hand I found Frank Stiles sitting in the parlour. I gave him a good cigar to smoke and had a nice pleasant chat with him. He looked over the little Princess bones and relics, and he was quite pleased with them and thought them very interesting. I then read your letter, and I think you are one of the dearest <u>craziest</u> little ladies I ever heard of. It made me laugh to see in your handwriting such a threat as that you intended to come down to Charleston if I were taken ill. If such a misfortune occurs, it would kill me off in about five hours if I thought that you seriously entertained or would attempt such a thing. Don't think for a moment of such a mad cap trick. In the first place I don't think I shall catch the [*yellow*] fever, in the second place it is not spreading very rapidly, thirdly if I were taken ill I should be as well nursed as anyone in the city. As for Mr. Sass taking fever, that is just about as likely as Dr. Ogier taking it, and Herbert wont take it either. But I am tired of talking and writing about the stupid fever. To tell the truth if it would not kill me, I should be very glad to have it and become acclimatized. Two of your Florida letters came this evening and I read them with a great deal of interest. I think you were quite right in telling me about Herbert. I know he does not like me and he takes every opportunity of doing and saying disagreeable things behind me, and endeavouring to be rude to me when he thinks he can, but he is merely a boy. I hope he will behave well to you when you come down. If he does not we can very soon settle it, by going to some other place. All that can be very easily managed when you once belong to me. You may depend upon it Julie that we are both far too independent to stay in a place where we had to submit to the slightest discourtesy, and we could very easily find some other abode. I don't exactly know what Mr. Sass' policy is in keeping Stringfellow and everyone connected with headquarters about him. I presume he thinks that it is for Herberts interest, but I know very well that I was Herberts best friend. I put him in his present place and prevented him going to Va.

The news from Va this evening is very discouraging. Genl Lee confesses that Early has been driven back with some loss. We are bound to meet with disasters until some method is found of putting all the detached men, deserters, stragglers, and shirkers into the field. If the people only proved true to themselves we could drive the Yankees out of the country in the next six months. I am extremely glad that you liked my Mothers letter. I wish you would write to her yourself. Her address is, Lady Feilden, Feniscowles Hall, Blackburn, care of Messrs Fraser Trenholm & Co. Liverpool. I do wish you would get that likeness from your brother Ned. I should like much to send it to England.

I am told this evening that Mr. Davis passed on to Macon this afternoon in a special train from Branchville to Augusta. I suppose he is off to try and patch up the quarrels that evidently exist in that Western army. I hope he may be successful. I trust he is going to send General Beauregard there.[6] If he would do that it would be a great thing, as it would add to the confidence of the country which is now much shaken. You are a nice young lady wishing that I had never come to this country. Why it just suits me. I was intended to live in the midst of all these troubles for I can keep up my spirits under all circumstances.

I am sorry so many of your low country friends are leaving Greenville but I expect you will find the time pass quickly [*sic*] until I come up, which will be about the 25th of October, not more than a month. I don't care what happens I shall come up and marry you then, if no one else comes up with me. I expect Major Stringfellow will be back by that time. Even if he is not, I will come up. I would sooner give up my commission and turn into a civilian than disappoint you and myself again.

I hope the children will like their grey cloaks. By the way I have got plenty of that cloth here if you want any more of it. I am very well off for everything but shirts but I shall get some of them this winter. In haste believe me to remain dearest your affectionate

H.W.F.

I will add a line tomorrow

Sept. 23rd. Col Lay & Herbert have gone down on flag of truce this morning. They meet the Yankees on the other side of Sumter. The city is quite quiet as a truce exists from 8 A.M. to 12 A.M. All well.

H.W.F.

Fragment of a letter from H. W. Feilden to Miss Julia McCord:

. . . to command this Department, he also advised that Genl Ripley[7] should be at once relieved and put in command of a Brigade in the field where under strict discipline he might improve. His habits are so irregular and he has so many opportunities for indulging in Charleston, that I am sure the President will see the necessity of it, and send him off, probably to one of the vacant Brigades in the Army of Va. To fill Genl Ripley's place General B. has recommended that Col. Harris[8] be promoted to the rank of Major General and that the defence of Charleston be handed over to him. Col. Harris told me that, he had told General Beauregard, he would only accept the command under certain conditions, and one of them was that he should select his own staff, and not have Ripley's crowd palmed off on him. In that case he will apply for me as his A. A. Genl. It will be a capital thing for me if all this happens. It will give me my promotion to a Majority and put me in a better position where I shall not be liable to be ranked by every ignoramus who has got influence enough to be placed on the staff of the Dept of So Ca, Ga & Fla. Again Col. Harris is a splendid officer, just the man I should like to serve under.

Charleston with him in command would make a splendid fight. I believe if this arrangement is carried out it will suit both of our views. I don't know what will become of old Sam Jones. He is in very bad health & I should not be surprised if he went off on sick leave soon.

I must confess that I should not be sorry to separate my official connection with Majors Lay and Stringfellow, as long as I have no duty to with them. I can tolerate them very well, but in the office they are insufferable, especially Lay. Herbert wont come up to Summerville & if he is acclimated he had much better stay where he is as he will be decidedly more comfortable.

I shall I think be able to come up for the 27th of October and if I get 15 or 20 days leave the fever will certainly have left Charleston before it is time for us to come down. If I get on Col. Harris' staff we shall be delightfully fixed. This is all intensely private darling. In haste with love to all your ever affectionate

H.W.F.

Henry W. Feilden to Miss Julia McCord

Charleston, September 25, 1864

Dearest Julie I received your letter of the 22nd last night. I am sorry that you allow the talking of old Mr. Huger[9] to affect your mind. Things are not in at all a desperate condition and if we are true to ourselves all will yet be right. As for reconstruction don't listen to such talk. It is impossible. Reconstruction means subjugation, and it is better for us to be killed than to submit to that. I confess the gloomiest portion of the picture is the willingness with which some of our people, talk of our being on our last legs. But after all I believe it is confined to a few who don't care whether they live under Yankee despotism, or the Queen of Madagascar provided they are allowed to retain their negroes. The Potter and Fuller blow up must be extremely interesting in the present stagnant state of Greenville politics. I expect old Potter will have to quit. He will be more than mortal if he can successfully resist the artillery of Miss [Lina's] tongue.

Now a little about our affairs. I dined last night or rather afternoon with the Crafts. W. Porcher, Mr. Wm & Mr. Frank Miles were there, and a very pleasant little party we had. I enjoyed it very much and spoke of you very kindly. I told you about General Beauregards expected arrival. Well he telegraphed last night that he was coming today. Mr. Sass and I went down to meet him. He arrived by the 8 oc train in the morning accompanied by Col Harris and Col Roman.[10] The latter went to the Rhetts, Colonel Harris is staying with Mr. Sass and the General with Mr. Wagner. General Beauregard is looking very well, in the best of spirits, full of hope, and declares that the Army of Va is invincible under any circumstances. Rain, starvation & privation has no effect on them, always ready to fight. The last joke our men have on the Yankees is to get up in the trenches and during the fighting to bellow like oxen, in order to remind them of Hampton's late cattle raid. I am perfectly delighted with <u>my General</u>. Five minutes talk with him would make the crankiest person cheerful, and your cousin Wm. Miles is little behind him. On the Genls arrival this morning we went to breakfast at Mr. Wagners. Some ten sat down. Mr. Miles, Judge Magrath, Genl Jones, Mr. Sass, myself and others, a very pleasant party. All day long the bell of Mr. Wagners house was ringing and numbers of gentlemen came to pay the General visits. I am sure his reception must have been extremely gratifying to him. If he was a prince in a European country more courtesy could not be shown to him. I remained in the house all day as he has none of his aides with him. At dinner this afternoon we had Genl B., Judge Magrath,[11] Lt. Beauregard, Capt. Warwick, Major Huger, Mr. Wm. Miles, Col. Harris, General Jones, and myself. I sat at the end of the table and had to do the carving. Mr. Wagner will insist on my helping him to entertain tomorrow morning. There will be ten at breakfast, and the same at dinner and so on until the Generals friends have all seen him.

General B. has not as yet been ordered to take the command of the Army of Tenn, though it is extremely probable that such will be the case. He is at present on a tour of inspection in this Dept & he will do us all an immense deal of good, and things will soon be set to work in a proper manner. There are some very delicate matters to arrange which I think he will do satisfactorily. One of them (entre nous) is a terrible row that Jones has got into with Ripley. I think the days of that old scoundrel are numbered, and a worse old dog does not hold a position of importance in the Confederacy. [*He was really a splendid officer but drank like the proverbial fish! I knew old Rip well when he was afterwards in quasi exile, and many a dinner we had together in London. He was a most amusing old Reprobate. H.W.F.*] When the quarrel between Jones and Ripley is settled I will let you know all about it as I am involved in it too. I shall have plenty to tell you for sometime to come.

The Army of Tenn has moved to a position which enables them to draw their supplies from Alabama and at the same time to threaten Sherman's rear. If Hood has brains enough which I doubt things will improve in Georgia.

Mr. Wagner showed me his Nassau letters today. Some wine for our wedding will be shipped in the [Fox], and the wire for the Greenville telegraph, in a few weeks. After the arrival of the wire I expect the line will be in operation. That will be a great comfort for the Greenville people. Goodnight my precious darling. Love to all. Your ever affectionate

H.W.F.

Sept. 26th Your letter of the 23rd received last night. Who taught you little lady to have no confidence in General Beauregard. I will write tonight. We are all well and in very good spirits.

Your loving
H.W.F.

General P.G.T. Beauregard to President Jefferson Davis

head quarters
Department of South Carolina, Georgia and Florida
Charleston, S. C. Septr 26th 1864

I arrived here yesterday, will await your orders, meanwhile will inspect defences of this place & confer with General Jones.

G. T. Beauregard
General
To President Jeff. Davis
Macon Geo.

Operator there will please forward immediately to other point if necessary.
G. T. B.

Henry W. Feilden to Miss Julia McCord

Charleston, September 27, 1864

Dearest Julie I have just received your long, charming, delightful letter of the 24th and 25th. It has been a real pleasure to me to read it tonight. I received it down in the office but did not open it until I got home. I am glad to see that you are in a little better spirits little lady than when you wrote your last. I am in first rate. I have been very busy all day in attending to my work as well as General Beauregards, and have had double duty to attend to but I enjoy working for him so much that I always esteem it a pleasure. Since he has been here everything moves like clockwork and all the offices have put on extra steam. I go in every morning to your cousin Theodore's and arrange with him who is to be at breakfast and dinner. Ten or twelve people come to each meal. He always wants me to go be there but I wont go, it is too great an undertaking, and he is obliged to rest content with my assistance as a general adviser. I have never been to Summerville to sleep because my own idea is that changing the air must be the very best plan to catch the fever. I only wish darling you were as little concerned about it as I am. I thought General

Jones had the fever. On Sunday night he left Wagners feeling very unwell and he afterwards had chill and fever but Dr. Ogier put him in a mustard bath, patched him up and the next day he was better. He went up to Summerville and I have not seen him since. He is a man of rather a weak constitution and "entre nous" so scared of the fever that he would die to a certainty if he was attacked with it. I think the fever is spreading slowly but it is too late in the year to have a fierce epidemic. If I was taken ill Frank Miles and Gilchrist have promised to take care of me. I should therefore be right well attended to. I am very glad you have sent me the ring impression. [*For size of wedding ring made from a sovereign.*] I will put it in to Mr. Haydon's[12] hands immediately and I am sure he will make a nice job of it.

Herbert has been coming to his senses these last few days and has behaved to me very well. He will improve in time though he is terribly childish for his years. Mr. Wagner wanted him to go and meet Genl B. at breakfast this morning but he obstinately refused, much to the annoyance of his father.

I should not be surprised if Genl Beauregard asked me to join his staff if he goes to Tenn. He is so very cordial and courteous to me. It would be a great thing for me, but I shall refuse it on your account unless we could make some arrangement that we should be married first. But don't make yourself uneasy little pet. I shall do nothing that will annoy you. Don't be afraid of it and perhaps the General may not be ordered to the Army of Tenn. and probably he wont ask me to join him if he is, so the disagreeable question will never arise.

I never mentioned a word dearest about Mr. M's letter. I have too much sense ever to breath[e] about anything of that kind to anyone. I am one of those who would never tell my mother or sister a single thing about my wife's private affairs. I consider all these things as resting entirely between ourselves. I have really got more common sense in these matters than most men have.

You will still write darling about Adele [*King*] depend upon it. I will never give you cause to complain in that quarter. I am the least addicted to flirting of any man I ever saw. I really haven't any taste for that specie of amusement. I cannot pretend. If I really paid attention to a woman it would be real and not a flirtation. My wife need never be afraid of any misbehaving in that manner.

Poor Mrs. [Jervie].[13] I did not mean to say anything unkind about her but she is tricky and selfish and very material. I think you told me that her husband (the first one) was a bad character. Now a woman cannot be married to a bad husband without seeing a very great deal of the worst features of a man's character. Of course she forms her estimate of mankind from that, and she does not give credit to the fact that there can be good and unselfish men in the world.

I believe I shall be able to come up about the 24th or 25th of October. Of course it depends a great deal upon the fever and Stringfellow's return. I should not like to induce him to come to Charleston before a frost. He is very much afraid of it and moreover has a young wife and two children entirely dependent upon him for support. I will come up whenever I can, and I daresay I shall be able to get a 20 days leave. If so we can spend a short time in Columbia with your friend Mrs. Starke or any other place that you may elect to go to.

I gave your love to my Mother and I am sure she will be delighted to receive it. Don't bother yourself about writing to her now. Wait until we are married and then we can write the letter conjointly.

I expect we have just as good women in the Confederacy as Mrs. De Montfort and Madam Salisbury,[14] but I think it hardly time for the Southern women to take the field. There are plenty of men in the land and if they will do their duty we shall whip the Yankees. [*I think this refers to some Northern ladies who had been gadding about forming a Woman's Legion. H.W.F*]

I hope "Bona" turned out to be a good little pig in the kitchen.

Sometime ago I sent out for a lot of things for the Genl and others amongst other things the grey cloth. I sent out two bales of cotton but that did not quite pay for them, and as usual when you send for friends I should have been left to pay the balance had not Mr. Cobia kindly offered to send me out a couple more bales on board the 'Syren'[15] now in port. If they get out safe it will pay for the things and have a balance to me, credit so that this winter we can send for some more little things from Nassau.

Bye the way about Captain [Hier] I have not bought his house yet. The lawyer I engaged to look into the title says that there are two mortgages on it which must be settled before I can buy it. I hope Captain [Heirs?] will settle this when he comes down and let me conclude the bargain (don't mention this though).

I leave this portion of my letter blank in order that I may have room to add a little tomorrow in the office. Goodnight darling.

Your loving H.W.F.

Sept. 28th Dearest I began this letter at home last night. So many people were talking around that I do not know whether you will be able to make any sense of it. We are having lovely weather & I should like much to go out and have a days partridge shooting but it would not be prudent. Neither have I the time to spare. I see advertised some linen cambric handkerchiefs by a late arrival. Do you want any darling.

Yours ever
H.W. F.

All well here. Capt [*Pliny*] Bryan[16] is better. *[He died of the fever after all.]*

Miss Julia McCord to Henry W. Feilden
Greenville, S.C., October 5, 1864

So you have at last gone to Summerville, & will I hope get my letter directed there, tomorrow. I took tea at the Chisolm's[17] last night, & when I returned home found a letter awaiting me from Herbert. He says you left Charleston the day he wrote, & that his father gave you a note to Miss Adele so he will probably have a very pleasant time. I think I shall write & ask her how she likes "The Paragon." This little piece of information I suppose he thought would give me infinite satisfaction, & no doubt prompted him to write, for he did not owe me a letter. I hope dearest you <u>will</u> have a pleasant time. I shall write & tell Herbert I have no fears where you are concerned & too much confidence in you to be annoyed, as he supposes I will be. The papers say that Gen Hardee[18] is to take command at Charleston. What becomes of Gen Jones? I was a little annoyed at first thinking what would be your fate, but remembering that you do not exactly belong to Gen Jones' staff. [*No! I was still on Genl. Beauregard's staff who was supreme commander of the Dept. Ga., S.C. & Fla. & Petersburgh.*] I supposed you would remain in the department & have wondered if this change would affect your promotion at all. What do you think of it, & how are you pleased to have Gen Hardee? So Beauregard is going to Georgia. I am delighted, for I expect great things of him & I trust now the horizon will brighten for us. We were extremely sorry to hear through Mr. Sass of the illness of both Mr. and Mrs. Gadsden,[19] the latter supposed to have yellow fever. I am relieved to think you are out of the city particularly as I hear one of the little negroes in the yard is sick with fever of some kind, but if you are not prudent now, you might just as well have staid in town. I am going to be very dissipated this week. Spent last evening out & am going tonight to Mrs. Jerveys <u>by an especial invitation</u>, & Saturday evening somewhere else. It is very solemn at home, so I go out to be enlivened as much as anything else. It is still cloudy & raining sometimes. I hope you have better weather down the country. I suppose I must think of you on Sunday looking particularly <u>spruce</u> walking to church with Adele. If I hear <u>much</u> I shall immediately get up a flirtation with Mrs. Jervey. I am sure you would be more afraid of her, than any young man up here. I wish I knew that good Col Harris. I would get him to keep me posted up as to your movements. Where are you going to stay at Summerville? I hope to hear from you dearest tonight, & long for a letter. I expect you will find Summerville a very tiresome place when you have been there a week unless you find <u>particular attractions</u> there. Write to me soon.

Affectionately, Julie

Henry W. Feilden to Miss Julia McCord
Summerville, S.C., October 11, 1864, 3 A.M.

My own darling Julie, I am sitting up with the old Colonel's remains [*Dear Major Genl Harris died of yellow fever. H.W.F. I was all alone in the house & with the coffin open & the windows open. I sat up with the body. H.W.F. I was so afraid of dogs or rats.*] which go down in the cars this morning to Charleston, where they will be temporarily interred in Magnolia Cemetery.

General Hardee returned from the city last night, and seemed to think better of his idea of sending us back again to the city. At all events he revoked the order sending me down, and as I have been mercifully preserved up to this time, I have no wish to run my head again into danger, so I shant return to the city of my own accord until we come together in November. I am writing dearest not because I have anything to say, but simply to relieve your mind of the impression that I was again going to risk my life in the city.

I don't like positively to say that I will be in Greenville by the 26th for our actions are so uncertain in these times, but you may depend upon me doing my best my own darling not to disappoint you this time if it lies within my power. For my part I don't care how private our wedding is. I really don't think these are times for festivities and rejoicing.

I did not know that Mr. Sass had sent you up any handkerchiefs. It was kind of him to think of doing so.

I hear nothing & do nothing up in Summerville so I can't send you one iota of news. All last week I was greatly confined to the house in attendance on the Colonel.

I have made the acquaintance of both of your neutral acquaintances Adele & Mrs. Geddings.[20] The former is a nice girl I think, or else a most consummate actor. She appears to be so girl like and innocent, which is extraordinary considering the moral atmosphere in which she has been raised.

Mrs. Geddings is allied I think to the genus <u>fool</u> and appears very vain and silly. She is losing her good looks very rapidly which is certainly I may say her only attraction. Does not sitting up at nights make me spiteful. God bless you darling. Love to my Greenville friends.

Your ever affectionate
H. W. Feilden

Miss Julia McCord to Henry W. Feilden
Greenville, S.C., October 12, 1864

We were all distressed to see the death of your friend Col Harris announced in the Columbia paper last night. He is a great loss to us. What a sad time you have had dearest. I am so sorry for it. I know your time has been much occupied as I hear from you so seldom. I hope you are still well, & are in no longer any danger of getting the fever. I look anxiously for a letter telling me so. I have not written for two days because I felt very unlike it & wished to hear again from you before I answered your last letter.

I am glad you are in Gen Hardee's staff so far as I am concerned but I am afraid you will find the condition of things very much the same as before.

We have had very cheering news lately. I do hope we will do something more soon which will put the Confederacy in good spirits. The Mr. Boyce[21] I spoke of is not the one who lives here, but his brother. That was a very good letter in the South Carolinian written to him about his letter. Such sentiments as he expressed should be put down immediately, & I think he ought to lose his place in the Legislature. The cold weather has abated considerably in the last two days. This morning it is delightful to me. I suffer dreadfully from the cold, & you know how intense it can be up here. I wish they could have a frost in Charleston to stop the fever. We have had it several times here. I do not think the wedding could take place in November, for many reasons. I think it will have to be postponed until the last part of the month about the 24th but there is no use in appointing a day, so far off, & until we can be more certain about it. The event certainly does not seem ever to draw nearer, but there are circumstances that we cannot control, and I have ceased to think of the matter for the present.

I hope you will not be rash dearest & go back to Charleston before it is perfectly safe. I suppose Col Lay feels uneasy about himself now, for he must have been a good deal exposed in Charleston. I think Herbert runs a great risk of taking it too. I wrote to him yesterday & made a particular request that he would be prudent. He is much distressed because Harrie will not write to him. I think the reason she does not, is because she has no private means of doing so. I have nothing very pleasant to tell you. You know what Greenville life is. Each day is pretty much the same & we have only "to beat, & beat the beaten track." The little family feuds & extraordinary rumours that you laugh at, the only excitements we have. I hope things will brighten around you soon & you will have no more such sad trouble in Summerville.

Excuse this short letter my dearest. I have two or three others to write this morning, a bonnet to trim for Miss V. & numerous other things to do. With much love

Affectionately
Julie

P.S. I will try & write a more satisfactory letter tomorrow & tell you the reason why I think it useless to make any arrangements for the 1st week of November.

General Thomas Jordan to General W. J. Hardee
Richmond, Va., October 12, 1864

Dear General

There is connected with the Department staff a young officer Capt H. W. Feilden A. A. Genl. whom I wish particularly to commend to your consideration as highly capable for the duties of the Adjutant General Staff, and as [sen] Inspector. He is of English birth & education, and has seen service in the British Army. At first, he was on inspection duty, but I had him transferred to my office, where he became my right hand man, and I am recommending him as a judicious, well informed, well trained staff officer.

Very sincerely your friend
Thomas Jordan
To Lieut. Genl W. J. Hardee

Henry W. Feilden to Miss Julia McCord
Summerville, S.C., October 13, 1864

My dear darling Julie, I intended to have written you in a long letter last night on my return from Charleston, but I was so tired and sleepy that I had to give up the idea. Mr. Browning is going down to the city this morning so I have got up and am sitting writing to you half dressed, so you need not be surprised if you only get a short note from me as I feel rather cold. I read your dear long letter over and over again before I went to bed and I am afraid you think that I am unkind and that I don't feel sorry enough for all the trials you have to bear on my account. I know that of late you must have had a very sad time, but it will soon be over, and I trust that I shall escape unhurt. I think darling the danger from fever is much exaggerated. You may depend upon it I have taken every precaution. Though I shall be sometimes obliged to go the city, yet in visiting the city in the day time Dr. Holbrooke told me that he thought the chances were one in a thousand that the fever did not take you. I think also that the disease is dying away in Charleston.

Mr. Sass is looking better and is decidedly more cheerful than usual. He tells me that Mary wants to be confirmed at the end of this month, so Mr. Sass and I will be able to come up together. I have not asked for my leave yet

Jacob Keith Sass (1813–65), a Charleston banker and churchman.
His son George Herbert Sass was a clerk at the headquarters of the
Department of South Carolina, Georgia, and Florida in Charleston.

Courtesy of the South Carolina Historical Society.

but I think I shall get it. I intend asking Colonel Roy[22] today. I am perfectly delighted with the change in affairs since Hardee took command. Everything moves like clock work and it is a pleasure to serve under him. He is strict and particular and a man must do his duty or he won't get on with him. He is just the sort of man I like to serve under. The soldiers call him Old Reliable, and I expect it is a [favorite] name for him. I like the members of his staff very much. They are nice gentlemanly men. I certainly prefer them greatly to General Jones crowd.

Tom Barker told me that he was going up to Greenville today and came to the office to see if I had anything to send up, but as Mr. Porcher had taken up the ring, I had nothing to send but my love which I preferred not doing by Tom Barker.

I shall go and call on the Jervie's [*sic*] this morning and give your message to Miss Mary. When I see Adele or Miss Addy as her Mama calls her I will give her your love, though I don't think she will appreciate it. I must not write more as it is time for Mr. Browning to be off. I have only written you this short line to let you see that I am always thinking of you darling & believe me to be your ever

affectionate H.W.F.

P. S. I will write a long letter today.

Miss Julia McCord to Henry W. Feilden
Greenville, S.C., October 19, 1864

My dearest

I am just as tired as I can be having been out & over the roughest roads all the morning paying visits. It is now very late in the day & as I am going out again as soon as dinner is over I will not be able to write you much of a letter. I received your two letters of the 13th last night. Your scold to the post master at Summerville was fruitless for I received them after I had already got the one written on the 14th but I enjoyed them just as much dearest for they were particularly affectionate & satisfactory & gave me great pleasure. You are very deceiving when you pretend to think I sent my love to Adele. You cannot get around me in <u>that way</u>. You know very well I <u>never</u> sent my love to her. Are you so fond of her that you must resort to such means of getting up a friendship between us? That was very cunning of you, but I am not so easily cheated. If you have given her my love please tell her it was a mistake.

I received the ring yesterday from Mr. Porcher. I think it is very handsome, & fits beautifully. I put it on my finger yesterday which Janie thought very shocking. I think this will be my last letter to you, for I feel now my own dear love as if it was impossible to write & nothing but a <u>sight</u> of you will come up to my expectations, so I do not care a great deal to get any more letters from you. I am sorry to tell you your worse [*sic*] fears about my <u>looks</u> will be realized, for in a quiet way I am <u>dreadfully</u> excitable & <u>that</u> breaks me down, so I am looking & feeling miserably <u>now</u> & by the end of the week I doubt if there will be left as much of me, as there is on an old mummy. My only consolation is that no one is expected to look well on such an occasion. I try not to think of the risk you run of taking the fever but I was <u>much</u> disappointed when I heard you were going back to Charleston during the day & feel as if I would be [provoked] as well as grieved if you get sick, though as it is not your fault, I will lay all the blame on the Gen. I hope Mrs. Hardee has arrived & put a stop to all such imprudence. I am going to the Davis' this evening to stay until tomorrow morning. Something quite unusual for me but they were so pressing in their invitation I could not get off. I am so anxious to consult you about something that I cannot decide about. I will have to wait until Tuesday night. It will be delightful to feel that there is someone whose interests are the same as my own & who can feel entirely with me, & to whom I can be <u>something</u>. I only wish I could be all I would be to you. If I <u>could</u> tell you all I have thought & felt & [resolved] about this, you would at least think I have made a good beginning. I do not know why it is but I cannot write you as I want to do, therefore I feel as if I had better say nothing until I see you. I hope then to be able to talk to you freely. Goodbye my own dearest. God bless you.

Affectionately
Julie

THE DEATH OF THE CONFEDERACY

December 21, 1864–April 6, 1865

Henry W. Feilden to Mrs. Julia Feilden, c/o J. K. Sass, Esq.
Charleston, S.C. December 21, 1864

My darling wife I write to you a few lines to tell you that I am one of the most miserable creatures in the Confederacy without you dearest. I have been completely lost without you all day.

I hope that you arrived safely in Columbia and that you were not desperately tired. I am sorry that the weather changed so cold today, it will make your journey uncomfortable. It has been blowing a gale of wind all day here and everything looks miserable and everyone dejected.

The "Kate Gregg"[1] with Captain [Murdeco] cannot get out tonight. The westerly wind is so strong as to keep the water low on the bar, and consequently she has to stay in port. Every day the chances of her getting out become slimmer.

The only bright spot in the desert of affliction is the return of the little "Syren" with the comforting news that she took out my bag of Sea Island cotton safe to Nassau. I will try and get another out this time. This will give us some little exchange in the hour of need.

The house looks miserable tonight. Herbert stays in the office and the establishment looks so cold and vacant that I have a great mind to remain all night in the office too.

I am very glad darling that you are off from Charleston. We are going to have sad times here. I understand that Genl Hardee and staff were at Hardeeville today. I have no official news of the evacuation of Savannah but I suppose it has gone.

This letter I am going to send to Columbia though I also intend to drop a little line to Greenville in case you go direct on.

My darling you must not get unhappy or dispirited on my account. You may depend upon it that I shall do my utmost to take care of myself for your sake, so do try and make yourself as easy as circumstances will permit.

I am so low spirited tonight that I can hardly write to you. Capt M. is sitting beside me and pouring into my ears his sorrows and afflictions. I am truly sorry for him. If he does not get out to Nassau I see no chance of his being able to make anything for his family and if he does get out there is the probability of our ports being closed and that he will be shut out from his family for the rest of the war. His position is truly sad and we ought to be thankful to God for all his mercies to us.

I hope someone met you at the depot. I am afraid Mr. Sass may have gone on to Greenville but any way the telegram will have been opened at the Bank and Mr. Newhall or someone would be there to meet you.

How I miss you dearest and all your kindnesses and attentions. I am nearly distracted at your going, but it was the right thing to do under the circumstances, for we shall soon have to undertake active operations.

You must try and make yourself as comfortable as you can at Greenville and write to me for whatever you want and don't spare your money in getting anything to make you more comfortable.

Herbert poor fellow is desperately in love and has got the blues. [Silvy] is as cross as two sticks and old Adam is as grave as a crow, and everything is at sixes and sevens. I am very thankful that you have taken off so many of my things, so that I can refit in case of accidents. I hope soon to get on Genl Beauregard's staff. I have a plan that I think will succeed. [Otey] will assist me in it. In that case my sphere of usefulness and duty will be enlarged, and in case of bad times coming I shall be able to make arrangements to send you into Texas. If things turn out as I expect you will probably be on the other bank of the Miss. by next summer. One thing you may be sure of and that is <u>you</u> have to be looked after, and I will resign my commission sooner than not to be able to do so.

When you get to Greenville give my kind love to all, and remembrances to friends. I am not writing tonight one tithe of what I should like to tell you my own precious wife. Leaving you is a great blow to me. I suffer just as much as you do darling.

It won't be very long I expect before I see you again. Goodnight my precious one and believe me to remain

Your ever affectionate husband
H. W. Feilden

Henry W. Feilden to Mrs. Julia Feilden
Charleston, S.C. December 21, 1864

My darling Wife, I have written to you tonight at Columbia. You may have gone straight on to Greenville I therefore send you this line direct to the latter place. I am too unhappy tonight to be able to write. Everything looks too miserable without you. Our bedroom has the most cold vacant look you ever saw. A cold wind has been blowing all day and everything looks miserable. Captain M. cannot get out tonight. I am afraid he won't be able to get out at all. He has been telling me all his troubles this evening. If he could only get his family to the north it would be a good thing. In that case he would be free to look after himself. His position is really distressing, and I am not surprised when he tells me that his mind has nearly broken down under his trials.

Tomorrow the papers will hear of the evacuation of Savannah. I believe you just got off in time. There will be a tremendous rush to the cars for sometime to come.

I will endeavour to get some more linen and some more coffee for you out of the next cargo. I believe the 'Syren' has some on board. I hope Mr. Sass will get the salt as I urged. It will be your only means of support in a short time for provisions will be awfully dear.

Mr. Sass instead of bringing up negroes to Greenville ought to cut down the number of darkies that he has to feed. I am very thankful that you have none of the wretches. The more I see of them the more disgusted I am with them, and I wish they were all free tomorrow so that the lazy brutes might have to find their living by work or die of starvation.

I will endeavour to send the money into Savannah by a flag of truce. The situation of the poor Cheves's must be distressing at the present moment. They don't know that I have help in store for them. Poor things I wish I could alleviate their minds tonight.

My dearest wife I feel your loss too sadly for my words to express but you know darling how much I love you. I shall live upon your dear letters. I am too tired to write any more sense tonight so adieu and with love to Miss M & Miss V and the children. Believe me to remain your

Ever affectionate husband
H. W. Feilden

P.S. The "Syren" came in last night. That is the ship that took out our bale of cotton.

H.W.F.

[This was a bale of Sea Island cotton which cousin Theodore Wagner kindly sent out from Charleston as a wedding gift for Julie. I daresay it fetched L 100 or more in Liverpool. H.W.F.]

Adele A. King to Henry W. Feilden
Summerville, S.C., December 21, 1864

Most decidedly I am a "non combattant," dear Capt Feilden, but I don't think my going to Charleston for a day will involve the certain fall of the city. I want very much to go to town next week, at least for the day, and I can not unless "the authorities" give me leave to visit my boot-maker. You are in this case the "authority" to whom I can most directly apply. Will you remember an old friend and give me a "permit"? I may not be able to go myself, and in that case will need to send my trusty maid Eliza.

Can you give me a pass for her too, and depend upon my discretion to make a wise use of it. I don't believe I am asking a great deal, if I am however, forgive my importunity, and give me what I want.

Mamma is in Columbia, so she cannot on this occasion join me in kindest remembrance to you and Julia. She cherishes fond thoughts of her sweet heart I know. Are you going to send her away immediately?

Excuse this hasty communication and believe me always yours truly,

Adele Allston King

I have just got a note from my Uncle urging me to go immediately to Greenville. Do you know any one who will be going next week? Of course I cannot go until I hear from Mamma, and that cannot be until next week I suppose.

Henry W. Feilden to General W. J. Hardee
Charleston, S.C., December 29, 1864

General

In conversation with you this morning you expressed yourself dissatisfied with the action taken by me in issuing the order extending the limits of the 2nd Mil. Sub. Dist. and I now beg respectfully to lay the matter as it occurred before you for your reconsideration, believing that when fully understood by you my course will meet with your approval.

I was instructed by Col Roy to refer during your absence in Savannah all matters outside of the general routine of the office to Genl Beauregard for his action, and to issue the orders received from him in your name.

Col Rhett the commanding officer of the 2nd Sub. District applied for the extension of that District, which application was approved and forwarded by Major Genl Ransom,[2] after which it was forwarded as instructed by Colonel Roy to the Head Qrs of the Mi. Dist of the West. This application was returned "approved with instructions to Lieut Genl Hardee to issue the necessary orders" which was done as directed by Col Roy i.e. in your name.

Immediately on your return from Savannah, Col Roy was informed by me of the action taken. He expressed himself satisfied, and here I consider my responsibility ended.

You expressed it as your desire this morning that any one issuing such an order could not remain in your office. If with the instructions given me I have erred in this matter, I would be pleased to have your official signification of the fact, that I may take steps to secure duty elsewhere as my presence in your office cannot be agreeable to you.

If on the contrary my course meets with your approval it will afford me pleasure to continue in your service. I have the honor to remain General

Respectfully
Your obednt Servant
H. W. Feilden
Captain & A. A. G.
To
Lieut Genl W. J. Hardee
Comdg Dept. S.Ca. Ga & Fla.

Note on outside leaf dated Dec. 30, 1864:

I take pleasure in saying that your explanation is entirely satisfactory, and that I would deeply regret to lose your services.

W. J. Hardee
Lieut G

Henry W. Feilden to Mrs. Julia Feilden
Charleston, S.C., January 5, 1865 10 P.M.

My darling wife your nice long letter of the 3rd came to me this evening and reading it has done away with a woeful fit of the blues from which I was suffering. I feel more & more every day my separation from you and if I continue to get worse every day as I am now doing, I shall be as thin as a lath. I really am a miserable creature. I have not a friend of any kind in this place. I go to the office in the morning, return at 3 oc, eat dinner in about ten minutes. Herbert is reading his Isabel's notes and preparing to go out and walk with her, and I return to the office. Today I took a walk as far as Legare St. picked a few violets and put them in my room to remind me of your dear self. A bachelor thinks he has plenty of friends and in consequence goes through the world in a free and easy selfish sort of manner, but the man who knows and appreciates a true woman's love, as I do <u>yours</u>, can never be contented away from her. Everything else in this world appears cold, selfish, hollow and insincere. At this moment I feel more lone, lost, and friendless, than I ever did before when turned loose in a new country for the first time, and not knowing a single soul in it, for then I could find acquaintances before night. Now I have no one to appreciate me. You must not base too many hopes on seeing me in Greenville very soon but you may depend upon it I will come up when I can. I suppose you will get the linen all right tomorrow evening when Major Lee's friend gets up to Greenville. This will obviate the necessity of your cutting up your under garments, which I should not like you to do, for you may require them before the war is over. I am glad you liked my letter to Genl Hardee. I think myself that it is a first rate one, and so the old General seemed to think also. I told you in my letter of yesterday that Dr. Cheves[3] bears his losses like a hero. He never refers to them, and is now engaged as an Asst Surgeon with Major Genl Wright.[4] He has passed however for full surgeon and he will soon receive an appointment to some regiment or hospital. While Dr. Cheves was here I treated him as politely as I could. He was evidently pleased with me, and when I mentioned to him that I wanted a negro he offered me one of his. He has a few left that were impressed by the Government for work at Savannah, and were withdrawn before the city fell. Our worthy old friend Adam is not fit for the field. Dr. Cheves tells me that the boy I expect to get is an admirably faithful fellow called "Marney." Perhaps you know him. The next time I write to Savannah I shall be sure to send kind remembrances to cousin Rache and Min. You will have seen by the Newspapers that Sherman has behaved very well in Savannah. Don't make your mind at all uneasy about the negro troops. I expect the Savannah people won't care a bit whether the city is garrisoned with white or black troops. I know it would make no difference to me for I lived in places where there were nothing but negro troops; Nassau for instance, and I noticed that people, Southerners, English & others seemed to enjoy life just as much as if all the troops on the island were white.

I will do all I can darling to try and get you a pair of shoes but I am afraid it will be a matter of great difficulty so few are coming in by the blockade runners.

Herbert gave me his letter to read before he sent it to Miss Malvina. I told him before he posted it that it would bring the old lady down from her high horse, but at the same time it convinced me that he has not a spark of real affection for the girl in him. I am sorry to say that Herbert is very deceitful, [*with the young ladies*] and I think it is owing greatly to the irregular reading in which he has indulged. You will see this wonderful Miss Isabel cast off some fine morning like the rest of his fancies. I have very little patience with Herbert in some of his tricks, and he is often very pert, but I think I snub him very hard sometimes. Today I pulled him down a little. He wrote something which I did not like on a paper and I told him to correct it. He said he was right and I was wrong. I replied that is a matter of perfect indifference to me, but do as I tell you. He did it, and when he brought me the paper I begged him before all the other young men in the office to lay down some general rules for my guidance in the office, as it was extremely disagreeable for me to be constantly corrected and instructed by him. He said no more after that.

I shall wear plenty of clothes in camp you may depend. I am not wearing flannel shirts because I have not felt cold enough, and I am happy to say that my tongue and mouth are much better.

If we can't hold Charleston I am very sure that we shall not burn it up because there are now in the city and there would be left behind some 15,000 poor men, women, children & negroes, who cannot possibly leave the city in any case, for they have no place to go, and would die of starvation. If it would do the slightest good you would be welcome to burn your house as far as I am concerned; but it would be a good deal like cutting off one's nose to spite the face. If Charleston is to be burnt out let the Yankees have the disgrace of doing it.

Sherman's army will commence active operations in South Carolina in a few days. Goodbye my precious darling. Give my love to all in the household and believe me to remain

Your ever affectionate & loving husband
H. W. Feilden

Fragment of a letter from Henry W. Feilden to Mrs. Julia Feilden:
Charleston S.C., January 19, 1865

My darling Wife, it seems like an age since I have heard from you and I doubt very much if you will get this letter for many a long day, but as Mr. Sass leaves tomorrow in the hope of getting to Columbia he may be able to send this through to Greenville. These dreadful freshets have been a very great disaster to us impeding the progress of our reinforcements and the withdrawal of our supplies &c. I thought at one time that you might have been able to come down here for a short time and when Herbert went up to Columbia on the 11th I sent you a note by him to that effect, but old Sherman on our coast and Porter at Wilmington have sent all my plans of that kind to the devil. The people are now dreadfully scared here, and many I am sure are sorry that they did not clear out before this. It cannot be very long before this City is attacked. I suppose we shall have to yield in the end unless strong reinforcements reach us of which I see very little hope at present. Sherman is now at Pocotaligo. He has taken the line of the Charleston and Savannah road & is moving up the south bank of the Combahee probably with the intention of striking the railroad at Branchville in which case we shall be cut off from all communications with Columbia and Augusta and have nothing but the N. Eastern road to rely on, so that if forced to evacuate Charleston we should have to look to North Carolina for refuge. In that case I shall endeavour as soon as I can be spared to make my way through the mountains to Greenville and if necessary take you to some safe place perhaps in Georgia. I enclose you the letter I got from sisters Charlotte and Mary. Mrs. John Cheves and Minna have gone to Augusta. Dr. Cheves went with them but I expect him back every day.

I hope you did not send me down any shirts by Edmund and I trust he has not been drowned along with my field glasses for I shall soon want them.

I send you by Mr. Sass $150 in gold. Take good care of them little woman and don't lose them. It will do to buy bread with at some future date. I will also try and get you some greenbacks. The loss of Fort Fisher & Wilmington as a port is a terrible blow to our cause.

Henry W. Feilden to Mrs. Julia Feilden
Charleston, S.C., January 30, 1865

My dearest Julie, your letter of the 24th received this morning. I am very happy in thinking that we are once more able to correspond. I wrote to you last by private hand. I believe Mr. Trescot was to take it up. I am afraid that postal communication will be [reversed] before you get this letter and you will wonder at my silence, but it was no use writing daily for the letters to accumulate in Columbia, but from today I will recommence the usual system of writing.

You must give up the idea of coming to Columbia. It is not safe now. Sherman is advancing on both Augusta and Branchville and I am afraid of him. If Branchville goes Columbia will be the next place threatened. I will endeavour to get up and see you in Greenville some way or other in that case.

I understand that Sherman burns everything as he leaves it behind. I suppose you have seen the peace rumours in the newspapers. I think there is something in it and I should not be surprised if we had an armistice in a few weeks. I hope it will come before Sherman takes this old place. But it is no use staking too great prospects of peace and happiness on the mere fact of three gentlemen going to Washington. The only reason that I can imagine for the Yankees listening to peace propositions is the fact that Europe is going to interfere in the matter.

I am much obliged to you darling for drying my clothes, and also for looking after the books. Put them on the shelves by all means.

I believe myself that we shall have peace and that you never will see the Yankee raiders at Greenville. If we do I vote that we beg, borrow, or steal enough money, to take us to the north & Canada this summer.

H.W.F.

Henry W. Feilden to Mrs. Julia Feilden
Charleston, S.C., February 10, 1865

My darling,
    I write you a few lines to say that we are all well here.

The plot however is thickening. The enemy landed about 4000 strong today on James Island. He drove in our pickets, but we hold him in check at our line of works. They reported to me, a few minutes ago, that Major Manigault was killed, but I think it is rather premature news.

The enemy were also operating today, on the Saltkehatchie, but we drove them back there; these are only demonstrations on the part of the enemy, made to cover Sherman's grand movement.

I am undecided what course Sherman will pursue; he may move on Augusta, Columbia, or Charleston. I think it is probable he may go to Augusta and Columbia first, and then gobble up Charleston afterwards. I am almost afraid this letter will not go through. I should not be surprised any moment, to hear that the enemy had cut the road, above Branchville; and our communications with Columbia.

Sherman's main body is now on the line of railroad, between Branchville and Aiken.

You see now that the peace rumours are all dissipated; I hardly expected such a finale. I thought old Lincoln would have temporized a little with our commissioners, but no. We have either to give in, or fight it out to the bitter end; I prefer the latter.

Mr. Philips[5] of the bank goes off tomorrow. I am sending up to you by him a beautiful volume of English, Irish, and Scotch Ballads, a very pretty portfolio, and about fifty photographs of English celebrities.

I suppose before many days pass over our heads, we shall have to clear out of this place.

We had Dr. Cheves, Dubose Porcher, & Mr. Price at dinner today. Col Lay is very sick again with an affection of the lungs; I do not think he will ever recover of it.

Genl Jordan is here. I have seen him several times.

As Herbert & I were going down George St. yesterday, we met Mrs. King and she made me promise to come and see her this morning. I promised to do so, but have not kept my word.

The crowd of Englishmen have not separated yet, and they bother me nearly to death.

I think I forgot to tell you that I paid that bill of Jones' for some $400 in Nassau. You seemed to be a little uneasy how I was to raise the funds.

I do hope Janie is better. We have not heard from Greenville since the 1st of Feb, ten days ago. I am longing darling to see your dear handwriting again, and still more to see your dear hand itself. My darling, I cannot think of you so far away without feeling very sad.

How I wish I could meet you again, but I do not like to think of leaving my post when we are fighting all around.

I have no news to give you, except wretched war news, and writing about that always gives me the blues. The Portfolio I send you up has a pretty little Sevres china picture on it. It represents Greuse's picture of the broken jug (a little damsel coming from the well with her cracked jug on her arm) from the Louvre.

I hope you have plenty to eat and drink up at Greenville. We still have lots of food here. I do wish some more coffee would come in. I must get you some more. And how about shoes, darling, can you get anything like shoes made up in Greenville. You must not get barefooted, though you told me you used to do so, with your sisters, on the beach.

Marney, the servant of Dr. Cheves gave [*lent*] me an excellent bay. He remembers you very well. You were quite right in supposing he belonged to Mrs. Richardson's [lot]. Goodbye my own darling. Excuse great haste. Give my love to all the household and believe me to be your ever affec

H.W.F.

Henry W. Feilden to Mrs. Julia Feilden
Charleston, S.C., February 13, 1865

My darling, Mr. Philips leaves today for Columbia and perhaps for Greenville. I send you by him the photographs and the portfolio. I will bring the ballads with me whenever I come up.

The fate of poor old Charleston is sealed. The enemy encompasses on nearly every side and a very few days now must see us evacuate.

I left on Saturday night with Genl H. in a special train & got to Orangeburgh about 3 oc in the morning. Genl H. gave his instructions to Genl Stevenson[6] and we returned to Charleston by 9 oc A.M. Sunday morning. I believe we were the last train that passed over the line, the Yankees striking the road shortly after we passed.

The state of affairs throughout the country is terrible. I can only trust in God preserving you from harm if such bad luck happens as the Yankees ever getting to Greenville. I wish you would endeavour to move to Flat Rock or some other safe point. You will however have Mr. Sass with you and he will guide your movements.

I will endeavour to get up to Greenville as soon as I can.

You may imagine how delighted I was to hear of Janie's recovery. Mr. Sass telegraphed us the news.

Goodbye my own darling. I hope I may see you soon, and believe me to remain your ever affectionate husband,

H. W. Feilden

Henry W. Feilden to Mrs. Julia Feilden, c/o J. K. Sass
Charleston, S.C., February 14, 1865

My darling, I do not know whether you will ever receive this note, as I am afraid the enemy are moving rapidly on Columbia. Things are culminating here, rapidly, to a crisis, and our exit from here cannot long be delayed. I am afraid to write fully on these matters, for I do not know into whose hands this letter may fall. I received yesterday your dear letters, dated the 2nd, 4th & 8th respectively. They all came in a bunch. The scolding you gave me in your letter of the 4th was thoroughly deserved my darling, and you may claim a divorce, the day I go in for another war, unless it is one of self preservation. Whenever I get through this one, I will devote the rest of my days to you my dearest.

I expect we are going to see hard times. I hope you, and all in Greenville, will be mercifully preserved. You must pray for me that I may be saved from danger. I cannot bear to think of leaving this dear old City, which we have defended so long and gloriously. I have given our house to an English family who will endeavour to save it for me. The "Coquette" went out last night. She had on board a great big bale of cotton for me, which will fetch in Nassau some $300. I have got a small amount of sterling there to draw on, enough to keep us from actual starvation for sometime after the war ends.

Frank Miles went off today to Columbia. He does not relish the idea at all, of falling into Yankee hands, but for my part I think Columbia is no safer than Charleston.

When I see Genl Hampton,[7] I will ask him who the gentleman was in Canada who wrote about you. When we go to see Niagra we can call upon him. I hope dearest, you will bear up under all these sad trials. You know this state of affairs cannot last forever. Peace will come sometime, and then we shall remain happy and contented in our quiet little establishment. I am giving up all love for getting on (as it is called) in the world and when peace comes will rest content in your love my darling. I hope you will get the photographs and the portfolio. Love to all the household. Believe me in great haste to remain

Your loving husband
H.

Henry W. Feilden to Mrs. Julia Feilden
Florence, S.C., February 28, 1865

My own Darling, I have a chance of sending a letter to Greenville and I seize upon the opportunity at once. I hope my precious one that you are safe and well, and all of Mr. Sass's family. We evacuated Charleston on Saturday morning the 18th. Columbia was occupied by the enemy on the 17th and the enemy left it on the 20th. I have just seen a gentleman from there. He tells me that Columbia is burnt to the ground and that it is an awful scene of desolation, the population starving.[8] Sherman then moved to Camden burning a large portion of that town.[9] His army is now moving on Cheraw.[10] Genl Hardee and our army are there. I came down from Cheraw by train the other day to this point to bring up rear of the army. I have been working night and day since I left Charleston, and have never taken off my clothes. I am wearing the same clothes that I left in. So you see I am a very fair specimen of a Confederate officer. I am very well and in excellent spirits. I hope you are the same. I am distressed of course at the amount of misery that I see around me. I am staggered when I think how God can permit such villains as these Yankees to wander over the country, burn our cities and turn out our women and children to perish of starvation. I hope and pray the day of retribution may come. I do not know my darling when I may see you again but I will write to you whenever I have a chance. I hope Mr. Sass got off safely from Columbia.

I am afraid he must have been unable to save the tin box containing the title deeds of our house and my other papers. I do hope and trust that you will be unmolested in Greenville.

I cannot write darling as fully as I should wish as I am afraid that the letter may fall into the enemy's hands. Up to this time we have had no regular fights only skirmishes. I shall be able to tell you of some wonderful sights when I see you again. When we evacuated Charleston it was a magnificent sight. It was before daylight. The cotton on all the wharves was on fire. The gunboats & shipping in the harbor were blazing. The long bridge and other points were great blazing fires. The N.E.R.R. Depot took fire and the flames spread and I have learnt since that the houses were destroyed as far down as Society Street, taking in Flyns church,[11] and down the east side of Meeting Street. I saw the Porchers at St. Stephens. I remained two days there bivouacking in the church. I saw Miss Laura Porcher, Dubose Porcher, Willy Dubose and many of your old friends. We burnt the bridge over the Santee as we retired. The enemy now occupy St. Johns Berkeley & St. Stephens. I hear the Yankees have stripped the inhabitants of everything even to their dresses. I do not know how much more we have to endure but as far as I am concerned I am a stronger Southern man at this moment than I ever was before, and I shall not give in till the very last moment. I am truly thankful that my health holds so good. I have been up night & day thro wet & fair. I long very much darling to see you again. God grant that it may not be a long time before I meet you again. My brains darling are rather muddled from want of sleep. You must not therefore expect a very lucid letter from me. Give my love to all in the household and believe me to remain my darling Julia your ever affectionate husband

H. W. Feilden
A. A. Genl.

Forgive a short letter & my great haste. Silvy & the servants were left behind. They behaved excellently till last moment.

HWF

Henry W. Feilden to Mrs. Julia Feilden

Camp near Fayetteville, N.C., March 12, 1865

My darling Wife, I received your letter of the 17th & 20th of Feb two days ago when we arrived at Fayetteville. You can hardly imagine how delighted I was to receive it my dear little wife. I am so glad to think that you are safe and well for the present. God grant that you may continue & remain so. I am glad that you liked your portfolio and the photographs. I have a beautiful book for you here someday I hope to bring it to you. The trunk we lost in Columbia had only one valuable thing in it viz a tin box containing my papers, the title deeds of my house, stocks, bonds, & letters & some valuable records however as you say it is a trifle in these times.

Now for a little about ourselves and our movements. Personally I have had a very pleasant time, except that I have been wet through for days at a time and sleeping out of doors night after night without taking off my boots.

As for our doings as an army I have not much to tell you except that we have been running from Sherman ever since we left Charleston and will continue to do so until we can join with Bragg & Beauregard then I suppose we shall turn and give fight.

We were driven out of Cheraw on the 3rd by the enemy. We had a little skirmish there as were burning the bridge behind us. Ned Parker had his mare killed under him there; 6 shots put through her.

We then retreated to Fayetteville pursued by the enemy, and got there on the 10th and evacuated it yesterday morning fighting the Yankees down the streets as our forces retired.

Herbert is very well & sends you and all much love. He is busily employed working in the office. You must tell his aunts not to blame him for not writing frequently. First of all there is no post, secondly about all his spare time is taken up like mine in cooking food and drying clothes. We have had wretched weather since we left Charleston but yesterday it brightened up and today is cheerful but the nights are cold.

The day before yesterday Hampton (who is with us) surprised Kilpatrick and captured his camp taking over 450 prisoners, releasing 150 of our men and damaging the enemy considerably. Our troops are in good spirits and will make a good fight at the very first opportunity we have of confronting the enemy.

I do hope the Yankees will not come to Greenville. If they do you may make up your mind to lose everything. All the reports I have from the rear of Sherman's army agree in saying that he leaves a howling wilderness behind him. Every horse & mule and all stock and every particle of food are taken and the house robbed of everything, frequently burnt down.[12] I can only hope that providence will vouchsafe to us a victory over him & that we may run him from here to the sea coast. I should like to see that day.

Will you give my kindest regards to Mr. Sass and love to the rest of the household. Tell them not to make themselves uneasy about Herbert. He is not at all likely ever to be shot as we keep our clerk and records away from danger. The only thing to look after is his health and up to this time he is thriving and looking fatter than when he started.

With best love to you my dear darling wife. Believe me to remain

Your ever affectionate husband
H. W. Feilden

Henry W. Feilden to Mrs. Julia Feilden
Charleston, S.C., March 13, 1865
16 miles from Fayetteville N Ca

My dear darling Wife, Captain Earle is sending a messenger to Greenville with letters so I take the opportunity of writing you a few more lines today. I sent you off a letter yesterday by Colonel Rutledge who was going to Columbia (or rather where Columbia used to be). I have nothing of particular interest to tell you. We are falling back slowly before Sherman, skirmishing with him. I hear the Yankees burnt down a large portion of Winnsboro when they left it.[13] This army of Sherman's is more atrocious than anything I have heard of in this war, except Sheridan in the valley of Virginia.[14] I hope that we may have a victory over this man Sherman. I should like to pursue him from here to South Carolina.

I wonder often what has become of [Mrs.] Rachel Cheves[15] & Minna and of your Mother & Sisters in law in Columbia. I am afraid if they remained there that they must now be perfectly destitute. I understood from Captain Earle he had written to Mr. Wm Beattie[16] to make up a mail for us. Do not lose the opportunity, but send me a long letter. One of Mr. Pinckney Walker's sons died this morning on the line of march of congestion of the brain.[17] I do not think any others you know have been killed or wounded. Henry Frost & Frank Huger were captured the other evening.

I will write you a long letter when I get to Raleigh. I am scribbling these few lines on the wet ground.

Tell Miss Victoria that the book I had for her was in the trunk at Columbia. Please give my kindest regards to Mr. Sass & my love to the others, and darling I trust that God will guard & protect you & bring me safe home again to you. Keep your spirits, my darling, and don't make yourself uneasy about me. I am very well and in excellent spirits. Goodbye my precious one. Believe me to remain

Your ever affectionate Husband
H. W. Feilden

Henry W. Feilden to Mrs. Julia Feilden
7 miles from Smithfield, N.C.
March 22, 1865

My precious darling,

I have got Herbert a leave of absence and am sending him home. I have received the letter from you since I left Charleston. The last was dated the 7th of March and I received it on the battlefield at Bentonville on the 19th inst.

I was very much surprised to hear of Mr. Sass death.[18] It astonished me very much. He was one of the last men I expected to be cut off suddenly. I am afraid anxiety in regard to the Bank must have brought on the disease that killed him. I have been so much employed ever since I heard of Mr. Sass death that I have not had time to speak to Herbert about it. Will you say to him for me when you see him that it is not intentional on my part, but that I was too tired and too much occupied with fighting to speak to anyone. Tell Miss Malvina & Miss Victoria also that they must excuse my not writing. I am really nearly worked to death. On the 16 inst we fought two of Sherman's corps near Aversboro [*sic*] and held him in check from daylight till dark, killing & wounding (prisoners report) [330 +], our loss about [200]. I had Billy wounded and the sleeve of my overcoat shot through.

We fought Sherman's whole army near here at a place called Bentonville on the 19th. On that day our corps drove his centre a mile & a half, capturing 4 guns. On the 20 & 21 we retired to our original lines and held him at bay. Last night we retreated in the direction of Smithfield. I expect our destination is Raleigh.

I am very well considering that I sleep out in the woods wet through at night and very often am in the saddle 24 hours at a time. Herbert I daresay has been very comfortable never having been away from the wagon train so I expect he will give you all a "couleur de rose" description of campaigning.

And now darling for a little business. Find out from Mr. [Thayer] what you have in the bank and pay your share of the house expense. If necessary use that gold for your expenditures, which I left with you. Whenever I come I will endeavour to put things all right.

If ever you want money write to Theodore Wagner and tell him to let you have some, and that I will give him exchange on England or Nassau for the amount. But I hope you be able to get on all right. I expect I [lost all.]

March 23. Herbert goes off this morning. I have only time to add one line my precious darling. I received two letters last night from you, old ones written in Feb last.

Herbert will give you all the news. Give my love to all & believe me to remain your ever affectionate husband

H. W. Feilden

Henry W. Feilden to Mrs. Julia Feilden
Camp near Smithfield, N.C.
March 23, 1865

My darling Wife, Captain Earle brought me your long and interesting letter of the 13th today. I was delighted to receive it. I have hardly read it through yet but I am so afraid of losing a chance of sending you a letter that I commence it at once. Herbert left this morning and I sent you a few hurried lines by him. I also sent you a little stud for fastening your collar, and a pencil case for Mary. Mr. Frank Porcher also left this morning for Greenville. Major Burnett Rhett is very well.[19] He commands the battalion of arty attached to our corps. Today is the first time since leaving Charleston that I have sat down to write a letter at a desk, and I am so busy with the accumulated correspondence of the last month that I doubt very much if this letter of mine to you will be a coherent one. I have been worked very hard indeed, and feel almost tired to death now. I have killed one horse with riding, had one shot, and another disabled, so that I am now dismounted. It is no use my buying any more for I cannot get enough food to keep the two crippled horses I have.

I am afraid darling that I shall not be able to come up to Greenville for a long time unless I get sick or wounded. I am not one of those who like to desert friends in trouble, and I cannot leave the army as long as the fighting is going on. I find the generality of men so lazy and indifferent and helpless. I had 3 or 4 clerks with me and the whole of them including Herbert did not give me any assistance. I never saw such a useless set in my life. Every one of them ought to have had a nurse to look after them.

I am so sorry my dear little wife when I think of you sitting so miserable, and disconsolate, thinking of me in Greenville. I feel confident darling that there are happier days in store for us, and that we shall get through all these present troubles. The prospect of our affairs is at present very gloomy. I am like Micawber though, looking for something to turn up.[20] I believe that eventually this army of Johnston's will be driven back to Virginia then when we concentrate with Lee, we shall in all probability strike both Sherman and Grant some terrible blows. We fought Sherman's whole army at Bentonville on the 19th, 20th & 21st and I do not think they fought with much vigor. I suppose Sherman had more than double our number. If we had been on equal terms we should have driven him into the sea.

Herbert will tell you of all our friends who have been killed or wounded or captured. By the way Ravenel Macbeth was wounded & captured again near Averysboro on the 16th.[21]

I think darling that you had better be saving of your money and not spend more than is absolutely necessary. Now that Mr. Sass is dead you must pay your share of the house expenses. I have advised Herbert to get rid of some of the servants and also of the carriage & horse. The strictest economy ought to be inculcated at once for I do not think Mr. Sass could have left much behind him. His real estate in Charleston is now in the hands of the enemy, and until that can be recovered, I am afraid his children will have very little to live on except some worthless Confederate bonds & notes. You must help them with your money and advice darling. As for myself I have lost nearly everything and will have to begin the world anew if I live through the war, but I think we have enough in England and Nassau to live on until the war ends. I hope now that we are coming nearer to the Railroad that I shall be able to write to you oftener. I do not think dearest that you ought to write me more than once a week, that is write a little every day if you like and dispatch a letter about once a week. I have written to you when I have had an opportunity but up to this date, we have had none worth mentioning. Though you have written to me so often I have only received four of your letters and three of them in the last 24 hours.

I am very sorry about the Lowndes. I am afraid Harrie will not come to any very good end. Don't let Herbert be too much with her. I think what you tell me about Mrs. Crafts is the most extraordinary thing I ever heard.

We are just going to change camp so I must conclude my precious darling. I do wish I could get one kiss from your sweet little lips. Goodbye my darling and believe me to remain

Your ever affectionate husband
H. W. Feilden

Henry W. Feilden to Mrs. Julia Feilden
Camp near Smithfield, N.C.
March 25, 1865, 10 oc at night

My darling precious wife, after a hard days work I sit down in my tent to write you a few lines. My fingers are so cold I cannot write very fast but I will endeavour to commence a letter to you which I will finish tomorrow if I am called away. I hope before this letter reaches you Herbert will be safe at home and that he will be a comfort to you all. Do endeavour to make him manly and independent, and think less of himself and more of his aunts and sisters. I know you have considerable influence over him. Do exert it for good as much as possible. This sad blow to the family may in the end be of great service to Herbert, if it only makes him exert the large share of talent he possesses for the benefit of his family. I will do all I can for them if I am spared and as long as we have anything left we ought to share it with them. You cannot think my darling treasure what happiness your letters are to me. You write so sweetly and affectionately that I love you if possible more and more every hour. I carry your letters in my pocket and when I get a quiet moment I read them over and over again, prizing them more than the greatest miser ever did his hoard of gold.

One of your letters dated the 6th of March I received in the battlefield of Bentonville on the 20th of March. You cannot imagine how it delighted me, and raised my spirits.

So many men now here with the army have left their families houseless and pennyless [*sic*] in South Carolina, and the exigencies of the service will not permit their going home. How fortunate we are by comparison. Oh, my precious one if we are only spared to meet again & live together what happiness it will be. I don't care how poor we may be. It will be the greatest blessing this earth can afford us. I have gone through all the wet and cold and hardships of this campaign so far without even feeling unwell. I think I am in better health than when I left Charleston. Sleeping in wet clothes and before camp fires seems to agree with me. I take good care to wear those flannel shirts that you remind me off [*sic*] in your letter.

I think you would like a short account of my proceedings since we left Charleston so I will endeavour to give it to you.

We evacuated Charleston the very same day as the Yankees under Sherman took possession of Columbia. Our orders were to go to Wilmington and unite with Beauregard and join him at Goldsboro N Ca. but in the meantime Schofield[22] took Wilmington, and our line of march was altered to Cheraw. The movements of our army were much hampered by the large amount of stores, guns and ammunition that we had to take along with us and by the time we got to Cheraw, Sherman, who had passed through Columbia & Camden was close upon us. We held our position at Cheraw until all our stores were across the Pedee [*sic*] River and everything of value to the army was got off. On the 2nd of March we evacuated Cheraw, the enemy following closely our rear guard. We in the rear had quite an exciting time getting off. I had to remain till one of the last and burn the Depot, and had to make tall running to get off. We had quite a brisk little skirmish, which was very entertaining, except to the poor fellows who got killed and wounded. Theodore Barker was amongst the latter number.[23] After leaving Cheraw we passed through Rockingham, Sherman following us and then we got to Fayetteville on the 9th. On the 10th Hampton struck Kilpatrick the Yankee cavalry leader a severe blow near Fayetteville capturing about 500 of his men, surprising his camp, releasing nearly 200 of our men, and Kilpatrick ran off in his shirt and took refuge in the woods. But we were still bound to retreat. Sherman was too strong for us. We left Fayetteville on the 11th closely pursued, and retreated towards Averysboro on the Raleigh road. On the 13th, 14th & 15th we skirmished with the Yankee advance and moved very slowly. On the night of the 15 we halted and threw up breastworks on the 16th. The 14 & 20th Army corps and Kilpatrick's cavalry attacked our lines commencing at early noon. The fight lasted all day. Our troops two Brigades of Hardee's corps say 5000 fought 20,000 obstinately and retained possession of our lines. We lost about 500 men. The prisoners captured next day reported the enemy's loss at about 3300. [*? absurd*]

This was a very gratifying little affair. It gave our men confidence, and showed them that they could fight Yankees as well as their brethren of the armies of Virginia and Tenn.

My poor horse Billy was here unfortunately wounded; unfortunately I say because the fight was nearly over at the time & the General and his staff had withdrawn from the immediate line of battle. Genl H was sitting down against a tree, I was talking to him, a stray shot came over, passed through the sleeve of my great coat (near enough to jar my funny bone) and went into Billy's leg, fortunately not hitting the bone. He is recovering rapidly now I am glad to say.

After the fight at Averysboro we again had to retreat and on the morning of the 19th we joined Genl Johnston at Bentonville near Smithfield. Sherman was in front of us and Genl J. determined to attack him though I suppose he outnumbered us by 3 to 1.

Hardee commanded the right and right centre of our line. We broke the portion of the enemy's line opposed to the right centre of our army, but our left and extreme right made no impression. On our part of the line we captured three or four guns and ran the enemy about a mile and a half. During the night we fell back to our original position and held our works during the 20 & 21 against repeated assaults of the enemy. In these attacks he must have suffered very severely. On the afternoon of the 21st the 17th Army corps of the enemy flanked our line and got into our rear, but Genl Hardee's generalship and the gallantry of the troops namely the 8th Texas Cavalry and Cummings Brigade saved us from disaster. In this gallant charge against the 17th Army corps which Genl H. lead [*sic*] in person, his only son Willie was mortally wounded, and he died yesterday in Raleigh.[24] Genl H. [*Hardee*] left camp last night for Raleigh to bury his poor boy. He was as gallant a little fellow as ever fired a musket. He was a mere schoolboy. I am too sorry for the General.

What is to be our next movement I do not know and hardly care to surmise, as we all place implicit confidence in Genl Johnston & feel that whatever he orders will be the best.

That ultimately we shall beat Sherman, I have no doubt. [*I am afraid this was to cheer the women. H.W.F.*] The [Fabian] policy of retreating and making him attack us behind breastworks will ere long, bring him down to an equality with ourselves, and then for the day of retribution, remember Columbia, remember South Carolina will be our battle cry, and I can assure you the atrocities of <u>those people</u>[25] in South Carolina, will not be forgotten by our soldiers.

The accounts I have heard of the Yankee atrocities in S. Carolina are heartrending and appalling. I hope you may be spared any such suffering. As far as human foresight can judge Greenville is as safe a place as there is in the Confederacy.[26]

If it were possible for you to divide your valuables, and send one half to some place a long way off it would be advisable, but I cannot give good advice so far from the scene of action. I can only hope you people in Greenville may be spared. Goodnight my precious one. I am very tired, & will finish this letter tomorrow.

Henry W. Feilden to Mrs. Julia Feilden
April 2, 1865

My dear Wife, I learn that there is a man just leaving for Greenville so I write you a line to say that I am quite well. I wrote you a long letter which I sent off by mail yesterday. I daresay this will reach you first. I have not heard from you later than the 13th of March. I hope Herbert gave you the little stud I sent you. How I wish I could see you again dearest. Keep up your spirits and trust in God that he might preserve us and bring us safe back again together. Our army is in very good spirits and increasing in numbers. Sherman is at Goldsboro where he has concentrated with Schofield. His next move I presume will be on Raleigh. I suppose we shall not let him get there without a fight. I hope you have still got plenty to eat. I wish I could get back for a short time and see that you are well provided for.

I trust Herbert will assume the responsibilities that now rest on him and attend to his family. All my clerks have been taken away by Genl Johnston orders [*sic*]. Only one allowed, am keeping the place for Herbert. Consequently I am nearly worked to death. Love to all. Your ever affect husband

H. W. Feilden

Henry W. Feilden to Mrs. Julia Feilden
Headquarters, Hardees Corps
April 6, 1865

My darling Wife, I sit down to write you a few lines today to have a letter in readiness whenever the opportunity occurs for sending it off to Greenville.

I have no news to give you of anything good for our cause. On Saturday the 1st of April, Grant broke through Lee's lines before Petersburgh [*sic*], on Sunday the 2nd the President and cabinet evacuated Richmond. I hear Lieut Genl A. P. Hill was killed and Major Genl Gordon, wounded. As a natural sequence if we abandoned Petersburgh we must have lost all our guns there.

I suppose Lee's army will fall back and join with us in N. Carolina, and I predict this summer will see us in Georgia. I expect Sherman will move at once from Goldsboro and advance upon Raleigh in order to get the railroad and cut off Lee from getting out of Va. We shall have some desperate fighting around Raleigh I am sure, and I am afraid in the end Sherman will gain what he wants unless Lee gets down from Va in time to join us.

I wonder what our leaders are going to do; a prolongation of the war appears nothing but a further useless loss of life. But the question arises whether death is not preferable to subjugation by the Yankees, and the association of a negro aristocracy. I am very thankful however that I have nothing to do with the settlement of this matter, and that there is no responsibility on my shoulders. I endeavour to think as little of our future as possible, and make myself happy by thinking if I am only spared to live with you after the war, I am ready to submit to the greatest trials and hard work. There must be plenty of places in this world, where we can hide ourselves away and be at rest.

I went out this morning and tried to find your brother Turquand[27] but there are so many Alabama regts in the service, it is like hunting for a needle in a bushel of hay. Your brother knows that I am on Hardee's staff & it would be much easier for him to find me than I, him. I hope you have made a belt or something to put your gold and jewelry in. If the Yankees come ever to Greenville they will rob you of everything. The experience of this war proofs [*sic*] that you can put no trust in any negro. They have invariably betrayed their masters and mistresses.

I wish I could get home to you for a sufficient length of time to look after your things and hide or bury some of them.

I hope to goodness I will be able to get to Greenville someday. I sometimes think I ought to resign from the army & look after you, but then again I am sure that as a South Carolinian you would sooner that I was in the field fighting for your liberties than staying at home looking after you. I could not resign with honor at such a junction as this, and I believe I am in reality a better [*as good a*] Southern man, though a foreigner, [*Britisher*] than most of the men born in the country.

We are having splendid weather and lovely moonlight nights. Last night some of the men came up to camp and sang "Home Sweet Home." They sang beautifully, and they succeeded in keeping me awake all night thinking of the burden of their song.

I hear today that Selma has gone.[28] I wonder how long it will be before the Yankees get all the places this side of the Miss.

Your letter of the 19th & 21st of March has just arrived and fortunately I have an opportunity of sending you an answer in return by a man who leaves for Greenville in the morning. It is a piece of good fortune that does not often occur. I sent off a letter by post this morning for Herbert containing two or three letters that came for him, and now I enclose them some more in yours.

Don't be at all afraid of my over exerting myself. I do nothing but what a man ought to do and your cousin Theodore is so accustomed to sitting still in an office that he is surprised at what amount a man can do, who like myself has been brought up from childhood to outdoor exercise.

I am very glad Mr. Wagner arrived safely at Greenville. He must have had a rough journey of it to Spartanburgh [*sic*]. Was it in joke or did he really mean it when he asked if you would like to go to England. I should like very much for you to go there not that I want to get rid of you, but I should be glad if you were out of this country for the next year for we are going to have terrible times. I should not mind going myself if I thought that my services could be of more use there than here, but such an idea on my part is preposterous for the enemy would never let me through their lines, and to tell the truth I would sooner be killed in this war than leave the country in its present distress of my own accord.

I expect when the war is over we shall find some of the colored ladies of the city living in our house, and I doubt very much whether we ever get it back again.

But you may make yourself easy on that score for if I live you shall have a home darling of your own. You must not think that I am downhearted. I am not, but I see things in their proper light. People in the army wonder at my good spirits, but for all that I cannot shut my eyes to our condition, though perhaps after all it is more philosophic to [try] and not to think but to float down with the current. I am sorry to hear Miss Malvina is unwell. Please give her my very kindest regards and say I hope she is quite recovered by this time. Mr. Charles Lowndes[29] is an excellent man for president of the Bank, if there is any Bank left. I am sorry to think that Mr. & Mrs. Cheeseborough met with such losses.[30] Please remember me kindly to them.

Mr. Wagner's experience of the negroes is very much on a par with that of all others. They almost invariably have betrayed their masters in this war.

I am sure the Middletons and Pringles must feel highly honored, at their colored people [*connections*] cutting such swells in Charleston. The color presented was doubtless of the 54th Mass. The original one belonging to that regt. I daresay you will remember it was in my possession and was captured at Battery Wagner in July 1863. I expected Dr. Geddings and Mr. Aiken[31] would take the oath of allegiance, and I have heard since that old Aiken is now Major & Macbeth[32] is in jail at Hilton Head. Though we are in the pine woods, yet you will perceive we keep "au fait" in the current news of the day.

I heard a hard story on the lovely Miss Booser, [*I have no recollection of who I refer to, perhaps some negro wench who ran off with a Yankee.*] that when she got to the coast she found her Yankee husband had got another wife in

[Mass.].[33] I don't know whether this is true but I think probably it will be the case.

I was surprised [words crossed out]. If we could only get one half of the men into the fields whose names we carry on the muster rolls we could have whipped the enemy long ago.

You ask me in your letter if I belong to the Masons. I do, but I am afraid you will not be able to get initiated into their mysteries for it is one of the fundamental rules in the order that no woman can be admitted, as they are not supposed to be capable of keeping a secret. Once upon a time a woman hid herself in a clock case, where a party of Masons assembled & she discovered their secrets. They therefore made her take the oaths and then as a precaution cut out her tongue and hands, so that she could not divulge the mysteries, either verbally or in writing.

Are you aware that in the black trunk I sent to Columbia there was half a bag of coffee for you. Don't think I came out of Charleston unprovided with coffee & tea. I brought out a bag of coffee, [60] lbs of tea and a bag of sugar. I think in all some $ [1000?] worth [words were crossed out], but I have distributed it right and left. Our mess has coffee for breakfast and dinner and tea at bed time.

Have the starch worked out of my shirts by all means, and if you feel very industrious do make me some stockings. Don't make them of too thick thread. The two pairs you sent me some time ago when I was in Charleston I could not wear. They were too coarse, and Marney [*The boy Dr. Cheves lent me.*] got the benefit of them. I am nearly sockless now and before I see you again I shall be barefooted. I hope you got your shoes made.

Please give my kind regards to Mrs. Elliott. I am not surprised at your being sorry for her at present, not having any experience, I cannot speak from personal knowledge, but should imagine her condition not very enviable.

You had better get the tin box from Mr. Thayer as soon as possible. It is much safer in your keeping than in the bank.

I have not seen brother Ned for a long time. He is away with his battery at Hillsboro with the rest of the reserve arty. When I see him I will give him your love.

I have seen a good deal lately of Dr. Cheves, who has now gone back to South Carolina, and when he went off I sent a beautiful book of ballads by him for you. You will be surprised to receive such a present from the pine woods of N. Carolina.

So many people are coming into the office that I am afraid I shall have to close my letter though I have a great deal more to tell you. I have even now two Major Genls pitching into me for not being able to tell them what became of certain papers sent to Richmond in Jan. last. So my precious darling goodbye. God bless you and believe me to remain your ever affectionate husband

H. W. Feilden

6

POSTWAR LIFE

May 1, 1865–July 4, 1920

Mary McCord to her sister Mrs. Julia Feilden
May 1, 1865

My dearest Julie,

What an age it is since I have heard from you. Not a line have I received from any of you since the 21st of last December, except a note from Capt Feilden, or rather I think two little notes. I have supposed you were in Greenville all this time, & the Capt with Johnson's [*sic*] army. Well everything has come to pass exactly as your [Croaker] sister Mary long ago foresaw. The Confederacy is dead, amen. What are you going to do with your ladyship? I have been teaching school (after all) with Mr. [Carson] for the last month and a half & I have a holliday [*sic*] now for a few days. I have been working hard, but don't think I will get much for my pains—have not received anything yet. Next week however there is to be a change. The public schools for white children are to be organized, and several female teachers are required to assist Mr. [Caner]. These ladies are to be examined by a board of trustees, and chosen according to their merits. Of course I know nothing about Mathematics, Mechanics and many of the ologies, therefore will not aspire to the highest honor or largest salary which is very good one. I should like to be drawing teacher, but doubt if I will be needed in that capacity as there is no love of art in these [?]. I suppose I will have to content myself with the primary & elementary department. I would greatly prefer planting corn to either the one or the other, but necessity has no [?]. I wish Miss Malvina &

Miss Victoria were here to give me advice & help. I never heard of poor Mr. Sass' death until a few days ago. What a dreadful loss to his family. Do say to Miss M how dreadful I feel for them.[1] We hear that Mr. Gourdin is dead also, but do not know if it is true. I never was so lonely in my life as I am this summer. I have no intimate friend, & our household is too busy to be communicative. I should die of melancholy if I did not have to work hard. I long to hear about all my friends. Willis [Keith] takes this to you, and we have permission to write. What has become of the [Cap] & Ned P and everyone I wonder. Sophy Dulles wrote very kindly to me & sent me various useful things through Anna [S.], also almost everyone is taking the oath now.

I hope you are well & cheerful dear Julie, though you must have been very anxious all this time. You must rejoice as we all do that there is prospect of peace once more. Do write & tell me about yourself as soon as you can. We are in the same house & will probably be here until November. Give much love to all in the house & to all friends elsewhere. God bless you my dear Julie.

Ever your affect
Sister Mary

Mrs. Hamilton has gone to the North. I long to go away, too.

Note on same letter from Charlotte Cheves to her sister Mrs. Julia Feilden:

Dearest Julie, I hope your husband has returned & that in time you may go to Europe—the best wish I can now make you. We long to hear from you. We have heard of no one for 6 months past. We are completely isolated & have a hard struggle for our daily subsistence. We are more fortunate in many respects than some, but our daily means of subsistence is very uncertain! We are all in the same house. I hope we may all meet again once more, & then we shall have much to tell of I can't write. I am [painting] all day and my hand is fatigued. We grieved to hear of Mr. S's death! I can't tell how much! It is desolate to be without male protection! I wish I could talk with you. We feel most anxious about [Rosalie, Turk & Janis]. I hope you are well. Farewell Dearest.

Yr loving sister C[2]

Henry W. Feilden to Mrs. Julia Feilden

Camp 20 miles north of
Charlotte N.C., May 4, 1865

My darling,

I and Captain Memminger[3] are marching with our wagon "en route" for Greenville. If we find no difficulty in crossing the Catawba and Broad rivers and do not break down on the way we shall arrive in Greenville on Wednesday night or Thursday morning.

I send this note by a gentleman who is riding through to Augusta and will strike the Greenville road at Ninety Six.

I have not heard anything about you for so long that I have been quite miserable. I suppose Col Campbell[4] told you he saw me near Greensboro. I had no idea he was returning to Greenville or should have written by him.

You are aware I suppose that the war has ended in this part of the country and that we have given in on this side of the Mississippi.

Considering the position we were in General Johnston made excellent terms with Sherman for the army, that is to say we are not to be molested by the Yankee govt and our personal property is respected. No one else in the country has any guarantee for either life or property except from the magnanimity of our enemies, which does not amount to much.

The feelings of indignation in the north against our late leaders is described by the Yankee officer as intense. Genl Schofield (a very old friend of Genl Hardee's) who now commands N. Ca. advised him to leave the country at once. My own opinion is that our prominent men will be treated with great severity if not executed.

Booth the murderer of Mr. Lincoln was caught and burnt to death in a barn by his pursuers. The death of Lincoln was looked upon by the [*our*] army as a great misfortune for the South. If he were alive we should have had no difficulty in getting terms. As it is Andy Johnson the new President is a cruel treacherous rascal of the blackest dye, burning with hatred against the South.

I feel very sad at coming home conquered instead of victorious. Give my love to Herbert and all the family and believe me to remain darling your ever affectionate husband

H. W. Feilden

Henry W. Feilden to Mrs. Julia Feilden
Charleston, S.C., May 30, 1865

My darling Wife,

Mr. Chisolm and myself arrived here last night safely and find ourselves this morning located at old Moses Chapman's, who proves himself the "friend in need" and therefore a "friend indeed."

I have not had time to look around me as it is not breakfast time yet and I got into the city late last night, but a glance out of the window plainly shows that times have changed. The house we used to live in [*Rutledge Avenue*] is occupied by a Mr. Redpath,[5] Yankee school teacher, several school marms, and several colored damsels. Herbert's old room which I can enfilade from the position I am now writing at. It is shared by a Yankee and a colored lady. I think her name is Miss Sedgenation [*cegenation*]. Chisolm's house is occupied by a Judge Cooler.[6] I hope though that he will be able to oust him. I hear our house [Legare Street & Battery] is occupied but by whom I know not. I am making friends with the mammon of unrighteousness and with that aid trust get the present incumbent out. If there is no yellow fever here and I can get back the house I think your best plan would be to come here. There is nothing to eat anywhere else. In Augusta things are very high. Coffee 75 cents a pound in specie and sugar 20 cents, but coffee is the same price here I understand.

I am in hopes that I will get Mr. Phillips to take this letter up to Greenville, but as the cars leave early I cannot write you as long a letter as I should wish.

A few words about the journey which was a very easy & tolerably pleasant one. We got to Ninty Six[7] all right on Thursday and rode about 16 miles & stayed at a planter's house there. The next day we rode through Edgefield and instead of going to Augusta we thought it expedient to get to Kalmia[8] near Aiken and see the Greggs and find out how the land lay. Mr. [Lemmans] insisted upon my staying with him at Kalmia, which I did and next day we went into Augusta, which is now a miserable place, the population scared to death of the Yankee garrison. That afternoon we met two Yankee officers going back to Charleston and they asked us to join their party which we agreed to do, and at six oc on Sunday morning we joined them at Aiken and rode halfway to Branchville during that day. Yesterday we got to Branchville at 10c got our horses on the cars and came into Charleston in grand style.[9] The two Yankees we traveled with, though regular down easters, acted as well as they could and were as kind and accommodating as possible. For instance they insisted upon paying all the expenses. We helped them to drink bottles of whiskey en route. At Branchville they got the U.S. officer to put our horses on the car and saved us 65 miles ride. By the way the 102 U.S. colored troops gave us lunch there. A nigger mess sergeant took our crowd in & gave us good coffee & sugar, hard tack & Northern bacon, and when the Yankee officer told the Sergeant we were rebel officers he said if that is so I would like to treat them ten times better than if they were Union officers. On getting into the city, our Yankee friends gave us a very good supper, ale, sherry, tea, fish, tomatoes, eggs, milk, blackberries & preserved peaches, but no more about good things at present or you will think me unkind. I hope darling you are well. I shall only stay here a few days. I shall be back in eight days or so. Give my kind regards to the old ladies, and love to Herbert. I have more to tell you than would fill a book. Goodbye though for the present, and believe me to remain darling ever your loving husband

H. W. Feilden

Henry W. Feilden to Mrs Julia Feilden
Charleston, S.C., May 31, 1865

My darling Wife,

I take the opportunity of Major Buist[10] going up to Newberry to send you a few lines to say how I am getting on. I think slowly but surely. I find no disposition on the part of the U.S. authorities to put any hindrance in the way of my getting the house, the only difficulty is that the owners are considered by the government to be those whose names appear on the city tax returns for 1860, or else you can show their titles [*sic*]. This is only reasonable for otherwise any impostor might come and claim the houses. I was speaking today to the estate commissioner and he said that if I could bring good oral testimony that the house belonged to me he would give me possession, though I cannot now pay the tax before the 1st of November. I do not apprehend any difficulty in getting the house.

I walked all around the city today. The harbour and the shipping looked beautiful. The condition of the city is not near as bad as represented, as long as one troubles nobody else. No one appears to trouble you. I wish I had you down here. I believe we could live down here for $100 a month very comfortably. You would have to do sometime without

[PART OF LETTER MISSING]

was [worried], but we shall be quite happy down here if we only can find something to live on. Kind regards to the family and believe me dearest to remain your ever loving husband

H. W. Feilden

Henry W. Feilden to Mrs. Julia Feilden
Orangeburg, S.C., July 12, 1865

My precious darling,

I send you up a budget of letters received last night on my return from Aiken where I had been driving a passenger to. I am well and hearty. I hope you are well darling. Col Yates[11] will hand you this letter and will also give you a personal account of myself.

We are getting on tolerably here. I only want a good stock of animals to do a good business.

I think we shall be able to get to Charleston in October. I am going there on Monday to get my black horse Julius and if I see a good chance will go on to Savannah. I must see Battersby before he leaves.

Do you want money darling. If you do let me know. I will send it up. All I can collect I am spending in mules.

I have not heard a word from home. I missed the chance of sending you up some white sugar by Frank Porcher. If it is to be bought in Greenville I advise you to do it.

I hope you got the cameos and liked them. Believe me my precious darling to remain in great haste your ever affectionate husband

H. W. Feilden

Henry W. Feilden to Mrs. Julia Feilden

Orangeburg, S.C., July 19, 1865

My darling Wife,

I have not been in Columbia for sometime. I expect there are several letters waiting there for me from you. I have not heard from you since I left. I hope you are well and getting on comfortably.

We are getting on tolerably here. Our stock of animals is increasing, and I think our trade will increase in a corresponding ratio. We have added to our hauling business a general commission agency which employs me more in Orangeburgh. I do not go out driving teams as formerly. We have negroes to attend to that. I look after the receipts of cotton and shipping of freight.

There is not very much business to be done here but enough to keep us until the fall. At present all the money we make is invested in buying mules etc so that we may increase our trade. I will send you up some money whenever a safe opportunity occurs.

I went down to the city on Friday last and came back yesterday. I brought up Julius [*A favorite black horse which I had ridden from Greenville to Charleston.*] and bought an ambulance there, for the passenger trade.

I saw Mr. [Cockings] in town who occupies our house. He is removing to a house in Broad St so that ours will soon be vacant. I will make some arrangements to have it occupied until we go down. I do not think it would be advisable for you to go to the city until October. I should like very much though if you get down here, and I am endeavouring to make some arrangements for that end, but it is almost impossible to get a room here. I do miss you so my precious darling.

I saw your cousin Theodore in the city. He is very well and sent you his love. Many people made enquiries after you.

There are very few ladies in Charleston and I doubt very much if society will ever be the same there, as it was before the war.

Mr. Theodore Stoney[12] is still in the city. I suppose Mr. Porcher got home safely and gave you my letter and parcel.

I find considerable difficulty in sending you letters now, so few people are traveling between Greenville & Charleston.

I do not know how we are to furnish our house this fall but I suppose we must be content with a couple of rooms at first.

I have not heard one word from home yet. I am very anxious to do so, as I am desirous of getting some money from England.

If I do not hear from you soon I shall be obliged to take a run up to Greenville and see what has become of you. I hope I shall not find that you have eloped. I am living a wretched life here. I have to sleep in a room so full of bugs that I never close my eyes at night. It is very hard that we should have been married for nearly a year and yet that we have not lived together for more than two months. I hope though that when we meet again we may never have to separate.

I cannot see any employment for Herbert, and I do not think that things will be much better in the fall. The country is in a dreadful condition, and I am afraid this generation will never see it prosperous again.

Please give my love to the Miss Murdens and the children. As for you my precious one please accept the very largest number of kisses & good wishes. I will try and see you soon. The scolding letter you wrote me never turned up at Chapman's. Someone else has read it. Goodbye dearest. Your ever affect. husband

H. W. Feilden

Henry W. Feilden to Mrs. Julia Feilden
Orangeburg, S.C., Aug. 1, 1865

My darling Wife,

I have written frequently to you but have only received <u>two</u> letters from you since I left Greenville. They were dated 9th & 10th of July. I know you have written a great deal oftener so I suppose my letters are like yours, not very regularly received. I wrote you a long letter already <u>today</u> and I sent it by the cars. I send this one by Mr. Peronneau who leaves for Anderson today.

It contained an account of my plan to get you down here. In case you don't receive that letter I will repeat the subject matter to you again. I expect to have a room or rooms here in the course of a week, and as soon as I am certain of it I will leave for Greenville. You must therefore be prepared to see me any day, and when I do come you must be ready to leave in a couple of days after. I shall make arrangements so that our baggage will accompany us. So darling say goodbye to your friends and pack up your things. On second thought perhaps it would be advisable not to say anything about it, until I come up.

I do not think you will find Orangeburgh any warmer than Greenville. You won't be very comfortable here, but more so than you are now, and then you will be so close to Charleston you will be able to go down and fix up the house.

I am writing you this note in a room full of people, all speaking & howling at the top of their voices so excuse my not sending you a very lucid letter.

I think I shall be up in Greenville nearly as soon as this letter. I have been working very hard to get a room. [Mrs.] E. L. Yates and I ran all over the town this morning to find you a place.

I have received many letters from home, will bring them up with me.

Please give my kind love to all and darling accept a great deal from me believing me to remain your ever affectionate husband

H. W. Feilden

P.S. My darling I am so unhappy away from you. I have spent a miserable time this last month. How I long to see you my precious one.

Henry W. Feilden to Mrs. Julia Feilden
96 M. T. O.[13] March 19, 1866

My darling, This day and about this very hour we were in the thickest of the first day's fight at Bentonville last year. A little after sunset a courier rode up to me and handed me a letter in a yellow envelope. A glance showed me that it was from you. I never enjoyed the sight of one of your letters more. It was a dear little love letter and I have that letter carefully put away and marked "received from my darling during the battle of Bentonville." As I read your dear little missive, so affectionate, so anxious, so tremulous for my safety, I could hardly believe that I was sitting on my horse amidst the uproar of a battlefield, surrounded by dead, wounded & dying men, the roar of battle in my ears, and its attendant horrors on every side. It was sad to think that perhaps for every one of those dead or dying men, some little heartbroken plaintiff voice was crying, praying. But somehow or other your letter did me good and I believe I did my duty better, when I thought of my honest true-hearted little woman far away.

Today I have been very busy writing to [Lawley] a sixteen page letter. Some of it is very good so much so that instead of posting it I will bring it down on Saturday and read it to you. It will interest you. I have also been attempting a Turkey trade and have half concluded a bargain for 12 hens $1.00, Gobblers $2.00. If I get them they will not cost more than 14 or 15 cent per lbs, one half the price of beef and much nicer though you will turn into a Turk yourself before you get half through them all.

I hope you have not died of fright since I left. I know it must be very painful to you to have to sleep in that large room alone but it is not going to last forever. What would you do if you were a widow?

Mr. Wm. Magrath is married.[14] The knot was tied this day last week. He left Aiken on Wednesday for I saw him on the cars on Thursday. He did not stay very long with his bride. Yesterday a bag of oysters came up for Mrs. W. J. Magrath. Proof presumptive in my mind that the report of his wedding is true. It is a nice mess for a man of his years to get into.

This is an outrageously dull place. I don't see or talk to any one except a few country bumpkins and their conversation is limited to niggers and guano & its relative merits to phosphate of lime. I have nothing more to say to you this evening my darling than to wish you every happiness and hoping that I will see you looking well & happy next Saturday. Believe me to remain

your ever affectionate husband
H. W. Feilden

Henry W. Feilden to Mrs. Julia Feilden
Williston, S.C.,[15] March 28, 1866

My darling, I hope you are better today. I feel very sorry for you being so sick, especially since I have a violent face ache today of the same kind as I have had twice before but not quite so violent. "A fellow feeling makes us wondrous kind."

Mr. Smith went to the city today. It is a great relief to get rid of him and I feel much happier alone. S. is very much of the same stamp as Captain Murden, but without exception the untidiest, dirty man I ever saw. He would get into bed with his shoes on and cover up the blankets with dirt. All his clothes, dirty linen included were strewn about the car, mingled with tobacco spit and multitudinous dirts. And oh! heavens! My recollections of the nights spent with him are fearful; he was so fat and unwieldy that when he rolled he took off all the blankets & then snored and grunted so loud that a sounder of hogs in the next car would have been kept awake. Just as often as I cleaned up the car he would in a quarter of an hour mess it up again. This morning after the cars left I swept and washed out my abode, beat every blanket, arranged a nice cotton mattress, nailed a sheet over the frame of the bed so as to give the place a neat look, then made up the bed, put my trunk and boots under the bed, washed the windows, hung up everything in place, got a box to put the firewood in instead of having it lying about the car, nailed up a blanket over the door between the office and sleeping room and arranged cords & rings to draw it up with, blackened the stove, fixed the roof so that it would not leak. I also rearranged my office, put all the papers straight which were in an awful condition. Borrowed a lamp and bought oil, and then a box of sardines and biscuits, and as soon as this letter is finished I will make tea and invite Mr. Browning the conductor. I did all this with my own fair fingers before the cars came back this afternoon and since then have unloaded freight, packed wagons, made out 4 freight lists and written several letters. Don't you think I have done an honest day's work. My car is now comfortable enough for a lady to live in.

I got a telegram from your brother Russell this afternoon telling me to meet him at the cars tonight. I suppose he means the cars tomorrow morning, if he is on his way to Charleston. I hope he will stay with you, and I will give him this letter to take.

goodbye darling
your ever affectionate Henry

P.S. You little exacting critical thing, I believe I have written you too long a letter. You will say this time that I am egotistical.

Henry W. Feilden to Mrs. Miles
Wells, Norfolk, England
June 2, 1899

My dear Mrs. Miles,[16]

I feel sure that we owe to your kind thoughtfulness, the files of the "Charleston News & Courier" May 10th, 11th, 13th & 14th, which came to hand last night. Julie and I are greatly indebted to you, and we have been reading these remarkable issues ever since they reached us.

In the mass of interesting information which we have been assimilating during the past twenty-four hours we were saddened to read the notice of William Porcher Miles's death. I can scarce realize that he was in his 78th year. I had not seen him for 34 years, and therefore, his presence was fixed on my mind as that of a man in the prime of life, full of wisdom, courtesy, and kindness. I have a pleasant recollection of him in my early days of sojourn in the Confederate States. When Mr. Jefferson Davis appointed me to a Commission in the P.A.C.S.[17] the President's nomination had to be approved by the Senate and Congress. Mr. W. P. Miles was my sponsor in the lower House and Senator Yancey undertook the same kind office in the Senate, as you may imagine, in the hands of such godfathers, my nomination was approved of without a word of dissent, though I was an alien.

After reading the accounts of the splendid Reunions of veterans, and what the old city did for them, you Charleston people may justly feel proud of yourselves. . . .

There are many interesting stories by old veterans in the papers sent, and I might have supplemented several of them with additional facts.

I am surprised that no mention was made of Colonel Harris, he was a real defender of Sumter and of Charleston. I think however, that Johnson has done him justice in his history of the Siege of Charleston.

The weather here is lovely at present, and reminds me of your beautiful Mays and Aprils when the roses with their wealth of bloom smother the city, and the mockingbirds sing in the early morn—in imagination I can hear them now.

In the Sass garden in Legare Street, there used always to be mockingbirds in the springtime.

Julie and I are very well. She rides a bike and thinks nothing of a spin of ten miles or more. She sends you her best love and many many thanks for the papers and I also should like to send my love to Mary if I dared to do so and not be deemed presuming.

Therefore to avoid personalities I send my warm good wishes to all the fair women and brave men of the dear old Palmetto State. May you all prosper, and hand down from generation to generation, the beauty, the bravery and nobleness of character, which I learned to love and have never forgotten from the days of old.

Yours very truly,
H. W. Feilden

Henry W. Feilden to Mr. A. T. Smythe
Burwash, Sussex, April 25, 1902

My dear Mr. A. T. Smythe,[18]

I was so sorry to be from home when Louisa went down to see Julia, but I am not my own master just at present, having to move an elderly uncle from this place to a new residence in Gloucestershire. I hope to be free middle of next week, and must see something of you. My uncle is 82, and of course needs help when shifting his effects.

In regard to an oil painting of Fort Sumter, I have long determined to return it to Charleston. It has a very interesting history.

There was a certain Lieut. Key, in the Engineers of the P.A.C.S., an artist of considerable merit. He was (or is if alive) a nephew of the author of the "Star Spangled Banner." I think I am right in this statement.[19]

For his name and initials please see introduction of Johnson's Defence of Charleston Harbour, wherin is published the order by General Beauregard, for certain officers to prepare a report on the siege of Charleston. . . . Key and I were detailed for this duty.

We collected a large amount of material, but the exigencies of war prevented our carrying out the plan, which has been so admirably accomplished by Major Johnson.

It struck me that an oil painting made at the time would be a most valuable reminiscence for posterity, and I urged Key to undertake the task, and as he was a refugee from Baltimore (I think), and of course being badly off,

I paid him, indeed I insisted on paying him, for he would have done it for nothing!

The canvas now in my possession was not actually painted under fire, and the smaller sketch was, for Key as Engineer, was frequently at Sumter on duty. Minor details were taken from photos . . . shortly before the surrender of Charleston. I happened to be back in the city, from General Hardee's staff, went to my lodgings and rolled up this picture, put it on board the last steamer leaving Charleston, and begged the captain of the ship to hand it over to the late Charles Prioleau in Liverpool, of the firm of Fraser Trenholm & Co. Subsequently Mr. Prioleau, returned it to me, and it has been ever since in my possession.

I only part with the picture, because I think it ought to be returned to S. Carolina and I shall feel glad, to think that my foster state (for my commission in the C.S.A. is [sic] given to me by Senate or Congress as a child of the Palmetto State) is in possession of this most interesting relic.

Yours most sincerely,
H. W. Feilden

Henry W. Feilden to Mr. A. T. Smythe
West House, Wells, Norfolk
May 17, 1902

My dear Smythe,

I have shipped the picture of "Fort Sumter" painted at Charleston in 1863, by Lieutenant John R. Key, of the Engineers, P. A.C. States, on board the "Minnehaha," and trust that it may recross the Atlantic in safety. If you turn to the introduction of Johnson's narrative of "The Defence of Charleston Harbour 1863–1865" you will see that Lieutenant Key and I, with Captain John Johnson and others were appointed by General Beauregard members of a Board to compile a military history of the Siege of Charleston. A certain amount of material for such a work was put together, but I fancy it was lost on the evacuation of the City in 1865.

I do not, however, think that a scrap of information gathered by that Board has been omitted from Major John Johnson's admirable narrative, which in my humble opinion is a model record of military events, and which must confer on the author the everlasting gratitude of the citizens of the Palmetto State.

Lieutenant Key, little more than a youth at the time was a painter of considerable merit, as the picture shows. It was at my urgent request that he undertook the painting, as I deemed it of great importance that some lasting memorial of Fort Sumter in 1863, should be preserved for posterity. The original sketches were made by Key in Fort Sumter, and the details worked out from photographs of Mr. G. S. Cook.

You may observe that the soldiers depicted are in the uniform of the First South Carolina Artillery, then commanded by Colonel Alfred Rhett. Towards the close of 1864, I sent this picture, through the blockade to Mr. Charles Prioleau, of the firm of Fraser, Trenholm & Co. in Liverpool; after my return to England Mr. Prioleau most kindly restored it to me.

It has remained for over thirty years one of my most valuable possessions, but my wife, a good daughter of the State, agrees with me that the picture should find its resting place, in the dear old City.

Yours most sincerely,
H. W. Feilden
The Hon. Augustine T. Smythe
Charleston, S. Ca.

Henry W. Feilden to Mr. A. T. Smythe
Burwash, Sussex, England
July 13, 1903

Dear Smythe,

Both Julie and I are charmed to receive the photograph of your good-looking son.[20] He looks a real young South Carolina gentleman just as I remember them forty years ago.

I like the little mare, she looks a good bred un, and the dogs are "sans reproche." His Aunt, who like all well bred women, has an eye for a smart young fellow, says that Austin is the exact likeness of his Uncle Turquand McCord, her brother, and I think that I can trace a strong family resemblance. . . .

I am very much obliged for the volume giving the Documentary History of the Confederate & Federal Navies off the Coasts of S. Car. during the war. I must admit that it was very dry reading, but I waded through each dispatch. I arose from the perusal with a very high opinion of the inventive facilities of the Southern men, and how much they did, with little or no mechanical resources. My old chief General Beauregard comes out well, in his able advocacy of the torpedo as the future weapon of naval battles. He was in that respect before his day. At this lapse of time, it is almost ludicrous to read the invectives that Admiral Dupont launched against the makers and users of those infernal machines! . . .

I do wish that your Senators and Congressmen would object to the war records being styled in the official volumes "War of the Rebellion." The term is incorrect. Sovereign States could not rebel. The appeal to the sword went against the Southern States, and the result has been a great consolidation of Federal power, but I will contend to my last breath that the commonwealth of S. Car., never <u>rebelled</u>.

We are sorry to hear that your daughter Susie[21] has been so far from well, but that Miss Jane McClintock is flourishing must be a great comfort to her.

Tell Sister Louisa that Julie has made the old shanty charming! Come and see it as soon as you can. With kindest wishes for you and yours from both, I am,

Yours sincerely,
H. W. Feilden

Henry W. Feilden to Mrs. Augustine Thomas Smythe
Burwash, Sussex, England
Sept. 24, 1909

My dear Louisa,

I have been away for a week, so that yours of the 7th which reached here on the 16th has only been opened.

You may well believe that I have been as greatly interested in the proceedings of Dr. Cook & Commander Peary as any of you over the water.[22]

That Commander Peary reached the spot on the surface of the globe, which we call Latitude 90, cannot be doubted. Peary's record is beyond question. He is the greatest of Polar explorers. He has covered a quarter of the Polar hemisphere with his gracks, so that laid down on a chart, they look like the lines of a spider's web—and for 23 years he had devoted his strenuous life to the accomplishment of reaching the Pole.

He had behind him the finest ship ever built for Arctic navigation, and his crew of Britishers (Newfoundlanders) under Bartlett, as good ice-sailors as any in the world. He had the resources of the United States to draw upon, and the scientific aid and advice of many of the greatest lights in America. Again it was a mere question of accident, bad weather, and the "Big Land" that prevented Peary from reaching the Pole in 1906.

Read his book "Nearest the Pole," and you must agree with me—I know Peary. He is, I feel sure, as honest as they make them. I have followed every incident of his many journeys, some of them over areas with which I am personally acquainted, and I never found the man to exaggerate, or write a word which I do not believe and in some cases I can, from personal knowledge, substantiate his statements.

Therefore I must give as my firm conviction that everything Peary states or writes is strictly the truth.

As things turned out, it is regrettable that Peary let Bartlett go back at the 88° but I quite understand his motive, at least I think I do. He did not wish, as a patriotic American, that the hoisting of the Stars and Stripes on the apex of the Earth, should be shared by a Britisher. I do not blame Peary at all. It seems to me very natural. He had the American public to consider.

As for Dr. Cook, what am I to say! It is not for me or anyone else to declare that a man of Arctic & Antarctic experience who has hitherto borne a most excellent character and reputation is a deceiver, or has deceived himself. If he reached the Pole, with his limited resources, it is miraculous. But it appears to me that if the Doctor has really done so, an examination of his daily log and observations by competent scientific men, must surely demonstrate the truth or falsehood of his statements. Therefore until deception is proved against the Doctor, I am not going to say he is anything but trustworthy. If there are many doubters of Dr. Cook's achievements, he had only himself to blame, in that in the first instance he did not give a matter of fact, business account of his proceedings. Either reporters did him injustice, or else in the excitement of the moment he gave himself away. Then in the first account he said he reached Cape Sharbo in North Devon in Sept. 1908 he was without food, fuel or ammunition, that they improvised with bows &

arrows, & lances, snared Musk-oxen, shot bears and wolves with arrows, and so forth, which is simply incredible. But that, perhaps, is embroidery, and really has not much to do with the question whether he did or did not reach the Pole over the ice from Cape Thomas Hubbard, 520 miles. Peary had 420 to overcome. . . .

This is a long-winded story and after reading it you will say this is no more than we knew before, and comes very badly from a man who has wintered within a mile of the same spot where the Roosevelt wintered 95–99, and has traveled along the coastline from whence Peary made his start this year. I know the extraordinary difficulties of getting over this Polar Pack. . . .

Our poor islands have seen their best day. As long as we were manufacturing masters of the world we could support a population out of all proportion to the area and production of the land. Now others are passing us, and we are, I believe, going from bad to worse. If I was thirty years younger I would seek a new home in Canada.

Affectionately yours.
H. W. Feilden

Henry W. Feilden to Mr. Augustine T. Smythe
Rampyndene, Burwash, Susssex
June 25, 1914

Dear Mr. Smythe,
      Yours of the 24th to hand.
      I have not followed the correspondence in the "Times," as I do not take that paper regularly.
      Somewhere in this house I have notes about the sinking of "Housatonic." It is 50 years ago, since she was sunk. Therefore I must repeat my memory before I am put on oath.
      The impression on my mind is that Lieutenant Dixon used a spar torpedo and what makes that suspicion almost a certainty is that the "Housatonic" lay in or just outside of Maffits Channel abreast of Sullivans I. . . . When she went down her masts stood up almost flush with the decks. I often looked at wreck from Ft. Sumter & Sullivan's Island. It seems to me that it would have

been impossible for any submarine to have got under the "Housatonic" in that shallow water.

You may remember that this infernal craft destroyed several crews.

The idea was to swing a floating torpedo astern, and dive under the ship hauling the floating torpedo against the [anchored] vessel.

They accomplished this inside of Charleston Harbour, but the Fishboat stuck in the mud, and the crew, "Georgians" (if I remember right) all perished, and when brought up the man hole was so small that the bodies had to be dissevered to pull them out. Then either Beauregard or genl. officers comdg. <u>discouraged</u> any further diving attempt, but permitted spar work.

McCabe sent me his paper on Custis Lee.

Yours sincerely
H. W. Feilden

Henry W. Feilden to [Mrs. Augustine T. Smythe]
Rampyndene, Burwash, Sussex
June 5, 1920

My dear Sister,

I hope you are well, for I have bad news to give you. My dear Julie had a seizure about a fortnight ago and remained unconscious for some 24 hours. When she partially recovered, recovering in a measure her speech, and the use of her right side and hand. Everything possible has been done for her, and both the doctor and I are pleased with her general improvement. She never had any pain. She now takes nourishment well . . . has day and night nurses, and I have been on the watch every day & night since she was taken ill. I consider her getting on well, but whether she will ever again be the active woman she has been all her life, remains to be seen. Of course age is against us, remember she is 82! About a month older than I am. On the whole she is a wonderful woman, and I think will come round. I was very much distressed at the thought of her passing without saying good-bye to me. But she is so much improved that she lies for hours with her hand in mine, and says that I am a dear good man, and so on. When she first recovered consciousness her mind wandered to her childhood, and she asked for her brothers Turquand,

Henry W. Feilden in June 1918. A note on the reverse states that
the photograph was taken at Burwash, Sussex, "after 6 hour spell at
garden work. Aged 80."

Courtesy of the South Carolina Historical Society.

Julius, Russell, sister Mary, [Richy], Miles & so on also for you, asking if they
were here? The intermediate 60 years seemed to have been forgotten.

Of course the seizure was due as it always is, to some lesion of blood on
the brain, but the cerebral hemorrhage must have been very slight, or she
would not so quickly have recovered consciousness and the full use of her
limbs. She takes nourishment well, and is kept perfectly quiet, so that she has
every chance.

I did not write to you sooner, because I wanted to tell you something
more or less definite. . . .

I am pretty well tired <u>myself</u> as with servants & nurses there are 6 women in the house, rather a serious undertaking for an old man like myself.

Your affectionate brother
H. W. Feilden

Henry W. Feilden to Mrs. Hannah Wright
Rampyndene, Burwash, Sussex
June 14, 1920

My dear Hannah,[23]

I am in great grief. I have lost your dear Aunt Julie, after 56 years companionship without a cross word between us. She had a seizure 3 weeks ago, but for 2 weeks rallied wonderfully and talked about you all. I am pleased that she saw David's photos, and she said what a dear little lad he was.

A second seizure came and she lived for a week unconscious, and passed away on Sat. 12 June. I was with her to the end, for she begged me 'never to leave her.'

I am too sad to write more. I have had a hundred letters and wires to answer, but I believe I have written to your mother.

Hannah Rhett I have written to and I daresay she will tell your mother as well.

Your affectionate uncle
H. W. Feilden

Excerpt, from a letter, [1920], from Henry W. Feilden
to John Bennett:

. . . The death of my beloved wife, your wife's Aunt, and my companion in joys and sorrows for 56 years has given me a bad shake, and I was in bed for ten days after the funeral, but am now allowed downstairs. . . .

Henry W. Feilden to Mrs. A. T. Smythe

Rampyndene, Burwash, Sussex

July 4, 1920 'Independence Day'

My dear Sister,

I have had such trying times that I have failed to write to you, for the immediate necessities kept me absolutely occupied. Also Hannah promised to write fully to you, which I trust she did. . . .

During the two weeks after her seizure during which Julie remained conscious, and could talk to me, she said she suffered no pain, only weariness, she took no interest in her surroundings. . . . She always held my hand and asked me never to leave her, which I complied with as I never left her for over an hour day or night from the time of her seizure, until she passed away. It is a very sad time for me, as the house is full from attic to downstairs with her things, and they have to be cleared under my superintendence. . . . She left a memo to whom she wished her jewelry to go, and I have divided that up. I'll send them before long. Now the result of my standing about day & night for 3 week, was to bring on a severe attack of Phlebitis in my right leg and I had to lie up for ten days in bed with my leg higher than my head. I am now allowed downstairs to rest on the sofa. Hannah is coming from town on the 13th to see me. She goes to Paris the 22nd.

Julie had so many warm friends; I think there must have been 150 letters to reply to from England, Scotland, Ireland even the Channel Islands. I answered each in my own hand-writing. . . .

It is very hard to part with a loving companion of 56 years. We had gone through so much together. I think on the whole she had a happy life. . . .

Crowds came to Julie's funeral and the wreaths were without number and most beautiful. She was such a beloved old lady.

As my doctor said to me it was a treat to have such a patient as Julie. She suffered much for some years from arthritis, but as he said never did she complain, and was always wise & witty, so that he got more good out of his visit to her than she did from his. Whence did the family brains come from? I suppose your father must have been a clever man. Of course I know your mother was an exceptionally able & clever woman, but sister Charlotte Cheves and sister Mary Magrath were also clever women. So there must have been a good strain in the McCord as well as the Cheves blood.

I am so [attached] to S. Ca. that Julie's death does not sever my love to the Palmetto State, and her dear womenkind. And one who like myself, followed the fortunes of the State from Fort Sumter to Va., and the final surrender of the last force of the Lost Cause, feels that I am an adopted child.

Ever your affectionate brother
H. W. Feilden

Henry W. Feilden to John Bennett
Rampyndene, Burwash, Sussex
July 8, 1920

Dear Mr. Bennett,

I sent off to-day the photo and correspondence about the Stono Ferry Engagement of the 20 June 1779 belonging to the Martin-Auliffe family.

I have been engaged during the past three or four days, in looking over correspondence of my beloved wife, your wife's Aunt Julie.

It has been a very painful task, for an old man over eighty to read over again the letters written at 25 to the girl he was engaged to, and married.

I find that she kept every letter that I wrote to her from 1863, to when the war closed, and we left Charleston in 1866. Fancy the dear creature, unknown to me, carrying all these notes and letters, carefully numbered and tied up, to India, Africa, the Mediterranean, and all the other stations we served in during my military career. For nearly sixty years she has carefully preserved them.

Some three or four months ago she did mention to me, that she had preserved all my letters, and that she never had the heart to destroy them, and said if I go before you, do not destroy them without looking at them, for though many of them are only the effusions between young engaged, and lately married persons, yet some of them are so interesting that I think they ought to be preserved.

I have glanced through them, about a hundred letters and notes written by myself to her. At least half of them I cremated as they were only intended for our two pairs of eyes, and contained descriptions of men & women, who

can only be names to our present descendants. Still I think some of my letters are of a little historical interest, and as you are the literary genius of our
family would you like to receive this small contribution to this histoire [?] of
S. Ca. and the Great War?

My heirs, utterly ignorant of S. Ca. & the War of Secession would cre-
mate them En blue.

I am enclosing you samples. The first is a most interesting letter from
General Beauregard, which I enclosed to my young lady then at Greenville,
and she has kept it in the letters and envelope—

In April 1864, Beauregard was ordered by the President to assume command at Petersburg, and defend the approaches to Richmond from the S.W.
He left Charleston on the 20th. Major General Sam. Jones having arrived
from Va. He B still retained the command of S. Ca. Ga & Fla. in addition.
General B sent for me to his room in Hd. Qrs. office. M.G. Sam Jones was
with him, and he said to Sam Jones, you tell me general you have not a single
staff officer until you can summon some, from Va & the Army of Tenn. I
shall leave you Captain F. for the present, he is young but efficient, and has
a very fair knowledge of the surroundings of Charleston. I said, Genl B. are
you not going to take me to Petersburg? His reply was, I am the best judge
of where you are most useful. You remain with Genl. Jones for the present. I
may send for you later. This accounts for my being the channel of communication between Beauregard at Petersburg, and Charleston as he appeared
to consider me still on his staff and directed me to communicate with him at
Petersburg.

Now will you refer to Johnsons' 'Defence of Charleston? Page 4. There
Major Wm. S. Basinger states that the report ordered by Genl. B. to be drawn
up was never accomplished owing to the Board having been dispersed. General B. writing from Petersburg ordered me to draw up a report from the
official file records in the Headquarters office Dept of S. Ca. Ga & Fla in
Charleston. This I tried to accomplish, and you may rest assured, I was
extremely gratified, when that eminent commander wrote re my report. "It
is lucid, concise & to the point giving I think a very fair & full account of the
operations referred to."

* * *

What became of this report of General Beauregard's after he had revised and
canceled it I cannot say. It may be now in the archives at Washington. The

rest of this letter is most historically interesting. Though engaged in desperate operations ~~fighting~~ at Petersburg, General Beauregard never for an hour lost touch with Charleston, and its defence. I received many communications from him, which were put amongst the records of the Dept. He always treated me, then a youngster, with such courtesy and consideration, that I revere his memory.

I have completely forgotten about this letter of Sept. 5th 1864 from General Beauregard until I came across it yesterday, amongst my wife's letters.

I think from your books that I have read, that you have a nice vein of humour in your composition. The description of a ride in Fla. will perhaps amuse you. Believe me all I saw is put down in perfect good faith, and admiration of the people I fell in with. But now a days speeding in a lightning train from Lake City to Tampa, to catch Tarpon, one would scarce believe that the country passed through is the same as described by me near sixty years ago. I am so broken with my cons, that I am five years older than I was 3 months ago, and do not think it likely I can pull through another winter. This is why I am bringing up these letters.

Yours Sincerely HW Feilden

Henry W. Feilden to an unnamed niece (explaining his two letters of March 1866):

Rampyndene, Burwash, Sussex
July 17, 1920

These two letters refer to a very curious experience of mine. Aunt Julie had returned to her house corner of Legare St. and Battery. She was expecting an addition to the family, and she declared she would not leave Charleston till it was over. I said we are wasting time here. I must go and do something. I met William Magrath (President S. Ca. & Ga. R.) in the street, and he said I want a man to go up on the line to the break between Augusta & Charleston, and take charge of the traffic, discharging & filling up. What will you give me? He said $100 a month (greenbacks). I said that is not much. He said the line cannot stand more. All right I'll go tomorrow, and I went. The two enclosed letters describe the surroundings. 'Fat Smith' was the booking clerk.

I took weekends in Charleston. Going up and down the line as a 'Dead Head.' I used to beg the conductor to let me run the show, so I went up and down the cars issuing tickets & getting the stuff, bringing it to the conductor who smoked & played poker in his crib. One Saturday Genl Hagood[24] came on board. He said what on earth Feilden are you doing here? I said learning my way about. I thought you would be back in England by this time. No, my wife is in Charleston. By some means or other it became known at Branchville that Hagood was on board. Arriving there, the station master said my wife has prepared lunch for the General. Of course he took me on his staff for the lunch, and he reckoned it would be better to take the real conductor as a hostage. So we went in to lunch, the Genl reckoning that the cars could not go on without the conductor. It was a good lunch, and an open pastry, with sliced lemon, lingers today in my memory, as a gift of Lucullus! I had been feeding for a week past on hominy & Hoppin John.

I think I stood the railway service for a month or six weeks, and then retired from the position of a railway magnate of the U.S.

H.W. F.

Fragment of a letter from John Bennett to Henry W. Feilden:
"Many Pines," East Flat Rock, N.C.,
July 25, 1920
H. W. Feilden, Esq.,
Ramyndene, Burwash, Sussex, England:

My dear Sir:—

It will give me the greatest pleasure to receive from the letters you refer to in your letters of July 8th, as remaining among Mrs. Feilden's correspondence, containing, not the simple personalia of such an intimacy alone, but comment on men and events, and enclosures of historical and biographical interest to us and to others . . . such letters as you shall select. I beg you to understand that there will be to me and to all of us far more than the abstract interest in their historical import. They will possess direct personal and affectionate interest for us, in addition to the historical value of your enclosures of official correspondence. Mrs. Smythe, who holds you in the deepest affection as linked with all the great memories of older days, is almost brought to regret that you could not have seen in us a repository for even those letters you refer to as "gossipy" chat of young people, dress, incidents and minor events of the period covered by the correspondence we refer to. She would have relished all such reference to other days, let descendants forget if they will. But such as you have selected I shall be only too glad to receive and properly to preserve, as family papers, or historical MSS as shall finally seem most fitting. I assure you that none shall go astray.

We read aloud your interesting and amusing account of your travel in Florida, (date Sept. 11, 1864); and I think, here and to-day, at this distance, were almost as glad in the recovery of the ring lost in the Indian princess's grave as yourself . . . though of course, that is impossible. What a picture of primitive Florida! Let us hope there may be other such liberal extracts from your journal, kept on your inspecting tours: they have much more than passing value: I know no duplicate of your account: viz., the Florida journey with Dick Long.

That these letters travelled with Aunt Julie . . . permit me to speak of her so; we always do here among us at home . . . to India, Africa, the Mediterranean and other stations of your service, adds but a closer interest to us, who are not without strong sentiment. I shall be happy to think that my wife shall have had any letters of mine sixty years, though it is impossible that I shall be there to know it. My father's correspondence with my mother, from New Orleans, to her in Southern Ohio, was destroyed by an irresponsible servant entire: to us an irreparable loss; to me, personally, more than a regret, My grandfather's papers were utterly lost in transit from Virginia to Missouri, when St. Louis was but late a half-French trade-post. Of Susy's grandfather we have, of course, his correspondence, prepared by Lousia Stoney. Of Maj. Augustine T. Smythe, her father, we have only a few letters from early days while he was yet a student in Columbia; Mrs. Smythe has destroyed many, for reasons similar to yours; what else remains is in her keeping. It is my regret we never were able to record properly the many personal reminiscences of the Great War and South Carolina's Reconstruction days Maj. Smythe at times was persuaded to tell. The value of such personal narrative of men and events to the student of history is very great; often far greater value than the studiously printed page when one is earnest for the facts and not the fictions of history.

I shall be only too glad, sir, to receive from you any letters and papers you shall choose to think of interest to your immediate English heirs, but which you think may possess personal or historic interest to us, and to myself, heirs of your reminiscence . . . if you will let me coin the term to fit the case. The enclosed letter from Gen. Beauregard, with your comment on Johnson's "Defence" and statement upon your "report" communicated to Gen. B. at Petersburg, and approved by him, is of significance worthy further commentary: with your permission I should be glad to reproduce Gen. B's letter with brief explanatory comment, in the South Carolina Historical Society's quarterly at first opportunity. I shall be interested to learn whether or no the report still exists at Washington. I do not believe it is in the published records of that great conflict . . . therefore fear it lost, destroyed. Nothing of this sort, i.e., Gen. B's letter to you, Sept. 5, '64, can be without value additional to its inherent interest. . . .

Of your recent loss, sir, may I say that if the affectionate regard and sorrow of those younger than yourself, and far removed, is kind, ours, and mine you have. For myself, I do not simulate attachments that I do not feel, and when I venture to sign myself to this long letter, affectionately yours, believe me, it is true.

I can say nothing to mitigate your loss but this . . . which is very little; but, sir, may I not say that we all, here, hold you nearer than you know, and so are touched by what touches you so deeply. . . .

NOTES

Introduction

1. Trevor-Battye, "Noble Englishman," Introduction:1. For more on British involvement in the Civil War, see Foreman, *World of Fire.*

2. Kipling and Pinney, *Something of Myself,* 112–13.

3. Hunter, *Cheltenham College Register,* 133.

4. Ibid.

5. Trevor-Battye, "Noble Englishman," 1:4.

6. Ibid., Introduction:11.

7. Ibid.

8. Hunter, *Cheltenham College Register,* 133.

9. Battye, "Noble Englishman," 2:1–2.

10. Ibid., 2:2.

11. Ibid.

12. Battye, "Noble Englishman," 2:2–4.

13. Ibid.

14. Henry Wemyss Feilden to Eliza Whigham Kennedy Feilden, March 4, 1863, Henry Wemyss Feilden Papers. Hereafter all letters cited are held in the Henry Wemyss Feilden Papers of the SCHS unless otherwise noted.

15. Ibid.; H. W. Feilden to Mrs. Miles, June 2, 1899.

16. H. W. Feilden to E. W. K. Feilden, March 4, 1863.

17. Ibid.

18. Ibid. In 1862 Maj. Gen. David Hunter (1802–86), commander of the Department of the South, issued an order abolishing slavery in his department (Beaufort, South Carolina, and environs, captured and occupied early in the war), but it was immediately rescinded by President Lincoln. Hunter's early efforts to raise black troops also were overruled by Lincoln. The black men who formed the First South Carolina Colored Infantry in 1862 were inducted involuntarily, and some observers noted the distressing scenes that occurred when they were taken from their homes. Edward L. Pierce, a U.S. Treasury agent, wrote: "On some plantations the wailing and screaming were loud and the women threw themselves in despair on the ground. On some plantations the people took to the woods and were hunted up by the soldiers. . . . I doubt if the recruiting service in this country has ever been attended with such scenes before." Sifakis, *Who Was Who in the Union,* 327; Donald, *Lincoln,* 430; U.S. Department of War, *War of the Rebellion,* ser. 2, 2:57.

19. H. W. Feilden to "Phil," April 16, 1863.

20. Cannon, *South Carolina Genealogies,* 3:83–84.

21. DuBose, "Reminiscences," 35.

22. H. W. Feilden to Julia McCord, April 20, 1864.

23. *War of the Rebellion,* ser. 1, 35, part 2: 427.

24. H. W. Feilden to Julia McCord, April 29, 1864.

25. H. W. Feilden to Julia McCord, April 20, 1864.

26. H. W. Feilden to Julia McCord, May 19, 1864.

27. H. W. Feilden to Julia McCord, May 23, 1864.

28. H. W. Feilden to Julia McCord, May 28, 1864.

29. H. W. Feilden to Julia McCord, May 19, 1864.

30. H. W. Feilden to Julia McCord, August 24, 1864.

31. H. W. Feilden to Julia McCord, August 25, 1864.

32. H. W. Feilden to Julia McCord, August 28, 1864.

33. H. W. Feilden to Julia McCord, September 1, 1864.

34. H. W. Feilden to Julia McCord, August 28, 1864.

35. H. W. Feilden to Julia McCord, September 11, 1864.

36. H. W. Feilden to Julia McCord, May 23, 1864.

37. Ibid.

38. H. W. Feilden to Julia McCord, June 30, 1864.

39. H. W. Feilden to Julia McCord, September 27, 1864.

40. H. W. Feilden to Julia Feilden, December 21, 1864.

41. H. W. Feilden to Julia Feilden, February 14, 1865.

42. H. W. Feilden to Julia Feilden, January 5, 1865.

43. H. W. Feilden to Julia Feilden, January 19, 1865.

44. H. W. Feilden to Julia Feilden, January 30, 1865.

45. H. W. Feilden to Julia Feilden, December 21, 1864.

46. H. W. Feilden to Julia Feilden, April 6, 1865.

47. H. W. Feilden to Julia Feilden, February 10, 1865.

48. H. W. Feilden to Julia Feilden, February 13, 1865.

49. H.W. Feilden to Julia Feilden, February 14, 1865.

50. H. W. Feilden to Feilden, February 28, 1865.

51. H. W. Feilden to Julia Feilden, March 12, 1865.

52. H. W. Feilden to Julia Feilden, March 22, 1865.

53. H. W. Feilden to Rudyard Kipling, March 26, 1911, University of Sussex, SxMs 38, 15/12, Feilden ALS.

54. H. W. Feilden, "An Episode of 1865," July 19, 1920, typescript copy, Henry Wemyss Feilden Papers, 2.

55. Quoted in Trevor-Battye, "Noble Englishman," Chapter 2:101.

56. H. W. Feilden to unnamed niece, July 17, 1920. The Feildens remained childless for the remainder of their lives.

57. Trevor-Battye, "Noble Englishman," 2:101.

58. Thornton, "Notes on Feilden," 1.

59. Ibid.

60. Ibid.

61. Thornton, "Notes on Feilden," 2.

62. Nares, *Official Report;* Nares and Feilden, *Narrative of a Voyage.*

63. Nares, Official Report; Nares and Feilden, *Narrative of a Voyage;* Hunter, *Cheltenham College Register,* 133.

64. Nares and Feilden, *Narrative of a Voyage,* 99.

65. Nares, *Official Report,* 47.

66. Thornton, "Notes on Feilden," 1.

67. Hunter, *Cheltenham College Register,* 133.

68. Trevor-Battye, "Noble Englishman," Introduction 4–5.

69. Ibid., 9; Thornton, "Notes on Feilden," 2.

70. Thornton, "Notes on Feilden," 2.

71. Kipling and Pinney, *Something of Myself,* 112–13; Thornton, "Notes on Feilden," 2.

72. Trevor-Battye, "Noble Englishman," 1:11.

73. Ibid., 1:11–12; Thornton, "Notes on Feilden," 2.

74. W. Feilden to John Bennett, July 8, 1920.

75. Aubyn Trevor-Battye (1855–1922), a British naturalist and friend of Feilden, began a biography of him and finished two chapters prior to his own death. Ella May Thornton, longtime Georgia state librarian, compiled a significant collection of Feilden material in hopes of writing a biography of him.

76. Kipling and Pinney, *Something of Myself,* 112–13.

77. Bennett, "McCords of McCord's Ferry," 189.

78. W. Feilden to John Bennett, July 8, 1920.

79. John Bennett to W. Feilden, July 25, 1920.

Chapter 1. The Adventure Begins

1. Eliza Whigham Kennedy Feilden (d. 1888) was the wife of John Leyland Feilden (1821–1915), whom she married in 1851. She was the author of a famous diary of her experiences in Natal published in London in 1887 as *My African Home.* Mosley, *Burke's Peerage,* 1:1404; Daymond, *Women Writing Africa,* 128.

2. Confederate general Pierre Gustave Toutant Beauregard (1818–1893) commanded the Department of South Carolina, Georgia, and Florida, which was headquartered in Charleston, from 1863 to 1864. Lt. Gen. Thomas Jonathan (Stonewall) Jackson (1824–1863) commanded the Second Corps of the Army of Northern Virginia following the Seven Days' Campaign. Warner, *Generals in Gray,* 22–23, 151–52.

3. Italian phrase meaning careless idleness or the sweetness of doing nothing.

4. A line from the *Odes* of Horace, a Roman lyric poet.

5. On January 31, 1863, the Confederate ironclads *Chicora* and *Palmetto State* attacked vessels of the Union fleet blockading Charleston Harbor. The Union ships *Mercedita* and *Keystone State* suffered extensive damage during the battle, and Confederate authorities used this victory to claim that the Union blockade of the port

had been lifted, when it was in fact only temporarily interrupted. Two days prior the Union gunboat *Isaac Smith* attacked Confederate shore batteries along the Stono River before running aground and being captured by Confederate forces. Long, *Civil War Day by Day,* 317.

6. James Alexander Seddon (1815–80) of Virginia served as the Confederate secretary of war from November 1862 until February 1865. Wakelyn, *Biographical Dictionary of the Confederacy,* 379.

7. Stonewall Jackson had many admirers among the British. The beautiful bronze statue of Jackson unveiled in Richmond, Virginia, in 1875 was financed by English admirers. Cooke, *Stonewall Jackson,* 514-20.

8. The striking prayerful attitude of this devout man was noted by a number of observers during the war. Jackson's chief of staff and biographer, Robert Lewis Dabney, wrote: "More than once, as one of his favorite brigades was passing into action, he had been noticed sitting motionless upon his horse, with his right hand uplifted, while the war-worn column swept, in stern silence, close by his side, into the storm of shot. . . . Recognizing the sovereignty of the Lord of Hosts, he interceded for his veterans that 'the Almighty would cover them with his feathers, and that his truth might be their shield and buckler.' The moral grandeur of this scene was akin to that when Moses, upon the Mount of God, lifted up his hands while Israel prevailed against Amalek." Dabney, *Life and Campaigns of Lieut.-Gen. Thomas J. Jackson,* 110.

9. Milledge L. Bonham was governor of South Carolina from 1862 to 1864 and an antebellum congressman from Edgefield. Harrison, *Biographical Directory of the American Congress,* 866.

10. Secessionville was located across the Ashley River from Charleston on James Island.

11. On March 3, 1863, the U.S. Congress passed the Enrollment Act, which called for the enlistment of all able-bodied men between the ages of twenty and forty-five. At the same time, Congress passed a financial bill to aid the nation's economy by allowing the government to issue treasury notes. McPherson, *Battle Cry of Freedom,* 600–601.

12. Abraham Lincoln's Emancipation Proclamation of January 1863 was viewed by some in Great Britain as an incitement to slave uprisings. British foreign minister Lord Russell predicted "acts of plunder, of incendiarism, and of revenge" as a result of it. The proclamation freed only those slaves under Confederate control and none under Federal authority. Donald, *Lincoln,* 379.

13. Sifakis, *Who Was Who in the Union,* 327; Donald, *Lincoln,* 430; *War of the Rebellion,* series 2, 2:57.

14. Another Englishman, Charles Dickens, echoed this sentiment in a letter he wrote to a friend in 1862: "Every reasonable creature may know, if willing, that the North hates the Negro, and that until it was convenient to make a pretence that sympathy with him was the cause of the War, it hated the abolitionists and derided them up hill and down dale." Storey, *Letters of Charles Dickens,* 10:111.

15. On April 7, 1863, nine Union ironclads under the command of Flag Officer Samuel Du Pont attacked Fort Sumter at the mouth of Charleston Harbor. Confederate batteries on Fort Sumter and Fort Moultrie returned fire, damaging several of the Union vessels and forcing them to retire. The worst damaged was the USS *Keokuk,* which was hit ninety times by Confederate guns and sank the following morning. Long, *Civil War Day by Day,* 335–36.

16. The *Keokuk* was an unusual ironclad vessel that suffered from poor armor protection. It sank the day after it participated in the attack on Fort Sumter. Tucker, *Civil War Naval Encyclopedia,* 338.

17. Col. Alfred Moore Rhett (1829–89) was in command of Fort Sumter at this time. Allardice, *Confederate Colonels,* 321.

18. The *New Ironsides* was one of three experimental Union ironclads produced to counter the threat of the CSS *Virginia* and is considered to have been the most powerful Union vessel of the Civil War. Tucker, *Civil War Naval Encyclopedia,* 473.

19. The *Warrior* and *Black Prince* were the two earliest British armored and iron-hulled warships. Neither vessel had turrets but instead fired broadsides like traditional naval vessels. Greene and Massignani, *Ironclads at War,* 35.

20. Vicksburg, Mississippi, and Port Hudson, Louisiana, were two cities critical to the Confederate defense of the Mississippi River. In mid-April 1863, Union troops were attempting to capture the former. Long, *Civil War Day by Day,* 331, 333, 338.

21. Feilden is referring to Confederate general Joseph E. Johnston (1807–91), who commanded the Department of the West in 1863, and Confederate general Braxton Bragg (1817–76), who commanded the Army of Tennessee at the same time. Wakelyn, *Biographical Dictionary of the Confederacy,* 259–60; Warner, *Generals in Gray,* 33.

22. Union major general Benjamin Franklin Butler (1818–93) also was known as "Beast Butler." Confederate president Jefferson Davis declared Butler an outlaw deserving of capital punishment after he executed a civilian in New Orleans and committed other notorious offenses there. Warner, *Generals in Blue,* 60–61.

23. Union forces captured Port Royal Sound, the surrounding Sea Islands, and Beaufort following the Battle of Port Royal Sound on November 7, 1861. Their victory provided the Union with army and naval bases to conduct operations against the South Atlantic coast of the Confederacy. Rowland et al., *History of Beaufort County,* 445–58.

24. Gen Beauregard. Warner, *Generals in Gray,* 22–23.

25. Maj. Gen. Samuel Jones (1819–87) was assigned to the Department of South Carolina, Georgia, and Florida in 1864. Warner, *Generals in Gray,* 165–66.

26. Robert Habersham may have been Julia McCord's banker in Savannah.

27. Jacob Keith Sass (1813–65) of Charleston was the president of the Bank of Charleston, treasurer of the (Protestant Episcopal) Grand Council, and treasurer of the domestic missions of the Protestant Episcopal Church of the Confederate States of America. Bishop Charles Todd Quintard wrote of Sass in his memoir: "He was one of the noblest laymen of the Church, of large heart and mind, full of love for

Christ and the Church—abundant in labors, earnest-minded and pure-hearted." Sass, *Story of the South Carolina Low Country,* 3: 936; Elliott, *Doctor Quintard,* 118–19.

28. George Herbert Sass (1845–1908), a native of Charleston, was the son of Jacob K. Sass. He was transferred from the Charleston Light Dragoons and assigned to bureau duty, having been deemed unfit for active service due to medical reasons. After the war he was a lawyer and an author who wrote under the pen name "Barton Grey." Wauchope, *Writers of South Carolina,* 342–43; Emerson, *Sons of Privilege,* 137.

29. Harriet Lowndes is probably Harriet Kinloch Lowndes (b. ca. 1842), the daughter of William Henry Lowndes (d. 1865) and Mary Esther Middleton. Chase, *Lowndes of South Carolina,* 23.

30. Probably Charlotte Bull Barnwell Elliott (1810–95), the wife of Episcopal bishop Stephen Elliott (1806–66), who is mentioned by Feilden in later letters. Barnwell, *Story of an American Family,* 157, 231.

31. Joseph A. Hincks (born 1841) of New Orleans. He was assigned to duty in the adjutant general's office under General Beauregard for a while during the siege and bombardment of Charleston and later served in Ferguson's Light Artillery. Evans, *Confederate Military History,* 13:447.

32. Brig. Gen. Thomas Jordan (1819–95) served as a staff officer under General Beauregard during the siege of Charleston. Warner, *Generals in Gray,* 167–68.

33. Maj. Robert Cogdell Gilchrist (1829–1902), a Charleston lawyer. He was retired from active service because of a wound but then assigned to be judge advocate general of the Department of South Carolina, Georgia, and Florida. Evans, *Confederate Military History,* 6:596–98.

34. Assistant adjutant general.

35. Probably Charles Royal Brewster (1808–85). A native of Maine, he came to Charleston in 1831 and began the practicing law in partnership with B. F. Dunkin. Way, *History of the New England Society,* 151–54.

36. Stephen Elliott (1806–66), a native of Beaufort, South Carolina, was the first Episcopal bishop of Georgia and later the presiding bishop in the Protestant Episcopal Church in the Confederate States of America. Barnwell, *Story of an American Family,* 157–59, 199–200.

37. Malvina Murden (d. 1890) operated a school in Charleston with her mother, the poet Eliza Crawley Murden, and sisters. Her sister Octavia was the wife of Jacob K. Sass. Tison and Stoney, "Recollections," 209.

38. Probably Francis Turquand Miles (1827–1903), a physician and medical educator of Charleston and Columbia. He was captain of Company B of the First Battalion, South Carolina Infantry, and later served as an army surgeon. National Archives, Compiled Service Records, First (Charleston) Battalion S.C. Infantry (Gaillard's Battalion), M267, roll 150; Waring, *History of Medicine in South Carolina,* 267–68.

39. William Izard Bull (1813–94), a planter and politician, owned Ashley Hall Plantation on the Ashley River near Charleston. Bailey, *Biographical Directory,* 231–32, Vol. 1; Bull, "Ashley Hall Plantation."

40. Possibly Annie Cuthbert Heyward (1838–86), daughter of Thomas Savage Heyward (1815–89) of Beaufort District. Heyward, *Heyward,* 110–11.

41. On May 5–7, 1864, Union and Confederate forces participated in the battle of the Wilderness in Virginia. Long, *Civil War Day by Day,* 493.

42. Simon Pure was a virtuous character in an early eighteenth-century play. Brewer, *Dictionary of Phrase and Fable,* 1143–44.

43. John Russell ran a bookstore that hosted an informal literary group in Charleston during the 1850s and 1860s. Hart and Leininger, "Russell's Bookstore Group."

44. This could be Isabella Middleton Cheves (1826–1912), the widow of Charles Manly Cheves, or Rachel Susan Bee Cheves (1821–88), the wife of Dr. John R. Cheves, both of whom were cousins to Julia McCord, or Julia's sister Charlotte (1818–79), who was Mrs. Langdon Cheves Jr. Cannon, *South Carolina Genealogies,* 1:385–86; 3:66, 83.

45. *Macaria, or, Altars of Sacrifice,* by Augusta Jane Evans, was a best-selling novel published in Richmond, Virginia, in 1864.

46. Julia's sister Mary Eliza McCord (1825–1903), who later married Andrew Gordon Magrath (1813–93), one of the wartime governors of South Carolina. Cannon, *South Carolina Genealogies,* 3:83.

47. John Fitzhugh Lay (1826–1900). A native of Virginia, he became assistant adjutant general to General Beauregard in April 1862 and was later on the staff of General Jones and General Hardee. After the war he moved to Florida to raise oranges but later returned to Virginia. His brother was Bishop Henry C. Lay. Allardice, *Confederate Colonels,* 234. The land to which Feilden refers probably was located near Lake Panasoffkee in present day Sumter County, Florida. Feilden would visit the site during his inspection tour of the state from August to September 1864. H.W. Feilden to Julia McCord, September 11, 1864.

48. Edward Lightwood Parker (1828–92) was Julia's brother-in-law. Her late sister Emma (1830–51) married him in 1850. During the war he served in the Marion Artillery. Cannon, *South Carolina Genealogies,* 3:83; Parker, *Genealogy of the Parker Family,* 49.

49. Penina Septima Moses (b. 1846) was the daughter of Maj. Raphael Moses from Columbus, Georgia. She married her cousin William Moultrie Moses (d. 1878) in June 1865. Rosen, *Jewish Confederates,* 333; Stern, *Americans of Jewish Descent,* 150–51.

50. A collection of narrative poems about ancient Roman history and myth composed by Thomas B. Macaulay (1800–59), an English historian, politician, and poet. First published in 1842, the collection includes a ballad called "Horatius," which contains the famous lines: "Then out spake brave Horatius, the Captain of the gate: / To every man upon this earth death cometh soon or late. / And how can man die better than facing fearful odds, / For the ashes of his fathers, and the temples of his gods."

51. The Ogeechee River is in Chatham County, Georgia. Abate, *Omni Gazetteer,* 3:242.

52. Bonaventure Plantation near Savannah. Wilson and Johnson, *Historic Bonaventure,* 9.

53. Isaac DuBose Porcher (1832–66) of Ophir Plantation was the son of Thomas Porcher (1766–1836) and Elizabeth S. DuBose. He married Maria Marion Palmer (not Parker). Towles, *World Turned Upside Down,* 996, 1001.

54. Patrick R. Cleburne (1828–64), a native of Ireland, was promoted to the rank of major general on December 20, 1862. In the Atlanta campaign, he defeated Union forces at Pickett's Mill in Georgia on May 27, 1864. Wakelyn, *Biographical Dictionary of the Confederacy,* 139; Long, *Civil War Day by Day,* 510.

55. Union major general William Tecumseh Sherman (1820–91) began his infamous march through Georgia in the spring of 1864. Warner, *Generals in Blue,* 441–43; Long, *Civil War Day by Day,* 495.

56. Jacob K. Sass lived at 23 Legare Street in Charleston. Smith, *Dwelling Houses of Charleston,* 221–22.

57. George Smith Cook (1819–1902) was a well-known photographer in Charleston. Teal, *Partners with the Sun,* 22–23.

58. Langdon Cheves (1848–1939) was Julia's cousin. After the war he worked as a field engineer in Georgia but later returned to Charleston, where he became a lawyer and historian. "Langdon Cheves."

59. Jane M. Lucas was the wife of Robert Hume Lucas (1825–1915) of Charleston. After the war she and her husband moved to California, where she died in 1895. Schwab, *Newspaper Extracts,* 146; Lucas, *Lucas Memorandum,* 72.

60. Adele Allston King (1844–89). She married John Middleton in December 1865 and was widowed in 1868. She married George Trenholm Kershaw in 1877. Pease, *Family of Women,* 242–45; Cannon, *South Carolina Genealogies,* 3:132–33.

Chapter 2. Defending Charleston

1. This may be John Hanckel (1821–86) or Allen Stuart Hanckel, both of whom were involved in blockade-running enterprises in Charleston. Nepveux, *George A. Trenholm,* 103, 118; Barnwell, *Story of an American Family,* 135.

2. The "Bee store" was located in a row of townhouses at 101–107 Bull Street in Charleston beyond the range of the Federal shelling. During the war the William C. Bee Company sold goods brought in through the blockade. Architectural File, 101–107 Bull Street, SCHS.

3. The wife of Brig. Gen. Beverly Holcombe Robertson (1827–1910), who was assigned to the command of the Second District of South Carolina in October 1863 and remained in that post for the remainder of the war. Evans, *Confederate Military History,* 4:656–58; Warner, *Generals in Gray,* 259–60.

4. Bartholomew Rochefort Riordan (d. 1897), a native of Virginia, was an editor of the *Charleston Mercury* newspaper in Charleston during the war. He married Mary (Minnie) Mitchell Whaley (ca. 1844–1902). Patey, *Whaley Family,* 35; Sass, *Outspoken,* 38.

5. Maj. Charles S. Stringfellow (b. 1837) of Virginia served as adjutant general and chief of staff for Gen. Samuel Jones. Evans, *Confederate Military History,* 4:1192–93.

6. John Archibald Campbell (1811–89) was a native of Georgia who practiced law in Alabama. He served as an associate justice of the U.S. Supreme Court before the war but resigned when Alabama seceded from the Union. In October 1862 President Jefferson Davis appointed Campbell assistant secretary of war, a post he occupied for the remainder of the war. Wakelyn, *Biographical Dictionary of the Confederacy,* 122–23.

7. Christopher Gustavus Memminger (1803–88) of Charleston was appointed secretary of the treasury by Jefferson Davis in 1861. He served in that post until his resignation in June 1864. Wakelyn, *Biographical Dictionary of the Confederacy,* 317–18.

8. Bishop Henry Champlin Lay (1823–1885) was the diocesan bishop of Arkansas during the Civil War. Perry, *Episcopate in America,* 147.

9. In June 1864 Maj. Gen. Samuel Jones quartered some fifty high-ranking Union prisoners, including five generals, in a house on Broad Street in Charleston to dissuade Union major general John G. Foster (1823–74), commander of the Department of the South, from continuing the bombardment of residential, nonmilitary areas of the city. Foster retaliated by requesting fifty Confederate officers, who were to be placed in a stockade prison in front of the Union forts in the harbor, under the fire of the Confederate batteries. When the imprisoned Union generals heard of Foster's intentions, they sent him a letter asking that the Confederate officers be treated humanely and assuring him that they were "as pleasantly and comfortably situated as is possible for prisoners of war, receiving from the Confederate authorities every privilege that we could desire or expect, nor are we unnecessarily exposed to fire." Fifty Confederate officers, mostly from the prison at Fort Delaware, were sent to Charleston, but soon thereafter an agreement of exchange was reached by the two governments, and both groups of prisoners were freed within three weeks. Joslyn, *Immortal Captives,* 17–22.

10. From June 15–18, 1864, the majority of the Union Army of the Potomac assaulted Beauregard's forces at Petersburg. Lee arrived with the remainder of the Army of Northern Virginia on June 18 to reinforce Beauregard. Long, *Civil War Day by Day,* 522–24.

11. The Congaree Hotel in Columbia was located at the northwest corner of Richardson and Lady Streets. Hershman, *Columbia City Directory,* 55.

12. Theodore Dehon Wagner (1819–80) was a signer of the South Carolina Ordinance of Secession and a partner in the prominent blockade-running mercantile firm of John Fraser & Company. He lived at 54 Rutledge Avenue. May, *South Carolina Secedes,* 221; *Census of the City of Charleston,* 221.

13. David Flavel Jamison (1810–64) was a prominent attorney, planter, historian of Orangeburg and Barnwell Districts, and president of the South Carolina Secession Convention. In 1862 he became the presiding judge for the military court of

Beauregard's Corps. He died of yellow fever in September 1864. May, *South Carolina Secedes*, 164–65.

14. Thomas Lewis Ogier (1810–1900) was a Charleston physician. He was a surgeon in the Confederate army and later the medical director for the Department of South Carolina, Georgia, and Florida. Waring, *History of Medicine in South Carolina*, 280.

15. Jamison was the author of the *Life and Times of Bertrand Du Guesclin*, which was published in London and brought in through the blockade.

16. Julia McCord's mother was Emmeline Wagner, the first wife of David James McCord. Cannon, *South Carolina Genealogies*, 3:83.

17. Maj. Gen. Lafayette McLaws (1821–97), a native of Georgia, "commanded the District of Georgia against Sherman's advances." Wakelyn, *Biographical Dictionary of the Confederacy*, 300; Warner, *Generals in Gray*, 204–5.

18. On June 27, 1864, Confederate forces under Gen. Joseph Johnston defeated Union forces under Maj. Gen. William T. Sherman at Kennesaw Mountain outside Atlanta. Long, *Civil War Day by Day*, 529.

19. Brig. Gen. Gideon Johnson Pillow (1806–78) was sent to Georgia in June 1864 to "interrupt the enemy's line of communications." Maj. (later Lt.) Gen. Nathan Bedford Forrest (1821–77) also was in Georgia at the time and was victorious at the battle of Brice's Crossroads. Hughes, *Life and Wars of Gideon J. Pillow*, 282; Warner, *Generals in Gray*, 92–93, 241; Long, *Civil War Day by Day*, 519.

20. Maj. Gen. Benjamin Franklin Cheatham (1820–86) was a distinguished Confederate corps commander in the Army of Tennessee and played a prominent role in the battle of Kennesaw Mountain on June 27, 1864. Warner, *Generals in Gray*, 47–48; Long, *Civil War Day by Day*, 529.

21. Dr. Charles Todd Quintard (1824–98) was a physician and Confederate chaplain and later an Episcopal bishop and a founder of the University of the South. In the summer of 1864, he was in Georgia with the army of Lt. Gen. John Bell Hood (1831–79). Quintard's diary does not mention a visit to Charleston but does state that he was in the company of Bishop Henry C. Lay at this period. Elliott, *Doctor Quintard*, 87–88.

22. Confederate lieutenant general Leonidas Polk (1806–64) was a graduate of West Point and resigned his commission in the U.S. Army to become an Episcopal priest. He later was named the first Protestant Episcopal bishop of Louisiana. He was killed at Pine Mountain, Georgia, on June 14, 1864, while commanding a corps of the Army of Tennessee. His funeral took place in Atlanta, not Augusta. Wakelyn, *Biographical Dictionary of the Confederacy*, 349–50; Warner, *Generals in Gray*, 242–43.

23. Feilden is referring to a sermon that Stephen Elliott gave in Savannah on April 8, 1864 titled *Gideon's Water-Lappers*, to mark a day of fasting, humiliation, and prayer established by the Confederate Congress. The title refers to a passage in the Old Testament book of Judges, 7:1–8, in which God directed Gideon, the military leader of Israel, to choose his soldiers by observing the men who were vigilant enough to lap water like a dog, with their eyes turned up and away from the water.

Elliott preached that the Confederacy needed "earnest, single-minded, self-sacrificing men . . . who, when the trumpet sounds to conflict, will not bow down upon their knees to drink, but will lap water as a dog lappeth, in their haste to press forward to their duty." Gideon was sent to fight a large Midianite army with only three hundred men. Elliott's sermon encouraged the Confederate people, who were fighting an enemy with superior numbers and resources, to rely on God's providence.

24. Union brigadier generals Truman Seymour (1824–91), Alexander Shaler (1827–1911), Henry Walton Wessells (1809–89), Eliakim Parker Scammon (1816–94), and Charles Adam Heckman (1822–96) were all brought to Charleston as prisoners of war and were exchanged in August or September 1864. Warner, *Generals in Blue*, 226–27, 421–22, 432–33, 434–35, 551–52.

25. Probably Theodore Dehon Wagner.

26. Susan Petigru King (1824–75), the wife of Henry C. King, was the youngest daughter of James L. Petigru. She was "famous for her wit and repartee" and was "well known as an author of considerable ability." Wauchope, *Writers of South Carolina*, 223.

27. Jacob K. Sass.

28. A French phrase meaning "at all costs" or "come what may." Fennell, *Stanford Dictionary of Anglicised Words and Phrases*, 291.

29. Burton, *Siege of Charleston*, 286–89.

30. Victoria Murden, sister of Malvina Murden.

31. Brig. Gen. William Booth Taliaferro (1822–98). "After the battle of Fredericksburg he was ordered to General Beauregard at Charleston, his subsequent military career being in South Carolina, Georgia, and Florida." Warner, *Generals in Gray*, 297–98.

32. On July 3, 1864, Union troops launched an unsuccessful amphibious assault at dawn from Morris Island against Fort Johnson on James Island. The failed attack resulted in Confederate forces securing 140 Union prisoners. Long, *Civil War Day by Day*, 532; Burton, *Siege of Charleston*, 286–87.

33. Maj. John Jenkins (1824–1905), a native of Edisto Island, South Carolina, served in the Third South Carolina Cavalry. "Mjr. Jenkins participated gallantly in many of the brisk encounters with the enemy on South Carolina soil, including the fight with the gunboats off North Edisto inlet [and] the affair on John's Island in February 1864, and the fighting there from July 2 to July 10, 1864." Evans, *Confederate Military History*, 6:678–79.

34. Burton, *Siege of Charleston*, 288–89.

35. The Marion Light Artillery began as an independent artillery organization for coastal defense in 1861 and ended the war in North Carolina in Rhett's Brigade. National Archives, Compiled Service Records, Capt. Parker's Co., Light Artillery (Marion Artillery), M267, rolls 103–4; Kirkland, *South Carolina C.S.A. Research Aids*.

36. On July 4, 1864, Johnston withdrew his Army of Tennessee to the Chattahoochee River, northwest of Atlanta, to escape a flanking movement by Sherman's Union forces. Long, *Civil War Day by Day*, 533.

37. Pvt. William E. Porcher, Company B, Second South Carolina Cavalry, was killed in action on John's Island on July 7, 1864. Kirkland, *Broken Fortunes,* 280.

38. On July 9, 1864, Confederate and Union troops engaged in a pitched battle on John's Island that was later referred to as the battle of Bloody Bridge. Burton, *Siege of Charleston,* 294–95.

39. Fort Johnson and Fort Simkins were Confederate fortifications on James Island. Fort Johnson was located "on the tip of the island facing Fort Sumter." Fort Simkins was an earthwork battery. Hayes, *James and Related Sea Islands,* 112.

40. Union major general John Gray Foster (1823–74) was "given charge of operations against Charleston in May 1864." Sifakis, *Who Was Who in the Union,* 141.

41. A letter found in the *Official Records of the War of the Rebellion* gives examples of the Union war on Virginia's civilian population during the summer of 1864. On July 5, 1864, Maj. T. O. Chestney reported to his commander: "About the 13th of June last a regiment of negroes, commanded by Colonel Draper, of Massachusetts, arrived at Pope's Creek, in Westmoreland County, Va., accompanied by about fifty regular U.S. Cavalry . . . some of the negro troops went to the house of a Private George, of Ninth Virginia Cavalry, and committed rape upon his wife, who had just been confined with a babe only six weeks old. She is now almost a maniac, and begs that someone kill her. This atrocious crime can be verified by a number of witnesses. . . . In Warsaw, Richmond County, the negro troops attempted to ravish white ladies, but were foiled by the assistance of female slaves. . . . The troops then went up to Layton's, in Essex County, in their boats, landed and commenced destroying all kinds of property . . . after which they embarked at Tappahannock and went to Point Lookout. On their way down the river they deliberately shelled private residences, which were inhabited only by women and children." U.S. Department of War, *War of the Rebellion,* ser. 1, vol. 40, pt. 3, 743.

42. Feilden is referring to the actions of the Marion Artillery at the battle of Bloody Bridge on July 9, 1864.

43. William Henry Lowndes (1817–65). His daughter Harriet was "the present object of Herbert's adoration." Chase, *Lowndes of South Carolina,* 23.

44. Feilden is probably referring to Capt. J. W. McAlpine of the Second Confederate Engineer Corps. Evans, *Confederate Military History,* 7:239.

45. Charlotte McCord (1818–79) married Langdon Cheves Jr. (1814–63). Cannon, *South Carolina Genealogies,* 3:83.

46. Gen. Ulysses S. Grant.

47. Dr. Samuel Choppin of Louisiana was a surgeon on General Beauregard's staff. Welsh, *Medical Histories of Confederate Generals,* 118.

48. Gen. Samuel Cooper (1798–1876), a native of New York, resigned as adjutant general of the U.S. Army in March 1861 and was appointed to the rank of brigadier general in the Confederate army. On May 16, 1861, he was promoted to the rank of general, which made him the senior officer in the Confederate army. He served as adjutant and inspector general in Confederate service throughout the war. Warner, *Generals in Gray,* 62–63.

49. James McNair Baker (1821–92) of North Carolina became a successful lawyer in Lake City, Florida, and later a judge. In November 1861 the Florida legislature elected him to serve as a Confederate senator. Warner and Yearns, *Biographical Register*, 11–12.

50. William Battersby (1820–83) was an English cotton broker who settled in Savannah in the mid–nineteenth century. His house, located at 119 East Charlton Street, was a Greek Revival, Charleston-style dwelling with a parterre garden. This historic home still exists and is known as the Battersby-Hartridge House. Beney, *Majesty of Savannah*, 74.

51. The town of Quitman is located in Brooks County, Georgia, a county on the border of Georgia and Florida. Abate, *Omni Gazetteer*, 251. Vol. 3.

Chapter 3. Wartime Florida

1. Andrew Low was a wealthy British cotton broker who lived in Savannah. During the war he was arrested and imprisoned "on suspicion of collaboration with the Confederacy." Low hosted many famous people in his home (now a house museum), including Gen. Robert E. Lee and William Makepeace Thackeray. Low's son married Juliette Magill Gordon, who founded the Girl Scouts of the U.S.A. Toledano, *National Trust Guide to Savannah*, 20, 44, 147.

2. Feilden's paternal grandfather was Sir William Feilden (1772–1850), First Baronet Feilden of Feniscowles, Lancashire. Pine, *New Extinct Peerage*, 204.

3. The 1855 *Charleston City Directory* lists a W. M. Wilson as a porter in the Bank of Charleston.

4. Napoleonic exile Prince Achille Murat (1801–47), nephew of Napoleon Bonaparte, settled in Florida in the early 1820s. He later lived in New Orleans and is buried in Tallahassee. Burnett, *Florida's Past*, 102–5.

5. In the early 1840s, William F. Russell was one of the first settlers on the Indian River at St. Lucie Sound, an area, according to the U.S. Congress, "overrun and infested by marauding bands of hostile Indians." Rights, *Portrait of St. Lucie*, 35–36.

6. Turtles.

7. *Deo volente* (God willing).

8. Probably Rev. Edward Reid Miles (1824–85), brother of Francis Turquand Miles. Cannon, *South Carolina Genealogies*, 3:182.

9. This likely refers to Julia's sister Charlotte (Mrs. Langdon Cheves Jr.).

10. This song, better known as "Swanee River," was composed by famed American songwriter Stephen Foster (1826–64).

11. Brig. Gen. John King Jackson (1828–66), a native of Georgia, commanded the District of Florida for a while after July 1, 1864, and later helped defend Savannah under Lt. Gen. William J. Hardee. Warner, *Generals in Gray*, 150–51.

12. Feilden probably means Capt. John Jackson Dickison (1816–1902), who commanded a company of cavalry (Company H, Second Florida Regiment) for three years. Evans, *Confederate Military History*, 16:252–53.

13. The battle of Olustee, February 20, 1864, was the largest battle fought in Florida during the war. Long, *Civil War Day by Day*, 466.

14. Capt. S. A. Moreno, assistant adjutant general in the Military District of Florida. See Evans, *Confederate Military History*, 16:192.

15. Union major general Quincy Adams Gillmore (1825–88) commanded the Department of the South. On August 21, 1863, he sent an unsigned note to General Beauregard demanding the immediate surrender of Morris Island and Fort Sumter. If Beauregard refused, Gillmore stated, he would open fire on Charleston. Beauregard angrily replied to Gillmore, accusing him of "barbarity." After the initial bombardment, Gillmore agreed to give Beauregard until 11 P.M. on August 23 to move noncombatants out of the range of his guns. Phelps, *Bombardment of Charleston*, 27–34; Warner, *Generals in Blue*, 176–77.

16. These forts guarded Mobile Bay, Alabama. Fort Powell was evacuated in early August after a bombardment by the USS *Chickasaw*, which then bombarded Fort Gaines. Fort Morgan was surrendered to the Federals after a fierce bombardment on August 23, 1864. Long, *Civil War Day by Day*, 552, 559.

17. Maj. Gen. William Henry Chase Whiting (1824–65) spent much of his wartime service in North Carolina, where he "developed Fort Fisher at the mouth of Cape Fear River into the strongest fortress in the Confederacy." Warner, *Generals in Gray*, 334–35.

18. Confederate major general Dabney Herndon Maury (1822–1900) was in command at Mobile, Alabama, during this period. Warner, *Generals in Gray*, 215–16.

19. V. Adm. David Glasgow Farragut (1801–70) commanded the Union naval forces in the battle of Mobile Bay and is known for allegedly crying out, "Damn the torpedoes, full speed ahead!" Sifakis, *Who Was Who in the Union*, 133.

20. U.S. admiral John Dahlgren (1809–70) commanded the South Atlantic Blockading Squadron from July 1863 to 1865. Sifakis, *Who Was Who in the Union*, 103.

21. Lake Panasoffkee.

22. Richard Call Long (b. 1846) served in the Fifth Florida Cavalry Battalion. Rerick, *Memoirs of Florida*, 607–8; National Archives, Compiled Service Records, 5th Batt'n Florida Cavalry, Microcopy 225, roll 5.

23. Richard Keith Call (1792–1862) was the territorial governor of Florida from 1835 to 1840 and again from 1841 to 1844. *Dictionary of American Biography*, 3:422–23.

24. Paynes Prairie.

25. This may be James Bryan Owens (1816–89), who was born in Barnwell District, South Carolina. He moved to Marion County, Florida, in 1853, where he and three brothers owned cotton plantations. During the war he served in the Confederate Congress. Wakelyn, *Biographical Dictionary of the Confederacy*, 336–37.

26. Col. Adam G. Summers raised cattle on pasture land west of Lake Weir, near the town of Summerfield, which is named in his honor. He also owned a mansion on Lake Weir. Waitley, *Best Backroads of Florida*, 175.

27. Members of the Branch family were among the early pioneers of Sumter County, Florida. Newell-Eitel, *Ties That Bind,* 22.

28. Members of the Tompkins family of Sumter County helped to establish the town of Bushnell. Newel-Eitel, *Ties That Bind,* 36.

29. Marietta Alboni (1826–94) of Italy was, according to her obituary published in the *New York Times* on June 24, 1894, "the most celebrated contralto" of the nineteenth century.

Chapter 4. Departmental Changes

1. Blanche Harriet Juanita Georgina Feilden (d. 1930) was Feilden's older sister. In 1871 she married Sir William Ridley Charles Cooke, a baronet. Mosley, *Burke's Peerage,* 1:885.

2. Charles Kuhn Prioleau (1827–87) was a Charleston native who moved to Liverpool in 1854 and was a partner in the commercial house of Fraser, Trenholm & Company. During the war he was a financial agent for the Confederate government. For a few years after the war, Prioleau lived in Bruges, Belgium, and conducted business as a banker. He died in London and is buried at Kensal Green Cemetery. "Historical Sketch of the Prioleau Family," 80, 98–100.

3. William Porcher Miles (1822–99) was the brother of Rev. Edward Reid Miles and Francis (Frank) Turquand Miles. Born in Walterboro, South Carolina, he was an attorney, planter, college president, Confederate congressman, and a U.S. representative. Miles spent his later years in Louisiana as a planter. See Cannon, *South Carolina Genealogies,* 4:184–85.

4. This is Theodore Dehon Wagner (1819–80), a partner in the Charleston firm of John Fraser & Company. At a memorial meeting of the Charleston Chamber of Commerce in 1880, one of his friends characterized him in eulogy: "In commerce, a king; as a citizen, a veritable Brother Cherrylbe in real life; never tired of kindly acts; never so happy as when engaged in the good offices of charity, or in extending his open, generous hand to thousands requiring help . . . and who found the richest reward of a useful life in loving companionship and unselfish regard for the welfare of others." Wagner's memorial in St. Michael's Church in Charleston reads in part: "He delivered the poor when they cried, and the fatherless who had none to help them." Charleston Chamber of Commerce, *Memorial Meeting,* 19; Jervey, *Inscriptions on the Tablets,* 30.

5. Lt. P. C. Warwick was assistant adjutant general and aide-de-camp to Maj. Gen. Samuel Jones. National Archives, Compiled Service Records, General and Staff Officers . . . , M818, roll 25.

6. Jefferson Davis actually had embarked on a morale-building tour of the South following Sherman's capture of Atlanta on September 2, 1864. Feilden evidently was unaware that Beauregard had quarreled with and been reprimanded by Davis following the battle of Manassas in 1861 and that Davis had relieved Beauregard of command of the Army of Mississippi following his withdrawal from Corinth, Mississippi, on May 25, 1862. Beauregard did not assume command of the Army of

Tennessee as Feilden expected. McPherson, *Battle Cry of Freedom*, 366–67, 416–17, 806–7.

7. Brig. Gen. Roswell Sabine Ripley (1823–87) was a native of Ohio who married into the Middleton family of South Carolina in 1852 and soon afterward settled in Charleston. He was on duty in South Carolina in 1863 and 1864, and after the war he lived in England for a period. Warner, *Generals in Gray*, 257.

8. David Bullock Harris (1814–64), a native of Virginia, was highly regarded by General Beauregard, on whose staff he served as an engineer in 1861. Harris later became chief engineer of the Department of South Carolina, Georgia, and Florida. He was repeatedly recommended for promotion and was promised one by President Davis in October 1864, but he died of yellow fever in Summerville, South Carolina, on October 10, 1864, before formally being appointed as a general. See Allardice, *More Generals in Gray*, 118–19.

9. Greenville was a popular destination for Lowcountry refugees. One of these was Arthur Middleton Huger (1821–70), whose wife was Margaret Campbell King. "Old Mr. Huger" may have been a reference to him or one of his relations, possibly Alfred Huger (1788–1872). Cannon, *South Carolina Genealogies*, 2:60–62; Huff, *Greenville*, 139.

10. Col. Alfred Roman (1824–92) served on General Beauregard's staff from 1862 to 1865 as assistant adjutant inspector general. Like Beauregard he was a native of Louisiana, and after the war he authored a military biography of the general. Allardice, *Confederate Colonels*, 327.

11. Judge Andrew Gordon Magrath (1813–93) of Charleston was appointed judge of the Confederate District Court in South Carolina. After resigning from the court, he was elected governor of South Carolina in November 1864 and inaugurated the following month. Following the war he married Julie's sister, Mary Eliza McCord (1825–1903). *Dictionary of American Biography*, 12:203–4; *Cyclopedia of Eminent and Representative Men*, 130–32; Cannon, *South Carolina Genealogies*, 3:83.

12. This was Augustus H. Hayden of Hayden & Whilden, jewelers and dealers in military goods in Charleston. Burton, *Hayden & Gregg*, 10–11.

13. Feilden is probably referring to Caroline Howard Gilman Glover (1823–77), the widow of John Wilson Glover (1820–46), who owned Fontainebleu Plantation near Walterboro, South Carolina. She was the daughter of Rev. Samuel Gilman and Caroline Howard Gilman. Mrs. Glover married Lewis Jervey (1819–1900) on March 9, 1864. Cannon, *South Carolina Genealogies*, 3:43; Glover, *Col. Joseph Glover*, 126–27.

14. Feilden is probably referring to the Countess of Salisbury, who defended her husband's castle (Roxborough) against the King of the Scots in the fourteenth century, and Countess Jeane de Monfort, a female warrior in the War of the Breton Succession.

15. The *Syren* was a paddlewheel steamer operated by the Charleston Importing & Exporting Company. Her first run through the blockade took place in November 1863. She made a total of thirty-three runs and was considered the most successful blockade runner in the Confederacy. Wise, *Lifeline of the Confederacy*, 163.

16. Capt. Edward Pliny Bryan (1830–64), of General Beauregard's staff, was a Marylander who served the Confederacy as a spy, an expert in mine warfare, and an officer in the Signal Corps. He died of yellow fever in September 1864. In his memoirs Brig. Gen. Edward Porter Alexander noted the death of Bryan, "whom Beauregard had kept on secret service, and who had been blowing up Federal steamboats on the St. Johns River in Florida." Tidwell, *Come Retribution,* 87, 130; Alexander, *Fighting for the Confederacy,* 425; National Archives, Compiled Service Records, General and Staff Officers . . . , M818, roll 4.

17. This is the family of Robert Trail Chisolm (1798–1883), a refugee from Charleston. His wife was Lynch Helen Bachman (1828–1906), the daughter of Rev. John Bachman. Chisolm, *Chisolm Genealogy,* 63; Huff, *Greenville,* 139.

18. Lt. Gen. William Joseph Hardee (1815–73), a native of Georgia, replaced Maj. Gen. Samuel Jones in the command of the Department of South Carolina, Georgia, and Florida in October 1864. In February 1865 he ordered the evacuation of Charleston. See Warner, *Generals in Gray,* 124–25, 166.

19. This is probably Rev. John Gadsden (1833–1902) and his wife, Emma Julia Boyle Gadsden (1836–1905). Reverend Gadsden was an Episcopal priest who became the principal of the Holy Communion Church Institute (later known as Porter Military Academy) in Charleston. Thomas, *Historical Account,* 764; Hampton, *Tombstones and Tablets,* 13, 71.

20. Feilden could be referring to the wife of William H. Geddings or of John Frederic Geddings (1829–87), who were Charleston physicians that served in the Confederate States Army medical service, but there were other residents of Charleston by that name who may have taken refuge in Summerville. Waring, *History of Medicine in South Carolina,* 238–39.

21. James Petigru Boyce (1827–88), a Baptist minister and educator, founded a Baptist seminary in Greenville, where he was a resident from 1855 to 1872. He had several brothers, but Julia is most likely referring to his cousin William Walters Boyce (1818–90), a native of Charleston who practiced law in Winnsboro, South Carolina. He served in the Confederate Congress and became an opponent of the Davis administration. In 1864 Boyce published an open letter that advocated a peace convention of all the states. O'Neall, *Annals of Newberry,* 99–101; Bailey, *Biographical Directory,* 1:169–70; *Dictionary of American Biography,* 2:523–24; Warner and Yearns, *Biographical Register,* 27–28; Boyce Family History and Genealogy Files.

22. Lt. Col. Thomas Benton Roy (1838–1910), a Virginian, transferred from the staff of General Beauregard to become the chief of staff for Lt. Gen. William J. Hardee, who "trusted Roy completely and treated him like a son." Hughes, *General William J. Hardee,* 209; *Confederate Veteran,* 19:209.

Chapter 5. The Death of the Confederacy

1. The *Kate Gregg* (formerly the *Stag*) was a blockade-running steamship owned by the Atlantic Steam Packet Company of Charleston. She ran from Charleston to Nassau and back. Wise, *Lifeline of the Confederacy,* 253, 307.

2. Probably Maj. Gen. Robert Ransom Jr. (1828–92). See Warner, *Generals in Gray,* 253.

3. Dr. John Richardson Cheves (1815–69) was the brother of Louisa Cheves McCord, the stepmother of Julia McCord Feilden. His wife was Rachel Susan Bee. The Cheves family genealogy states that Cheves earned a medical degree but never practiced medicine; but in fact he did serve as a surgeon in the Confederate army, and before that, using his knowledge of chemistry, he was in charge of "engineering obstructions and torpedo defense in Charleston Harbor." Cheves lost a number of close relatives in the war, including a brother, Langdon Cheves Jr., who was killed in action in July 1863, and a son, Edward Richardson Cheves, who died in battle in Virginia in June 1862. The "losses" Feilden mentions, however, may refer to Cheves's rice plantation in Georgia, Grove Point, which was burned and plundered in 1864 by Sherman's army. Cannon, *South Carolina Genealogies,* 1:385–86; McCord, *Louisa S. McCord: Political and Social Essays,* 30; Beney, *Majesty of Savannah,* 94.

4. Ambrose Ransom Wright (1826–72) was promoted to the rank of major general in November 1864 and commanded the forces of Georgia, his native state. Warner, *Generals in Gray,* 345–46.

5. J. E. Phillips was a teller for the Bank of Charleston in 1865. There was also an L. M. Phillips who was a bookkeeper at that time. Clark, *History of the Banking Institutions,* 205.

6. This is Maj. Gen. Carter Littlepage Stevenson Jr. (1817–88). See Warner, *Generals in Gray,* 292–93.

7. Lt. Gen. Wade Hampton (1818–1902) of South Carolina. Warner, *Generals in Gray,* 122–23.

8. David P. Conyngham, a New York newspaperman traveling with Sherman's army as a correspondent, described the burning of the city as an eyewitness: "I trust I shall never witness such a scene again—drunken soldiers, rushing from house to house, emptying them of their valuables, and then firing them; negroes carrying off piles of booty . . . officers and men reveling on the wines and liquors, until the burning houses buried them in their drunken orgies. I was fired at for trying to save an unfortunate man from being murdered. . . . Shrieks, groans, and cries of distress resounded from every side. Men, women, and children, some half naked, as they rushed from their beds, were running frantically about, seeking their friends, or trying to escape from the fated town. A troop of cavalry, I think the 29th Missouri, were left to patrol the streets; but I did not once see them interfering with the groups that rushed about to fire and pillage the houses." See Conyngham, *Sherman's March,* 330–31.

9. Paul Trapier (1806–72), an Episcopal minister, lived in Camden, where his home, Kamchatka, was thoroughly pillaged by Federal soldiers. His wife left a memoir of the town's ordeal, noting the terrible abuse of the black women of the area: "I could fill pages with accounts of the misery these raiders left in their track. Their treatment of the slaves . . . was atrocious. A gentleman in our neighborhood assured us that not a female slave on his plantation (with a single exception) was allowed

to retain <u>that</u> which should have been dearer to her than her life. This exception, a brave married woman, stood at the door of her house with a log of wood in her hand, and said she would dash out the brains of any man who came near her." Stokes, "Sherman's Army," 118.

10. John Bachman (1790–1874), a Lutheran clergyman and famed naturalist, was in Cheraw when Sherman's army occupied the place and described what he saw in a letter written in 1865: "Officers, high in command, were engaged tearing from the ladies their watches, their ear and wedding rings, the daguerreotypes of those they loved. . . . A lady of delicacy and refinement, a personal friend, was compelled to strip before them, as they might find concealed watches and other valuables under her dress. A system of torture was practiced toward the weak, unarmed, and defenseless, which, as far as I know and believe, was universal throughout the whole course of that invading army. Before they arrived at a plantation, they inquired the names of the most faithful and trusted servants; they were immediately seized, pistols were presented at their heads; with the most terrific curses, they were threatened to be shot if they did not assist them in finding buried treasures. If this did not succeed, they were tied up and cruelly beaten. Several poor creatures died under the infliction. The last resort was that of hanging." Dr. Bachman, an elderly man, was robbed and so severely beaten by one of Sherman's soldiers that one of his arms was paralyzed for the rest of his life. Davis, *Rise and Fall of the Confederate Government*, 2:601–2.

11. The Second Presbyterian Church was called Flinn's church, after its first pastor, Rev. Andrew Flinn (1773–1820). *New Guide to Modern Charleston*, 78.

12. One of Sherman's aides, Capt. George W. Pepper, recorded his memories of the march through South Carolina in a memoir published in 1866: "Houses were burned as they were found. Whenever a view could be had from high ground, black columns of smoke were seen rising here and there within a circuit of twenty or thirty miles. Solid built chimneys were the only relics of plantation houses after the fearful blast had swept by. The destruction of houses, barns, mills, &c., was almost universal. Families who remained at home, occasionally kept the roof over their heads." Noted South Carolina author and historian William Gilmore Simms (1806–70) described the "march of the Federals" into South Carolina as being characterized by "scenes of license, plunder, and general conflagration." Pepper, *Personal Recollections*, 336–37; Simms, *Sack and Destruction*, 29.

13. W. W. Lord Jr., an eyewitness of the destruction of Winnsboro, wrote of it in his memoir: "[The] advance-guard of unofficered and undisciplined stragglers . . . rode along our little street without making any depredations or paying any attention to the closed shutters and doors of the frightened villagers; for the pioneers seemed to know that their conquering general—'Uncle Billy,' as they fondly called him—was to make his headquarters on that street. . . . Downtown, however, the torch was soon applied by the main body of the army, which had entered the village by another road, and the business portion of Winnsboro was at once wrapped in flames. Like truants out of school, these overgrown 'Boys in Blue' played snowball along the fire-lit streets with precious flour; made bonfires of hams and sides of

bacon . . . set boxes and barrels of crackers afloat on streams of vinegar and molasses that were sent flowing down the gutters from headless barrels; and fed their horses from hats filled with sugar, throwing what remained into the flames or the mud. In this wanton horseplay enough foodstuff was destroyed to have nourished the community abundantly for at least a year . . . the residential sections of the village were not neglected. All homes outside the sacred limits of the headquarters precinct were stripped of food and treasure." The soldiers also burned the Episcopal church in Winnsboro and exhumed and desecrated the body of a recently buried Confederate soldier, whose grave they thought might contain buried valuables. Lord, "In the Path of Sherman," 443–44.

14. Infantry and cavalry under the command of Gen. Philip Sheridan devastated the Shenandoah Valley of Virginia beginning in September 1864, burning crops and other properties under orders of General Grant that the area "cease to be a granary and a sanctuary for the enemy." A Confederate cavalryman from Virginia described the expedition thus: "Sheridan . . . was disgracing the humanity of any age and visiting the Valley with a baptism of fire, in which was swept away the bread of the old men and women and children of that weeping land. On every side, from mountain to mountain, the flames from all the barns, mills, grain and hay stacks, and in very many instances from dwellings, too, were blazing skyward, leaving a smoky trail of desolation." Long, *Civil War Day by Day,* 574; Myers, *Comanches,* 335–36.

15. This is Rachel Susan Bee Cheves, the sister-in-law of Julia's stepmother, Louisa Susanna Cheves McCord. Mrs. McCord lived in Columbia with her daughters (Julia's stepsisters) in a house that Gen. O. O. Howard confiscated for his quarters during Sherman's occupation and burning of the city. She later testified in a deposition: "Indicating the pre-knowledge of the soldiers of the coming horrors of that night . . . while the pillaging of my yards and buildings was beginning in the morning or early afternoon . . . a slip of paper was secretly brought me by a frightened servant girl; she said that a soldier had dropped it on the step and told her to bring it to me. It was a few words written in pencil and addressed to the 'Ladies of Columbia,' advising them to leave, if possible, for some place of safety; that a 'terrible fate' awaited them, and adding that he wrote this because he had kind friends among us." Despite General Howard's presence, the McCord house was pillaged and nearly burned by his soldiers. Cannon, *South Carolina Genealogies,* 1:382–86; McCord, *Louisa S. McCord: Poems, Drama, Biography, Letters,* 244.

16. Possibly William Beattie (1839–82) of Greenville. Whitmire, *Presence of the Past,* n.p.

17. This is Henry Pinckney Walker (1817–90), a native Englishman who was in the British consular service in Charleston. He was a strong supporter of the Confederate cause and had five sons. In late 1863 as he approached the age of military service, George, one of the younger sons (b. 1847), was sent to England to live with relatives there, but at least two of Walker's sons served in the Confederate army. The son Feilden mentions was Henry P. Walker Jr., who was born in 1845. See Henry Pinckney Walker Papers, SCHS.

18. In 1865 as Sherman's army was moving across South Carolina, the assets of the Bank of Charleston had to be hurriedly railroaded from Columbia to Greenville. "During the transfer, President Sass fatally over-exerted himself saving bank property from a fire, while, tradition says, he lost a serious amount of his own. In consequence of this labor of duty he died in Greenville on March 3, 1865. For twenty three years he had served the bank as teller, cashier and president. Reputed for his piety, his charities, and his great devotion to duty, his last sacrifice was but a fitting end to his life." See Stoney, *Story of South Carolina's Senior Bank*, 36.

19. Andrew Burnett Rhett (1831–79), the son of Robert Barnwell Rhett (1800–1876), was the commander of the Brook's Guard Artillery Company. Cannon, *South Carolina Genealogies*, 4:27; Hewitt, *South Carolina Confederate Soldiers*, 405.

20. Mr. Micawber is the ever-hopeful character in Charles Dickens's 1850 novel *David Copperfield*.

21. James Ravenel Macbeth (1839–93) was a captain of the First SC Artillery and the son of Charles Macbeth, the mayor of Charleston. He was "captured on Morris Island, July 10, 1863; was in prison at Johnson's Island for over one year and, after his release, was with the army at Savannah opposed to Sherman, and subsequently lost his left arm, and was shot through the leg at Averysboro, N.C." Macbeth, *Abstract of a Genealogical Collection*, 22–23; Ravenel, *Ravenel Records*, 68.

22. Union major general John McAllister Schofield (1831–1906). Warner, *Generals in Blue*, 426–35.

23. Maj. Theodore Gaillard Barker (1832–1917) was adjutant general of the Hampton Legion. "At Cheraw, February 1865, he was wounded by a fragment of a shell." Evans, *Confederate Military History*, 6:445–46.

24. William Joseph Hardee Jr., the son of Lt. Gen. William J. Hardee, served in the Texas Rangers and in General Wheeler's Cavalry. At the battle of Bentonville, he was mortally wounded in a cavalry charge. He died on March 24, 1865. Hughes, *General William J. Hardee*, 291–94.

25. Union troops.

26. Greenville was not visited by the armies of Major General Sherman, but in May 1865 after Lee's surrender, Federal troops in pursuit of Jefferson Davis raided the town. Caroline H. Gilman, a famous author, lived there as a refugee after her home in Charleston was hit by a shell, and she wrote an account of what happened in Greenville: "The raiders, about two hundred in number, went to Main Street and opened the Commissary stores, robbed the Bank, pillaged every article of clothing from the rooms of the Ladies' Association, and then proceeded to private houses and property." Among the valuables stolen by the soldiers was thirty thousand dollars in gold, the assets of the Bank of Charleston that Jacob K. Sass had hidden in a store in Greenville. Later that year Mrs. Gilman traveled eastward across the state back to Charleston, observing along the way "Sherman's Desolation . . . all ruin, ruin." Saint-Amand, *Balcony in Charleston*, 131, 137; Huff, *Greenville*, 144.

27. Turquand C. McCord (b. 1839) was Julia's youngest brother. He served in the Twentieth Regiment, Alabama Infantry. Cannon, *South Carolina Genealogies*, 3:83.

28. Federal troops under the command of Maj. Gen. James Harrison Wilson captured the city of Selma, Alabama, on April 2, 1865. Long, *Civil War Day by Day,* 664.

29. Charles Tidyman Lowndes (1808–84) was a Charleston businessman, banker, and planter. Lowndes became the sixth president of the Bank of Charleston, serving in that post from 1865 to 1872. Davidson, *Last Foray,* 220–21; Stoney, *Story of South Carolina's Senior Bank,* 36.

30. John Cheeseborough was a cashier with the Bank of Charleston. Clark, *History of Banking Institutions,* 204.

31. William Aiken (1806–87), a South Carolina planter and politician. "Although he opposed nullification and secession, he financially supported the Confederacy during the Civil War. After the South's defeat, he was arrested and transported to Washington where he was only briefly detained." Bailey, *Biographical Directory,* 1:40–41.

32. Charles Macbeth (1805–81), the mayor of Charleston. Macbeth, *Abstract of a Genealogical Collection,* 22.

33. Feilden is referring to Marie (or Mary) Boozer (1846–1908), the daughter of a Philadelphia woman who was married several times. The lady's second husband, Mr. Burton, was the father of Marie, but she was adopted by her mother's third husband, a Mr. Boozer of South Carolina. A beautiful, blue-eyed blonde, Marie lived in Columbia. Her mother was known as a Union sympathizer, and both women fled Columbia when it was burned by Sherman's army. During their flight north, they took refuge with one of Sherman's generals, Hugh Judson Kilpatrick, a recent widower and a notorious womanizer. Marie traveled with him into North Carolina, and Kilpatrick's biographer asserted that there was "no doubt" that the two were having an affair. During the South Carolina campaign, Kilpatrick also kept a Chinese girl with him as his mistress. Martin, *Kill-Cavalry,* 217; Selby, *Checkered Life,* 18–23.

Chapter 6. Postwar Life

1. Jacob Keith Sass was the brother-in-law of Malvina and Victoria Murden. Their sister Octavia Murden Sass died in 1862. Jervey, *Inscriptions on the Tablets,* 242.

2. Charlotte McCord Cheves (1818–1879), Julia's oldest sister. Cannon, *South Carolina Genealogies,* 3:83.

3. This is probably one of the sons of Christopher Gustavus Memminger (1803–88). Robert Withers Memminger (1839–1901) held the rank of major in the Confederate army. Two other sons also served: Willis Wilkins Memminger (1845–76) and C. G. Memminger Jr., who held the rank of lieutenant in February 1865. Trimpi, *Crimson Confederates,* 212–13.

4. Feilden probably is referring to Josiah A. Patterson Campbell (1830–1917), a native of Lancaster, South Carolina. Allardice, *Confederate Colonels,* 88.

5. Feilden is referring to James Redpath (1833–91), a journalist, abolitionist, and reformer. During the war he was a correspondent with the Union army, and in 1865 he was appointed superintendent of education in Charleston, "where he

had much to do with reorganizing the school system of the state, especially colored schools." *Dictionary of American Biography,* 15:444.

6. Feilden means Judge Dennis Nelson Cooley (1825–92). A native of New Hampshire, he was a lawyer appointed by Abraham Lincoln in 1864 as commissioner to South Carolina. In 1865 Cooley was appointed by President Andrew Johnson as the commissioner of Indian affairs. He was later a banker and a state senator in Iowa. *Portrait and Biographical Record of Dubuque,* 223.

7. Ninety Six is a town in Greenwood County, South Carolina.

8. Kalmia Landing is in Aiken County, South Carolina.

9. Many of the railroad lines in South Carolina had been rendered inoperable by the invading Union troops. A line of the South Carolina Rail Road Company, the route from Orangeburg to Charleston via Branchville, reopened on May 19, 1865. For a while it was operated by the U.S. military, until the property was returned to the South Carolina Rail Road Company. Fetters, *Charleston & Hamburg,* 140.

10. Maj. George Lamb Buist (1838–1907) of Charleston. Evans, *Confederate Military History,* 6:489–90.

11. Feilden probably is referring to Lt. Col. Joseph A. Yates. Evans, *Confederate Military History,* 6:198–201.

12. Feilden probably is referring to Theodore Stoney (b. 1826), a Charleston merchant. Porcher, "Porcher," 124.

13. "96 M.T.O." is possibly Millway Turn Out, a railroad turnout near a grist mill on Hard Labor Creek, in the area of the town of Ninety Six. Watson, *Greenwood County Sketches,* 201.

14. William J. Magrath (1817–1902) married Ellen Julia Williman, a young widow who died about two years later. Magrath later married Selina Emily Bollin. He was a lawyer and president of the South Carolina Rail Road. See Magrath Family Papers, SCHS.

15. Williston was a town on the railroad line in Barnwell County, South Carolina.

16. Mrs. Miles may be Jeanie Wardlaw Miles, who was the wife of Julie's cousin Francis Turquand Miles.

17. Provisional Army of the Confederate States.

18. "Mr. Smythe" is Augustine Thomas Smythe (1842–1914), husband of Julia Feilden's stepsister Louisa Rebecca McCord Smythe. He was a Charleston lawyer and a state senator. See Bailey, *Biographical Directory,* 1523–25. Vol. 3.

19. Feilden is referring to John Ross Key (1837–1920), the grandson of Francis Scott Key, who wrote "The Star-Spangled Banner." After the war John Ross Key continued to work successfully as an artist. A painting by him titled *Bombardment of Fort Sumter* is in the collections of the Greenville County Museum of Art. This painting was "in the collection of the Union League Club in Philadelphia since the late 1930s" and was purchased for the museum, so it may not be the same painting Feilden owned. *Appleton's Cyclopaedia of American Biography,* 3:530; Severens, *Greenville County Museum of Art,* 68–69.

20. A. T. Smythe had two sons living at this time, Langdon Cheves Smythe (1883–1941) and Augustine Thomas Smythe Jr. (b. 1885). Bailey, *Biographical Directory,* 1525. Vol. 3.

21. Feilden is referring to Susan Dunlap Adger Smythe, who in 1902 married the author John Bennett (1865–1956). Her daughter Jane McClintock Bennett was born in May 1903. Bailey, *Biographical Directory,* 1525; Greene, *Mr. Skylark,* 93–95.

22. There was a great debate in 1909 regarding whether Dr. Frederick Albert Cook (1865–1940) or R. Adm. Robert E. Peary (1856–1920) was the first to reach the North Pole. In some circles the debate continues to this day. Henderson, *True North.*

23. Feilden is writing to Hannah McCord Smythe (1874–1955), the daughter of Julia Feilden's stepsister Louisa Rebecca McCord Smythe (Mrs. A.T. Smythe). Hannah married Anton Pope Wright. Her son was David McCord Wright (b. 1909). Bailey, *Biographical Directory,* 1525. Vol. 3.

24. Johnson Hagood (1829–98) was a planter and lawyer from Barnwell County, South Carolina. He was a respected general in the Confederate army, and in the 1870s he was active in exposing the fraudulent financial dealings of the state's Reconstruction administration. Hagood became the governor of South Carolina in 1880. *Cyclopedia of Eminent and Representative Men,* 78–86.

BIBLIOGRAPHY

Archival Sources

Architectural File. #30–01 101–107 Bull Street. South Carolina Historical Society (SCHS), Charleston.

Boyce Family History and Genealogy Files. #30–04 Boyce. SCHS.

DuBose, William Porcher. "Reminiscences." South Caroliniana Library, University of South Carolina, #636 ("Copied from typed copy lent by Mrs. Joseph M. Bell, 1017 Bull Street, Columbia, S.C., 1946").

Feilden, Henry Wemyss. Henry Wemyss Feilden Papers, 1851–1949. #1025. SCHS.

Feilden, Henry Wemyss. Feilden ALS, SxMs 38, 15/12. University of Sussex.

Magrath Family Papers, 1865–1956. #1072. SCHS.

National Archives. War Department Collection of Confederate Records. RG 109. Compiled Service Records of Confederate Soldiers Who Served in Organizations from the State of Florida. Fifth Battalion Florida Cavalry. Microcopy 225, roll 5.

———. War Department Collection of Confederate Records. RG 109. Compiled Service Records of Confederate Soldiers Who Served in Organizations from the State of South Carolina. First (Charleston) Battalion S.C. Infantry (Gaillard's Battalion). Microcopy 267, roll 150.

Thornton, Ella May. "Notes on Henry Wemyss Feilden." Henry Wemyss Feilden Papers, 1915–1958. Hargrett Rare Book and Manuscript Library (HRBML), University of Georgia, Athens.

Trevor-Battye, A. "A Noble Englishman: Being Chapters in the Life of Henry Wemyss Feilden, C.B., Colonel, 1838–1921." Unpublished manuscript. Henry Wemyss Feilden Papers, 1915–1958. HRBML.

Walker, Henry Pinckney. Family Papers, 1836–1957. #1223. SCHS.

Primary Sources

Alexander, Edward Porter. *Fighting for the Confederacy: The Personal Recollections of General Edward Porter Alexander.* Chapel Hill: University of North Carolina Press, 1989.

Charleston (S.C.) City Council. *Census of the City of Charleston, South Carolina, for the Year 1861.* Charleston: Evans & Cogswell, 1861.

Conyngham, David P. *Sherman's March through the South, with Sketches and Incidents of the Campaign.* New York: Sheldon, 1865.

Elliott, Stephen. *Gideon's Water-Lappers: A Sermon.* Macon, Ga.: Burke, Boykin, 1864.

Fremantle, Arthur James Lyon. *Three Months in the Southern States.* Carlisle, Mass: Applewood Books, 2008.

Kipling, Rudyard, and Thomas Pinney. *Something of Myself and Other Autobiographical Writings.* Cambridge: Cambridge University Press, 1991.

Lord, W. W., Jr. "In the Path of Sherman." *Harper's Magazine,* February 1910, 438–46.

McCord, Louisa S. *Louisa S. McCord: Poems, Drama, Biography, Letters.* Edited by Richard C. Lounsbury. Charlottesville: University Press of Virginia, 1996.

———. *Louisa S. McCord: Political and Social Essays.* Edited by Richard C. Lounsbury. Charlottesville: University Press of Virginia, 1995.

Nares, George Strong. *The Official Report of the Recent Arctic Expedition.* London: Murray, 1876.

Nares, George Strong, and Henry Wemyss Feilden, eds., *Narrative of a Voyage to the Polar Sea during 1875–76 in H.M. Ships 'Alert' and 'Discovery.'* London: Low, Marston, Searle & Rivington, 1878.

Pepper, George. *Personal Recollections of Sherman's Campaign in Georgia and the Carolinas.* Zanesville, Ohio: Dunne, 1866.

Simms, William Gilmore. *Sack and Destruction of the City of Columbia, S.C.* Columbia: Power Press of Daily Phoenix, 1865.

Stokes, Karen. "Sherman's Army Comes to Camden: The Civil War Narrative of Sarah Dehon Trapier." *South Carolina Historical Magazine* 109 (2008): 95–120.

Storey, Graham, ed. *The Letters of Charles Dickens, Volume 10, 1862–1864.* Oxford: Clarendon, 1998.

Tison, John Laurens, Jr., and Samuel G. Stoney. "Recollections of John Stafford Stoney, Confederate Surgeon." *South Carolina Historical and Genealogical Magazine* 10 (1909): 20.

U.S. Department of War. *The War of the Rebellion: The Official Records of the Union and Confederate Armies.* Washington, D.C.: Government Printing Office, 1880–1909.

Secondary Sources

Abate, Frank R., ed. *Omni Gazetteer of the United States of America.* 11 vols. Detroit: Omnigraphics, 1991.

Allardice, Bruce S. *Confederate Colonels: A Biographical Register.* Columbia: University of Missouri Press, 2008.

———. *More Generals in Gray.* Baton Rouge: Louisiana State University Press, 1995.

Bailey, N. Louise, ed. *Biographical Directory of the South Carolina Senate, 1776–1985.* 3 vols. Columbia: University of South Carolina Press, 1986.

Barnwell, Stephen B. *The Story of an American Family.* Marquette, Mich.: Privately printed, 1969.

Beney, Peter. *The Majesty of Savannah.* Gretna, La.: Pelican, 2006.

Bennett, Susan Smythe. "The McCords of McCord's Ferry, South Carolina." *South Carolina Historical and Genealogical Magazine* 34 (1933): 188–89.

Brewer, Ebenezer Cobham. *Dictionary of Phrase and Fable*. London: Cassell, 1905.

Bull, Henry DeSassure. "Ashley Hall Plantation." *South Carolina Historical and Genealogical Magazine* 53 (1952): 61–66.

Burnett, Gene M. *Florida's Past: People and Events That Shaped the State, Volume 3*. Sarasota, Fla.: Pineapple, 1986.

Burton, E. Milby. *Hayden & Gregg: Jewellers of Charleston*. Charleston, S.C.: Charleston Museum, 1938.

———. *The Siege of Charleston, 1861–65*. Columbia: University of South Carolina Press, 1970.

The Charleston City Directory and General Business Directory for 1855. Charleston, S.C.: Gazlay, 1855.

Charleston (S.C.) Chamber of Commerce. *Memorial Meeting of the Chamber of Commerce of Charleston, S.C.: Tributes to the Memory of Augustus O. Andrews, Theodore D. Wagner, William M. Lawton*. Charleston: News and Courier Book Presses, 1880.

Chase, George B. *Lowndes of South Carolina: An Historical and Genealogical Memoir*. Boston: Williams, 1876.

Chisolm, William Garnett. *Chisolm Genealogy*. New York: Knickerbocker, 1914.

Clark, W. A. *The History of Banking Institutions Organized in South Carolina Prior to 1860*. Columbia, S.C.: State Co., 1922.

Cooke, John Esten. *Stonewall Jackson: A Military Biography*. New York: Appleton, 1866.

Cyclopedia of Eminent and Representative Men of the Carolinas. Vol 1. Spartanburg, S.C.: Reprint, 1972.

Dabney, Robert Lewis. *Life and Campaigns of Lieut.-Gen. Thomas J. Jackson (Stonewall Jackson)*. New York: Blelock, 1866.

Davidson, Chalmers Gaston. *The Last Foray*. Columbia: University of South Carolina Press, 1971.

Davis, Jefferson. *The Rise and Fall of the Confederate Government*. Richmond, Va.: Garrett & Massie, 1938.

Daymond, M. J., ed. *Women Writing Africa: The Southern Region*. New York: Feminist, 2003.

Dictionary of American Biography. New York: Scribner, 1928–36.

Donald, David Herbert. *Lincoln*. New York: Simon & Shuster, 1995.

Elliott, Sam Davis. *Doctor Quintard, Chaplain C.S.A. and Second Bishop of Tennessee*. Baton Rouge: Louisiana State University Press, 2003.

Emerson, W. Eric. *Sons of Privilege*. Columbia: University of South Carolina Press, 2005.

Evans, Clement A., ed. *Confederate Military History: A Library of Confederate States History, in Seventeen Volumes*. Wilmington, N.C.: Broadfoot, 1988.

Faust, Drew Gilpin. *Southern Stories: Slaveholders in Peace and War.* Columbia: University of Missouri Press, 1992.

Fennell, C. A. M. *The Stanford Dictionary of Anglicised Words and Phrases.* Cambridge: Cambridge University Press, 1892.

Fetters, Thomas. *The Charleston & Hamburg: A South Carolina Railroad and an American Legacy.* Charleston, S.C.: History Press, 2008.

Foreman, Amanda. *A World on Fire: Britain's Crucial Role in the American Civil War.* New York: Random House, 2011.

Greene, Jack, and Alessandro Massignani. *Ironclads at War: The Origin and Development of the Armored Warship, 1854–1891.* Cambridge, Mass.: Da Capo, 1998.

Hampton, Ann Fripp. *Tombstones and Tablets: St. Paul's Episcopal Church, Summerville, South Carolina.* Summerville, S.C.: Phantom, 1998.

Harrison, James L. *Biographical Directory of the American Congress, 1774–1949.* Washington, D.C.: Government Printing Office, 1950.

Hart, James D., and Phillip W. Leininger. "Russell's Bookstore Group." In *The Oxford Companion to American Literature.* New York: Oxford University Press, 1948, 659.

Hayes, James P. *James and Related Sea Islands.* N.p.: Privately printed, 2001.

Henderson, Bruce. *True North: Peary, Cook, and the Race to the Pole.* New York: Norton, 2005.

Hershman, J. T., comp. *The Columbia City Directory.* Columbia, S.C.: Steam-Power Press of R. W. Gibbes, 1859.

Hewett, Janet B. *South Carolina Confederate Soldiers, 1861–1865, Name Roster, Volume 1.* Wilmington, N.C.: Broadfoot, 1998.

Heyward, James Barnwell. *Heyward.* N.p.: Privately printed, 1931.

Huff, Archie Vernon. *Greenville: The History of the City and County in the South Carolina Piedmont.* Columbia: University of South Carolina Press, 1995.

Hughes, Nathaniel Cheairs. *General William J. Hardee: Old Reliable.* Wilmington, N.C.: Broadfoot, 1987.

Hughes, Nathaniel Cheairs, and Roy P. Stonesifer. *The Life and Wars of Gideon J. Pillow.* Chapel Hill: University of North Carolina Press, 1993.

Hunter, Andrew Alexander, ed. *Cheltenham College Register, 1841–1889.* London: Bell, 1890.

Jamison, David Flavel. *Life and Times of Bertrand Du Guesclin: A History of the Fourteenth Century in Two Volumes.* Charleston, S.C.: Russell, 1864.

Jervey, Clare. *Inscriptions on the Tablets and Gravestones in St. Michael's Church and Churchyard, Charleston, S.C.* Columbia, S.C.: State Co., 1906.

Johnson, John. *The Defense of Charleston Harbor: Including Fort Sumter and the Adjacent Islands, 1863–1865.* Germantown, Tenn.: Guild Bindery, 1994.

———. *Views of Fort Sumter, Charleston, S.C.* Charleston, S.C.: Walker, Evans & Cogswell, 1899.

Joslyn, Mauriel Phillips. *Immortal Captives: The Story of the Six Hundred Confederate Officers and the United States Prisoner of War Policy.* Shippensburg, Penn.: White Mane, 1996.

Kirkland, Randolph W. *Broken Fortunes: South Carolina Soldiers, Sailors, and Citizens Who Died in the Service of Their Country and State in the War for Southern Independence.* Charleston: South Carolina Historical Society, 1995.

———. *South Carolina C.S.A. Research Aids.* Pawleys Island, S.C.: Kirkland, 1992.

"Langdon Cheves." *South Carolina Historical and Genealogical Magazine* 41 (1940): 96–97.

Lebergott, Stanley. "Through the Blockade: The Profitability and Extent of Cotton Smuggling, 1861–1865." *Journal of Economic History* 41 (1981): 867–88.

Long, E. B. *The Civil War Day by Day: An Almanac, 1861–1865.* Garden City, N.Y.: Greenwood, 1977.

Lucas, William Dollard. *A Lucas Memorandum.* N.p.: Privately printed, 1985.

Martin, Samuel J. *Kill-Cavalry: The Life of Union General Hugh Judson Kilpatrick.* Mechanicsburg, Penn.: Stackpole Books, 2000.

May, John Amasa. *South Carolina Secedes.* Columbia: University of South Carolina Press, 1960.

McPherson, James. *Battle Cry of Freedom: The Civil War Era.* Oxford: Oxford University Press, 1988.

Mosley, Charles, ed. *Burke's Peerage, Baronetage & Knightage.* 107th ed. 3 vols. Wilmington, Del.: Burke's Peerage & Gentry, 2003.

Moulton, Michael P., and James Sanderson. *Wildlife Issues in a Changing World.* Boca Raton, Fla.: CRC, 1999.

Myers, Frank M. *The Comanches: A History of White's Battalion.* Alexandria, Va.: Stonewall House, 1985.

Nepveux, Ethel Trenholm Seabrook. *George A. Trenholm: Financial Genius of the Confederacy.* N.p.: Privately printed, 1999.

A New Guide to Modern Charleston. Charleston, S.C.: Walker, Evans & Cogswell, 1912.

Newell-Eitel, Karen. *The Ties That Bind: A History of Linden and the Linden Cemetery Picnic.* Linden, Fla.: Linden Cemetery Association, 2000.

O'Neall, John Belton, and John A. Chapman. *The Annals of Newberry: In Two Parts.* Baltimore: Genealogical Publishing, 1974.

Parker, William Henry. *Genealogy of the Parker Family of South Carolina, 1670–1935.* N.p.: Privately printed, 1935.

Patey, James Garner. *The Whaley Family and Its Charleston Connections.* Spartanburg, S.C.: Reprint Co., 1992.

Pease, Jane H. *A Family of Women: The Carolina Petigrus in Peace and War.* Chapel Hill: University of North Carolina Press, 1999.

Perry, William Stevens. *Episcopate in America: Sketches Biographical and Bibliographical of the Bishops of the American Church.* New York: Christian Literature, 1895.

Phelps, W. Chris. *The Bombardment of Charleston*. Gretna, La.: Pelican, 2002.

Pickett, W.D. "Col. T.B. Roy." *Confederate Veteran*. 19 (1911): 209.

Pine, L. G. *The New Extinct Peerage, 1884–1971*. London: Heraldry Today, 1972.

Porcher, Catherine Cordes, comp. "Porcher, a Huguenot Family of Ancient Lineage." *Transactions of the Huguenot Society* 81 (1976): 90–186.

Portrait and Biographical Record of Dubuque, Jones and Clayton County, Iowa. Chicago: Chapman, 1894.

Ravenel, Henry Edmund. *Ravenel Records*. Dunwoody, Ga.: Berg, 1971.

Rerick, Rowland H. *Memoirs of Florida*. Atlanta: Southern Historical Association, 1902.

Rights, Lucille Rieley. *A Portrait of St. Lucie County, Florida*. Virginia Beach: Donning, 1994.

Rosen, Robert N. *The Jewish Confederates*. Columbia: University of South Carolina Press, 2000.

Rowland, Lawrence S., et al. *The History of Beaufort County, South Carolina, vol. 1: 1514–1861*. Columbia: University of South Carolina Press, 1996.

Saint-Amand, Mary Scott. *A Balcony in Charleston*. Richmond, Va.: Garrett & Massie, 1941.

Sass, Herbert Ravenel. *Outspoken: 150 Years of the* News & Courier. Columbia: University of South Carolina Press, 1953.

———. *The Story of the South Carolina Low Country*. West Columbia, S.C.: Hyer, 1956.

Schwab, Carolyn, comp. *Newspaper Extracts from the Sausalito News, Marion County, California, February 12, 1885 to December 26, 1890*. Westminister, Md.: Heritage Books, 2006.

Selby, Julian A. *A Checkered Life: Being a Brief History of the Countess Pourtales Formerly Miss Marie Boozer of Columbia, S.C.* N.p.: S & H, 1915.

Severens, Martha R. *Greenville County Museum of Art: The Southern Collection*. New York: Hudson Hills, 1995.

Sifakis, Stewart. *Who Was Who in the Union*. New York: Facts on File, 1988.

Smith, Alice R. Huger. *The Dwelling Houses of Charleston*. New York: Diadem, 1974.

South Carolina Genealogies: Articles from the South Carolina Historical (and Genealogical) Magazine. 5 vols. Spartanburg, S.C.: Published in association with the South Carolina Historical Society by Reprint Co., 1983.

Stern, Malcolm H., comp. *Americans of Jewish Descent*. New York: Ktav, 1971.

Stoney, Samuel Gaillard. *The Story of South Carolina's Senior Bank*. Charleston, S.C.: SCNB, 1955.

Teal, Harvey S. *Partners with the Sun: South Carolina Photographers, 1840–1940*. Columbia: University of South Carolina Press, 2000.

Thomas, Albert Sidney. *A Historical Account of the Protestant Episcopal Church in South Carolina, 1820–1957: Being a Continuation of Dalcho's Account, 1670–1820*. Columbia, S.C.: Bryan, 1957.

Tidwell, William A. *Come Retribution: The Confederate Secret Service and the Assassination of Lincoln.* Jackson: University Press of Mississippi, 1988.

Toledano, Roulhac. *The National Trust Guide to Savannah.* New York: Preservation, 1997.

Trimpi, Helen P. *Crimson Confederates: Harvard Men Who Fought for the South.* Knoxville: University of Tennessee Press, 2009.

Tucker, Spencer C., ed. *The Civil War Naval Encyclopedia.* Santa Barbara: ABC-CLIO, 2011.

Waitley, Douglas. *Best Backroads of Florida: The Heartland.* Sarasota, Fla.: Pineapple, 2006.

Wakelyn, Jon L. *Biographical Dictionary of the Confederacy.* Westport, Conn.: Greenwood, 1977.

Waring, Joseph Ioor. *A History of Medicine in South Carolina, 1825–1900.* Charleston: South Carolina Medical Association, 1967.

Warner, Ezra J. *Generals in Blue: Lives of the Union Commanders.* Baton Rouge: Louisiana State University Press, 1992.

———. *Generals in Gray: Lives of the Confederate Commanders.* Baton Rouge: Louisiana State University Press, 1987.

Warner, Ezra J., and W. Buck Yearns. *Biographical Register of the Confederate Congress.* Baton Rouge: Louisiana State University Press, 1975.

Watson, Margaret. *Greenwood County Sketches: Old Roads and Early Families.* Greenwood, S.C.: Attic, 1970.

Wauchope, George Armstrong. *The Writers of South Carolina.* Columbia, S.C.: State Co., 1910.

Way, William. *History of the New England Society of Charleston, South Carolina, for One Hundred Years, 1819–1919.* Charleston: Society, 1993.

Welsh, Jack D. *Medical Histories of Confederate Generals.* Kent, Ohio: Kent State University Press, 1995.

Whitemire, Beverly T. *The Presence of the Past: Epitaphs of 18th and 19th Century Pioneers in Greenville County, South Carolina, and Their Descendants.* Baltimore: Gateway, 1976.

Wilson, Annie Marie, and Mandi Dale Johnson. *Historic Bonaventure: Photographs from the Collection of the Georgia Historical Society.* Charleston, S.C.: Arcadia, 2003.

Wilson, Robert. "Historical Sketch of the Prioleau Family in Europe and America." *Transactions of the Huguenot Society* 71 (1966): 80–101.

Wise, Stephen R. *Lifeline of the Confederacy: Blockade Running during the Civil War.* Columbia: University of South Carolina Press, 1988.

INDEX